THE
SILENT
TWINS

THE
SILENT
TWINS

by

Marjorie Wallace

PRENTICE HALL PRESS • NEW YORK

Published in 1986 by Prentice Hall Press
A Division of Simon & Schuster, Inc.
Gulf + Western Building
One Gulf + Western Plaza
New York, New York 10023

Originally published in Great Britain by Chatto & Windus Ltd.

PRENTICE HALL PRESS is a trademark of Simon & Schuster, Inc.

Library of Congress Cataloging-in-Publication Data

Wallace, Marjorie.
  The silent twins.

  Originally published: London : Chatto & Windus, 1986.
  1. Gibbons family. 2. Gibbons, June. 3. Gibbons,
Jennifer. 4. Wales—Biography. 5. Twins—Biography.
I. Title.
CT9998.G53W35   1986   942.9′009′92 [B]   86-12244
ISBN 0-13-810276-7

Manufactured in the United States of America

10 9 8 7 6 5 4

First Prentice Hall Press Edition

To Doris Wallace Harwood – a remarkable mother

Contents

ACKNOWLEDGEMENTS

First and foremost, I should like to acknowledge the courage of Aubrey and Gloria Gibbons, the parents of the twins, who trusted me and gave me unwavering help, even when it meant great sacrifice to themselves, their family and their privacy. Without their strength to carry through the decision that their daughters' story should be told, this book would not have been written.

I should also like to acknowledge the brave concern of Tim Thomas, the educational psychologist who first assessed the twins. It was his fears for their future which prompted me to take an interest in their story and, despite disapproval from less imaginative colleagues and at the risk of his job, he gave me and the Gibbons family every possible support. His wife, Susan, and his children had to suffer much unpleasantness, but they have always encouraged him.

My thanks are due to many people in and around Haverfordwest including Dr Evan Davies, Cathleen Arthur, the twins' special teacher, who lent me her thesis, and the police, who opened their files to me.

I am grateful to the governor and staff at Pucklechurch remand centre for allowing me access, to Dr William Spry, the psychiatrist for the twins' defence, Dr John Hamilton, director of Broadmoor special hospital, and to some doctors, nurses and social workers there. In particular, I should like to acknowledge Dr Boyce Le Couteur, who invited me to visit and encouraged my continuing contact with June and Jennifer, and Mr Douglas Hunter, social worker, who checked the chapter on Broadmoor.

I should like to thank Mary Senechal and Frances Angliss for their excellent help in the task of transcribing the diaries. Also Kim Bourne and Sally Baker.

Most important of all, I am indebted to Tom Margerison, whose firm judgements, patience and kindness have sustained me over the three difficult years of my involvement with the twins.

Illustrations

Introduction

As I looked out of the window
There I saw the bird sitting alone.
His feathers ruffled in the snow,
His beak firmly closed to the world.
Just like I was, but who was to know.
June Gibbons

Haverfordwest is an uninspired little town with spiky outlines, its houses stuck to the hills like the crusted spines of an ancient reptile. Set at the western tip of the Pembroke peninsula, the capital of West Wales, it embodies centuries of spiritless days of cloud and rain. Old streets and new housing estates merge effortlessly in the overall grey. The inhabitants too seem to have taken the weather into their souls, speaking in a soft squelching brogue and keeping their inner selves tightly shut against the elements. At the top of a hill, set between the abandoned racecourse and town, there is one of these postwar housing estates – nondescript terraces of two- to four-bedroom houses built for the families of 'other ranks' from the nearby RAF base at Brawdy. Although the grime on the pebbledash bears witness to many years of living, the estate retains the look of temporary dwellings. Almost every garden has remained a solid patch of green. Few trees have been planted, and fewer flowers.

In number 35 Furzy Park, the end house of one of the terraces, lived the Gibbons family, then the only black family on the estate. Aubrey Gibbons, a handsome man with considerable charm and a desire to please, worked as an assistant air-traffic controller at the base. Since leaving Barbados twenty years previously, he had built a safe, if not meteoric career with the RAF. His wife, Gloria, four years his senior, had brought up their five children, following her husband round a succession of RAF stations. They were a close, respectable family, pleasant to talk to but reluctant to mix with their neighbours. The children were all polite and well-behaved. There was nothing remarkable about the Gibbonses; they went about their daily business disturbing no-one. Nothing remarkable – except, of course, the twins.

June and Jennifer were identical twins (although Gloria had always believed otherwise). They were pretty and petite, with unusually fine features. They spent most of their time together in their bedroom above the living room, playing with dolls, even at the age of sixteen, chatting to one another and listening to the radio or tapes of pop music. Occasionally, they would put on some make-up, style their hair and stroll into the town. They would collect their unemployment benefit and return with books of stamps, pens, note pads and exercise books. Every day the postman would deliver to Misses J. and J. Gibbons a dozen or so letters, large brown envelopes and Jiffy bags. Gloria would collect them at the door, a look of increasing bewilderment on her face. What were her twin daughters up to?

Ever since they had left school, with only one CSE each to their credit, they had shut themselves away in their bunk bedroom, never coming down to meals, never even smiling at other members of the family or acknowledging their presence in the house. The girls were deeply attached to their family, and demonstrated it in dozens of small indirect ways, but they could rarely express it openly. At times there was so little contact, and they were so much engrossed with their own secret affairs, they were more like enemy soldiers billeted with the family. Day after day Gloria would find them either lying in their nightclothes on their beds or tapping industriously at the two typewriters they had asked her to buy from a mail-order catalogue. One day, as she delivered the post outside their locked bedroom door, Gloria's curiosity got the better of her. She opened a packet and, lifting out a thick yellow pamphlet, looked at the title: 'The Art of Conversation'. Close to tears, she read the words as though unwilling or unable to believe what was in front of her. For since they were small children June and Jennifer had refused to talk to anyone: to Aubrey, to their older brother and sister, even to her. Gloria thought back over the years of disappointment and worry. 'Oh, Twinnies,' she said. 'You really are trying now.'

I first heard of the silent twins in April 1982 when I was working as a writer for the *Sunday Times* and reported on their trial on charges of arson and theft. It was an extraordinary occasion. The twins, tiny and vulnerable, said not a word apart from a few grunts which the court interpreted as pleas of guilty. The unemotional legal pantomime went on around them without touching them. A doctor gave evidence; the lawyers made their submissions; the judge pronounced sentence. It seemed simple, unthreatening, but the calm tones of authority sentenced the frightened children to be detained in Broadmoor special hospital for an indefinite period.

It was partly the shock of the sentence that made me visit the twins' parents to investigate their story. But there was nothing much to say until Aubrey asked if I would like to see the twins' room. He opened the door to reveal a small room full of black plastic dustbin bags piled on the bunk beds, scattered over the floor, dumped on every piece of furniture. Aubrey opened a bag full of writings and drawings. 'The police took them and we've just got them back,' he explained. It was an extraordinary collection of diaries, typed manuscripts of stories, novels and poems, illustrated strips and books of drawings. Aubrey allowed me to load the black bags into the back of my car and I carried the treasure trove back to London.

There, I discovered from the diaries that at seventeen June and Jennifer had pooled their unemployment benefit to pay £700 towards the cost of printing June's first novel, 'Pepsi-Cola Addict'. Since then she had written dozens of short stories and poems and started three new novels. Jennifer had written three short novels and dozens of essays. Their stories were primitive in style, but full of energy and sensitivity.

Some time later I had a telephone call from Dr Le Couteur, a consultant psychiatrist at Broadmoor, who had read my article on the twins and asked for my assistance in trying to get them writing again. If I could stimulate their creative talents, he thought, they might start to communicate with people around them. Apprehensively, I agreed to visit them. I arrived at Crowthorne station, derelict and overgrown with graffiti, and made my way up the hill to Broadmoor special hospital.

The forty-foot brick walls spill over the hilltop, like a fortified town designed not to keep invaders out, but the inhabitants in. This is Britain's most notorious maximum security hospital. Inside there are exercise yards, prefabricated huts, substantial ward blocks, boiler houses, and crumbling 'villas' with iron-railed balconies and barred windows. Even the landscaped garden and vegetable plots are segregated by imposing walls, like terraces on the hillside. Everywhere there are locks and the noise of keys jangling on the belts of nurses. Rapists, child molesters, poisoners, stranglers, arsonists, and mass murderers are among the 500 inhabitants. I signed the visitors' book for the female wing and was promptly reprimanded for having dared to turn back a page to squint at the names of previous visitors.

Chastened, I queued as instructed with a handful of other visitors. A tiny man was shouting hysterically at the entry desk, demanding to see his wife. He was told she was unable to see him. He was desperately explaining to the nurse at the door that he had been travelling the whole day to see her. The nurse said it was impossible. The argument was still raging when a woman in blue nurse's uniform unlocked a gate and ushered our straggly group into a visiting room. A dozen or so card tables were set out with two canvas chairs at each. The only decoration was a show case of soft teddy bears with pastel pink and blue bows, cuddly rabbits, koala bears with surprised, round eyes and a few rag dolls in smocks and bonnets – an ironic display of innocence made by the hands of the country's most violent men and women.

'June Gibbons,' another officer announced. I looked up. Two nurses were supporting the rigid figure of a girl, as though she were a coffin propped against their shoulders. The girl did not move. Her eyes were downcast, her arms hanging heavily on either side. Her face held no expression, as though all life had gone from it. She was sat down at the table in front of me. A few feet away the nurses pulled out chairs to monitor our 'conversation'.

There wasn't much to overhear. For the first quarter of an hour I began to believe that June was unable to register anything I was saying. I talked on regardless, feeling more and more self-conscious. Since arriving in Broadmoor a month ago, June had not spoken to nurses, the doctors, the speech therapist or other inmates. She would talk only to her twin sister Jennifer, who had been separated from her, placed in a separate block and was undergoing 'intensive care'.

On this occasion, sitting across the bleak little table from the lifeless June, any contact seemed hopeless. But gradually, as I talked about her writing, I could see June's eyes flickering and her mouth edging into something resembling a smile. But her words were torn whispers, her whole being was strung between a desperate need to speak and some destructive internal command which forbade her such freedom. She would start to tell me something, then suddenly gag as though an invisible presence had put its hands around her throat. Who or what could hold such power over a human being, to compel her to lifelong silence and immobility? What inner force gave her the strength to reject everything and everyone offering help or affection? What had happened to allow a potentially attractive young girl to waste her youth, not just behind the walls of a prison hospital but behind her own private defences? For one moment, as her escorts came forward to take her away, June looked at me, half pleading and half amused at the indignity of her exit, and briefly I saw her clever, observant eyes and ironic smile. I felt like a detective on the trail of a murder story. Only in this case the 'body' was still alive and the murderer some person or power in her mind.

I was escorted across a tarmac court to the block then known as Lancaster House to see Jennifer. Lancaster House 1 is the female 'intensive care' unit for patients who have failed to co-operate or cannot be controlled on more open wards. The lower cells are bare with only mattresses on the floor, their doors often locked. Jennifer had attacked a nurse who had intercepted a letter for her twin sister, June. She was now under observation. Two sets of doors were unlocked and locked behind us and I was shown to a small room which was used for visitors, since those in intensive care are not allowed into the main block.

Jennifer was escorted by two nurses twice her size. She sat at the table opposite me. The nurses settled down close by to watch and listen. I brought out my briefcase with the brochures on the writing course I was showing her. Jennifer was interested. At first, she did not speak but made abrupt little noises and glanced meaningfully at the nurses. I took out paper and pencil and we conducted our conversation in writing. Then she began to talk. Her main concern, she told me, was that she had been separated from her twin and was desperate to be with her again.

With each visit, Jennifer and June gained confidence in me. They gradually thawed in the excitement of discussing their work and started to talk more freely. They spoke in anxious, staccato bursts like machineguns, which I gradually learned to interpret.

A friendship grew across the prison walls, cool and remote like that of cats, but with trust and respect on each side. They wrote to me and allowed me to have all their diaries – more than a million words of them. They were in prison exercise books, each page filled from cover to cover in the most minute handwriting I had seen, almost too small to be read with the naked eye. There was no space left on the page, just a dense mass of words, neatly and carefully formed, like tiny black stitches running in seams, four deep to the lines.

I examined the text more closely and gradually made out words, then lines, then paragraphs. Every sentence was written in such a compelling way that it was impossible not to finish reading an entry once it was started. I was sucked into the minutiae of the twins' daily routine, and absorbed by their thoughts, dreams, reflections and often startling imagery. When they felt cold and tired, so did I. My moods swung to their rhythms. So detailed and vivid are the descriptions, I was able to live through their experiences and understand something of their troubled minds. Gradually I was able to reconstruct the sad drama of their lives.

I have talked about the case to the twins' parents and family, to their teachers, to the psychologists, psychiatrists and social workers who tried to help them, to the American boys who seduced them, to the police who arrested them and the lawyers who sought to defend them. I have spoken, too, to members of the staff at Pucklechurch remand centre, and the doctors and staff at Broadmoor. My interviews have demonstrated the impressive accuracy of the twins' diaries, even to the most minute detail. Their reporting is impeccable and their judgements and interpretations sound. On several occasions where there was discrepancy between what I was told and the diaries, on further questioning my informant had to admit that the diaries were right and he or she was wrong. Because June and Jennifer proved so accurate on the parts of their saga I have been able to check with others, it seems likely the unchecked parts are no less accurate. I have therefore drawn heavily on them for the colour and detail in this book.

June and Jennifer emerge, through these diaries, as two human beings who love and hate each other with such intensity that they can neither live together nor apart. Like twin stars, they are caught in the gravitational field between them, doomed to spin round each other for ever. If they come too close or drift apart, both are destroyed. So the girls devised games and strategies and rules to maintain this equilibrium.

The mystery of the twins lies in these childhood games which they cannot relinquish without losing one twin or the other to the real world. Such games and rituals often embody sinister meanings which can lead the players into the darker side of life. There are penalties to be extracted, forfeits to be paid. Failure, punishment, even death await those who play too long.

This is the story of a mystic bondage by which the extremes of good and evil, which both June and Jennifer personify, have led to the possession of one twin by the other. It is about the waging of a silent war which neither could win: the struggle for individuality – the birthright for which Cain killed Abel, Jacob tricked Esau, the power struggle in which Romulus killed Remus.

CHAPTER ONE

Happy Families

Families are so tragic, full of moments of disaster . . . sometimes it's about love, mostly about hate. So that's why I could see the pretence, the pretence of a jigsaw family trying to think they fit into each other: that they've got all the correct pieces. *June Gibbons*

June Alison Gibbons arrived first in the world, a fact which came to haunt her as she grew older. Jennifer Lorraine Gibbons appeared just ten minutes later. It happened on 11th April 1963 at 8.10 am at Steam Point, the RAF hospital in Aden. Their mother, Gloria Gibbons, was well pleased to have doubled her family at a single stroke: two sisters for Greta, aged seven, and four-year-old David. Of course, it was no real surprise. The doctors had picked up the entwined echoes of two babies two months ago when they had done an ultrasound scan. Gloria lay back and allowed the busy routine of the hospital to engulf her.

She remembered her childhood in Barbados; the arrival of the youngest of her five brothers and sisters. She thought of her mother, dear Betha, still very close, hurrying off to play the organ in the local church. Her father had been a book-keeper at a sugar plantation, and then kept a grocery shop at St Philips. He was a strict Barbadian father, ambitious for his eldest daughter whom he wanted to become a teacher. He was determined she should not 'mix with bad company' and had sent her at the age of thirteen to a co-educational private school, the Industry High School.

Gloria was sensible and intuitive but not interested in academic subjects. She left school at eighteen, having failed her school certificate, and learned book-keeping and typing. At one stage she took a job as an infant teacher, but loathed it. Eventually, at twenty-two, she settled down into a job as telephonist at Seawell Airport, St Philips. There, two years later, she met the man of her dreams, handsome, debonair, nineteen-year-old Aubrey Gibbons.

Aubrey was the son of a carpenter, the eldest of six children. His home life was unhappy with his parents continually, violently quarrelling. But Aubrey was bright. He did well in primary school and learned to play the family piano, his father's most significant possession. At the age of eleven he won a scholarship to Harrison College, an expensive school meticulously modelled on the best English examples. Aubrey stayed with his aunt at St Michael's, close to the school, and soon proved himself a good scholar. He even had private lessons in Greek and Latin, and achieved good marks in Latin, chemistry, mathematics and modern languages. He was an all-rounder, keen on cricket, and at fifteen was playing the organ in the college chapel on Sundays. He eventually got school certificate in nine subjects.

But things at home were getting worse. The rows were interminable. His mother packed up and left home half a dozen times, but always she returned, miserable, defeated. Two of his brothers died. Then, when he was eighteen and set to take his higher school certificate, his mother died after giving birth to her seventh baby. Aubrey was desolate; guilty that he had been away, and filled with bitter hatred of his father, so deep that still, nearly forty years later, he will not write to or acknowledge him. All thoughts that he should fulfil his family's dreams to become a doctor or lawyer evaporated. He left school. 'I feel I failed,' he now admits. 'I was a disappointment for my family. I'm not what they wanted me to be.'

But at least he found a job quickly, as a meteorological assistant at Seawell Airport where he met Gloria. They were married on 8th December 1955. He was twenty-one and she was twenty-five. The following year Gloria had her first child, Frank, who died as a tiny baby. A year later Greta arrived, and nearly two years after that, David.

Advancement in the tiny meteorological section at Seawell was slow, almost infinitely so. It seemed quite well paid when he had started, but now with a wife and two children, Aubrey needed something better.

After long deliberation he decided to cut free from the Caribbean and emigrate to England to join Gloria's brother in Coventry. He arrived in January 1960, took the aptitude tests for the RAF and was accepted. Gloria and the children followed in July to start camp – following as Aubrey moved from base to base.

A service family's life is never easy; harried by continual moving from one temporary home to another, making do with other people's possessions, finding and losing friends at every move, suffocating in the social claustrophobia of a military base. For Gloria, it was that much more difficult because she was black and there were then few black families in the RAF.

It was different for Aubrey. Harrison College had taught him the ideals of the English gentleman. Now, as a member of the RAF, he set about showing he was as English as any of them, or more so. He enjoyed a drink and discussion with the boys. He played cricket for the base's team. He wanted, needed, to be liked and accepted. But already Aubrey's yearning for social respectability was having its effect on the family, which saw less and less of him. He involved himself very little with the children. Like many Barbadian men, he felt his contribution to family life began and ended with providing shelter. Everything else was up to Gloria.

She had a tough time, alone with two babies and two small children in a service apartment with few friends and little support. June, although the older, was the weaker of the twins and in the early months Jennifer outstripped her at all the milestones of development – sitting, crawling, walking. Even as babies, Gloria noticed, they wanted to do everything together. She breast-fed them for the first months and they exhausted her by their struggle to feed at the same time.

Just before Christmas 1963, Aubrey was posted to a base at Linton, on the river Ouse in Yorkshire. There, the twins grew into toddlers, charming their family, smiling and laughing. It was an easier time for Gloria with Greta and David both attending school. The twins were full of life and played happily together, deeply involved with one another, but they were late talking. By the time they were three years old they were only able to put together the simplest two- or three-word sentences and even the few words they knew were indistinct. But Gloria was not greatly worried. She knew that twins were often late talking, and in every other way they were healthy and happy.

In 1967 she became pregnant again, and in the following year her fifth child, Rosie, was born. June and Jennifer were at school now but still did not speak much. At the end of their first year the teacher wrote in her Service Children's Report about June: 'At first rather unsettled and inseparable from her twin sister. Has settled better since. Is a little more independent. If upset will cry for a long time. Will not talk to me. Talks to other children.' A year later the report was a little better. 'June is beginning to write but still lacks confidence to speak or read.' The teacher added an observation which was to follow the twins' progress throughout their schooling: they 'tend to be too content to do very little. They show very little initiative or imagination.' The school decided to send the girls for weekly speech therapy, but it does not seem to have helped. They brought home exercise books filled with sounds and words they were meant to practise, but never did. Gloria clung to her belief that they were just a little backward and would catch up in their own way. In any case, with five children to care for, there was little time for practising grunts and whistles. So by the time they were eight, although their school reports refer to them as reading fluently and writing, the twins were still not speaking. 'Jennifer,' says her report, 'has no oral response, but writes diligently.' June is 'still silent and won't converse. Both of them are very shy.'

This charitable explanation became the acceptable excuse for the twins' odd behaviour. It followed them to their next school at Braunton, Devon, where they went when Aubrey was posted to RAF, Chivenor, in 1971. The twins, then eight and a half years old, found themselves in a new environment with no familiar faces, and little sympathy among their peers for children who did not speak properly and had black skin. They were laughed at in class and bullied and baited in the playground, thus forced to cling even more tightly to the safe world of each other, to strengthen the walls of their twinship and to withdraw behind them. They stopped trying to communicate with outsiders and, even within the family, became more isolated. Gloria and Aubrey would hear them chatter endlessly to one another and to their dolls, but could only make out an occasional word. It was as though they had deliberately distorted their speech into a secret code to prevent others from understanding it.

Private languages used by twins are not unknown. A French film director made a film about the secret language of a pair of twins in San Diego, California, in 1977. From early childhood, these twins had invented a 'code' which sounded so foreign that at first people thought they had developed a new language. Like the Gibbons twins, these two girls, who called themselves Poto and Cabengo, spoke rapidly in staccato bursts. By slowing down the tapes and analysing them word by word, their secret 'language' turned out to be ordinary English mixed with German (their family was bilingual), but spoken fast and with many repetitions and such altered stress on individual syllables that the words took on the opposite emphasis to normal. In the case of Poto and Cabengo, once their game was discovered and they were separated and placed in different schools, they abandoned their own language and spoke normally.

With June and Jennifer, there was no such easy outcome. Their lack of speech to outsiders and their high-speed 'patois' between themselves were only symptoms of the more serious conflict which soon dominated their lives. No-one knows when it began, whether it started in infancy, or in their first school, or at Braunton, but by the time they were eleven the battle lines had been firmly drawn both against the outside world and internally, between twin and twin.

Aubrey was by now becoming concerned about the twins. They had never spoken to him or their older brother and sister, beyond a few monosyllabic replies. He would be reassured for a time by friends, family and teachers that it was just a matter of time and they would 'grow out of their shyness', but he was never really convinced and felt an expert should examine his twin daughters. He was worried, too, because there was to be another disruption in their lives. The Chivenor base was to be transferred to Haverfordwest in West Wales. Many of the servicemen were worried about the schooling of their children and, to reassure them, a deputation of Haverfordwest teachers and educationalists visited Braunton and talked to the parents. One of the speakers was Tim Thomas, the educational psychologist for Pembrokeshire. Aubrey Gibbons stayed behind after the talk and discussed the twins' problems with Thomas, a likeable, caring man, then in his early thirties. He thought they should go to a normal school where they should be separated and that adolescence would resolve their problems. Aubrey was reassured and felt the girls would get any treatment they needed in their new school.

The Gibbonses gradually settled into their Welsh surroundings. Aubrey, by now a corporal, commuted each day to the base at Brawdy where he was working as an assistant air-traffic controller. Greta, who was seventeen and had two O levels, managed to get into Haverfordwest Technical College for a secretarial course. David and the twins went to Haverfordwest County Secondary School, along with fifty or sixty other 'Brawdy people' – the children of servicemen at the RAF station and the nearby US Navy base. Rosie went to the local primary school.

But tensions were rising at home. In Devon, when they were eight, the twins still used to reply, although laconically, to some of Gloria's direct questions. 'What did you do at school today, Twinnies?' she would ask. 'Nothing much,' one or other would whisper, then bound away, giggling. In Haverfordwest that response would have seemed loquacious as the girls lowered their curtain of silence. They turned the Gibbons' chatty family table into a Trappist refectory. Direct questions asked at mealtimes received no acknowledgement except an occasional nod. The twins took no part in family discussions but bowed their heads, eyes fixed on their plates, their faces without expression, tight and drawn in denial of the world around them. To Aubrey, Greta and David they would not utter even a syllable, but they did talk and play with Rosie, the baby of the family.

Aubrey had tried to teach the girls draughts, a game at which he was champion for the county of Pembroke. They seemed to enjoy it, but though they would laugh when someone made a mistake, still they did not speak. Aubrey was gradually becoming impatient with them; they were an intrusion on the family and a threat to his self-esteem. But rather than allow his anger to lash out, he withdrew from the silent civil war that was tearing his family apart, and spent more time away from home.

At school, the twins' silence was noticed immediately. The headmistress, Beryl Davis, who prides herself on getting through to children, asked them to her office to get their names and ages for the school records. 'They stood one behind the other, as in a queue,' she recalls. 'They would look at your chest, straight through you and would not answer. It was most unnerving. Then June would whisper a muffled reply. I thought that given a little time they would thaw out.' But the twins remained frozen. No teacher or pupil ever heard them talk. They were never known to go to the lavatory, did not eat at school and were always together.

They had no friends, partly because of their different behaviour, and partly because they were the only black family in the school. 'They were pretty little girls,' remembers Michael John, one of the teachers at the school, 'their hair in plaits, their skin glowing with cleanliness. They were dressed alike in the school uniform – grey pleated skirts, white shirt and navy tie. I asked one her name. She said nothing. One of the boys said: "She's ignorant. She doesn't speak to anyone." ' But this sort of behaviour did not bring them favour with teachers or pupils. They were accused of 'dumb insolence' by teachers and bullied by the other children.

Because of the bullying, the twins were allowed to leave school five minutes early. 'One day I was in with the school secretary, whose window looks out on the playground,' says Cyril Davis, their headmaster, 'and there were the twins doing a kind of goose-step, walking ten yards one behind the other, very slowly as though in some strange stately procession. "Do they always walk like that?" I asked the secretary. "Yes," she said. I couldn't believe it and jumped in my car to see how long they would keep it up. I followed them through the town, still doing their dead march, one following the other.'

The twins made only one friend, Diane Williams, an asthmatic, religious girl, the youngest of eight children of an ardent Pentecostal Christian family. Diane and the twins would go shopping and walking in the town on Saturdays, or occasionally they would go to the Williamses' house in Baring-Gould Road for tea. 'They were beautifully dressed, always clean and tidy,' says Mrs Williams. 'They were good little girls, too. But whenever I entered the room they would go quiet. They never spoke to me and if anyone came to the house they would disappear.' They did speak to Diane. 'They were quite normal to me,' she recalls, 'but I never saw them talk to their parents. Their speech was a bit fast and strange, but I soon got used to it and we chatted away. They weren't happy. I felt sorry for them.'

Predictably, without speech, June and Jennifer did not do well at school. Both were put in the remedial band but in 1976 June was doing so well she was transferred to the B band where she came thirteenth in general English, third out of seventy-four in history and fourteenth out of seventy-two in geography. Her mathematics was very poor. Jennifer was less successful and remained in the remedial form close to the bottom of the class. The school operated a scheme for assessing the children's social abilities in which each teacher gave a rating for certain personal qualities. June emerged as the more balanced and likeable as well as the more intelligent twin, but was found 'sadly lacking in self-confidence and sociability'. Jennifer was rated low in co-operation but had one surprising quality, noted by all the teachers – leadership.

The staff were driven to distraction by the twins' behaviour, their lack of speech, their failure to react. When attacked they would stand facing one another, one arm on the other's shoulder, huddled together to protect and give strength to one another. 'They were like bits of straw in the eddies of a stream,' says Michael John, 'you'd find them huddled together in back corners out of the flow of life. They were always apart from everyone else, trying to be invisible, yet they attracted attention in a way I disliked. I've had 6000 children go through my hands in thirty years and I've encountered only four I felt were evil. One was a boy who raped the daughter of a best friend, another eventually shot a boy, a third was found guilty of rape and assault. The fourth was Jennifer. I felt that June should not be allowed to mix with her or come under her influence. The bad one would not have been so bad had she not been able to draw strength from her twin, and the other would have been normal.'

Whatever the views of individual teachers, the extraordinary thing is that the school took no action. 'They never stepped out of line,' says Cyril Davis, the headmaster. 'They never broke any rules and we had no disciplinary problems.' Nor had the school been alerted by reports or a follow-up from Tim Thomas, the educational psychologist whom Aubrey had spoken to in Braunton. Davis claims that after two years of getting no human response from the twins the staff were desperate and he summoned the parents. Gloria defended her twins with the usual argument: 'They're just a little shy.' Davis claims that he got no hint from Gloria that the twins did not speak at home and assumed they behaved normally there. 'The parents couldn't account for the twins' silence in school,' he says. 'Their attitude was "What does it matter if they're learning OK?" '

There the matter might have rested had it not been for a perceptive school medical officer, Dr John Rees, who visited the school for routine tuberculosis vaccinations. June and Jennifer queued up with the other children, moving carefully, anxious not to do anything which might draw attention to themselves.

'It's a bit like a cattle market, hundreds of kids, shuffling past you. "Does it hurt, doctor?" Giggles. Reactions of all kinds. I remember the day I first came across the Gibbonses,' recalls John Rees. 'There were these white arms and suddenly there was a black one. That was unusual. There were very few coloured people in that part of the country. I grasped the arm in my usual friendly fashion, with one hand, needle in the other, and was about to make my usual jolly quip when I looked up and saw the child staring straight ahead of her.' The quip died on his lips. He gave her the vaccination but even as he did, detected no response. 'It was not like the casualties I had seen in the army, not like anything I had experienced in my life before. There was nothing there. The word "zombie" came to me then and does now. The little negress looked through me as though she were in a trance.' Two or three down the line, he saw another black arm. He looked up and there was the same impassive face, the same trancelike stare. His usual ebullience could not cope with the degree of unease with which the twins filled him.

Dr Rees was so disturbed by the sensation of their 'dead' arms he asked for an appointment with Cyril Davis, the headmaster. 'He had about 1500 children at the school and didn't seem to have much information on the twins,' says Rees. 'At least, not the kind of information I was interested in. He told me they were a "funny pair and didn't communicate much and didn't talk to the teachers". They hadn't been referred to the school welfare officer because they were well behaved and kept themselves to themselves. I recall the headmaster said they were doing the work all right. I asked permission to see the parents and my office made an appointment with them.'

Rees drove to Furzy Park and was pleasantly surprised by the interview. He found Aubrey and Gloria both intelligent and helpful. They both spoke well and took equal part in the discussion. They told him the twins seldom spoke but would come in from school and rush up to their bedroom where they would 'twitter away' in a language so fast that Gloria could not understand. What surprised him was how such otherwise perceptive parents were not 'unduly worried' by their daughters. Later he heard that West Indian families expect strange behaviour in twins, and he thought their lack of concern was probably cultural. He asked their permission to refer the twins to Dr Evan Davies. 'I passed that particular buck on to him,' says Rees. He wrote to Davies:

The present home situation is that the twins mix very little with the family except at meals, preferring to go together to their bedroom where they will read and play. Very occasionally they will visit friends' houses, but not to parties, and one girl of their age will visit them in their home now and again. When the girls talk to each other the parents can only recognize the occasional word, but can make no sense of the conversation. On returning home from school they volunteer nothing, but will answer questions more or less intelligibly.

Gloria had clearly not been able to tell Dr Rees the full extent of the girls' speechlessness. But she did admit that, after discussing the problem with their local GP, Dr James Bowen, he had examined them and suggested they might be tongue-tied. Tongue-tie is a congenital defect in which the tissue which connects the tongue to the base of the mouth is 'overgrown', making full movement and control of the tongue difficult and hence causing speech defects. Relatively minor surgery can cut away excess tissue, giving the tongue more freedom of movement. Certainly, the twins were somewhat tongue-tied, since they could not protrude their tongues beyond their lips. Dr Bowen had referred them to the surgical outpatients' department at the Withybush hospital in Haverfordwest in May 1976, six months before Dr Rees became involved, but nothing had yet been done.

The idea of a physical cause for the twins' behaviour was a comfort for Gloria and Aubrey and much less threatening than the alternative hypothesis that they had simply decided not to talk. But John Rees noted: 'Both babies were breast fed without difficulty, which would tend to preclude any tongue-tie sufficient to seriously interfere with speech.'

Rees sent his observations on the twins to Dr Evan Davies, Consultant Child Psychiatrist for Dyfed, who invited the family along to his clinic at the County Health Office, Haverfordwest. Dr Davies is a reticent Welshman, well qualified and innately cautious. He was born in 1933, trained as a doctor at the Welsh National Medical School in Cardiff, was swept into the army for his national service and then took up psychiatry. In 1966 he had become consultant child psychiatrist in Haverfordwest with responsibility for 56,000 children in the area.

Dr Davies knew the problems of elective mutism for he saw a case perhaps every two years, and he was not keen to become involved. Elective mutism is a rare condition where a person chooses not to speak, although physically able to do so. It usually occurs in only children of overprotective mothers, or can follow emotional trauma, often only for a short period. Although twins are late in talking, there are only a handful of recorded cases of elective mutism in twins.

It was late November 1976 when Gloria, June and Jennifer Gibbons, muffled in winter clothes, arrived at the clinic to play out their charade with Dr Davies. It took some time for them to remove their coats and settle down. The girls appeared to move only if he turned his back or left the room. He could hear the rapid shuffling which ceased the moment he turned round to find them with demure expressions and downcast eyes. He did not intend to be drawn into this odd little game they were willing on him, so he carefully avoided turning away from them. He ran through the girls' history, asking the appropriate questions. Not a flicker of interest or understanding crossed the girls' faces. There was no communication.

Embarrassed by the silence and eager to plead for her daughters, Gloria answered all the questions in a crescendo of detail, swamping Davies so that he could elicit nothing from the twins, and could not even be sure they could speak fluently when not overheard, as their mother claimed. Davies described the interview in a letter to Rees:

While I was unable to engage them in any verbal exchange, they did reply to questions with an almost imperceptible nod. With some encouragement they drew for me and Jennifer appears to have a degree of artistic talent. Although June was the smaller twin, she appears to be the dominant member and usually initiates activities.

Evan Davies seems to have got it wrong. Every other observer of the twins regards Jennifer as the leader. 'The trouble was I could never tell them apart,' Davies now admits. 'I had the feeling I was being presented with a difficulty partly because they were unlike children I had ever seen. I attributed my failure to the cultural gap.'

Davies was sure the Gibbons twins were elective mutes and that they probably had a speech impediment that prevented them from speaking fluently and that had triggered their mutism. The case, he recognized, would be even more difficult than the usual elective mutism because the twins would get strength from one another. 'Treatment under these circumstances,' he wrote to Rees, 'presents a considerable challenge which I am reluctant to accept.' Instead, he referred the case to Miss Ann Treharne, chief speech therapist at Haverfordwest.

Up to this point nobody was absolutely sure whether the twins were physically incapable of speaking or were, as both Dr Rees and Dr Davies believed, perfectly capable of speech (although probably with some impediment) but simply chose for psychological reasons not to

CHAPTER TWO

Mocking Birds

It was more comfortable just nodding heads. Words seemed too much; if we were suddenly to talk, it would be too much of a surprise. June Gibbons

Eight days after their fourteenth birthday, on 19th April 1977, the twins arrived in Pembroke to start at their new school. The Eastgate centre is a grimy stone Victorian Gothic church school perched beside a mammoth roundabout to the east of the town, rocked by juggernauts on their way to Pembroke Dock. Behind the school the tarmac playgrounds, bounded by a stone wall that follows the line of the old town walls, tumble steeply downhill into the green lap of playing fields. The school was converted in 1972 when the special education centre was set up to cater for those children whose behaviour was too disruptive for any other institution. Inside the main building, there has been a transformation. Everything is casual and open plan. There are two adjoining classrooms and an area off the main classroom which acts as a library, an expensive investment in the dozen or more disturbed children the centre serves.

The teacher in charge at Eastgate when the twins were there was John Harry, an ex-art and pottery teacher, an agreeable man in his mid-thirties, who is remembered as always anxious to please. The twins' special teacher was Cathleen Arthur, then in her late twenties. She was a very different character from John Harry, ambitious, forceful and enthusiastic, a 'bonfire' type of woman as one colleague describes her, with 'jet black hair and smouldering eyes'. She was the daughter of a successful local farming family who had sent her to Dr Williams School in Dolgellau, a well-known Welsh girls' public school, now closed. She was a bright student and became head girl. From there she went to the Central School of Speech and Drama in London where she met her husband, Tim Arthur, and married him in a Druid-style ceremony on Primrose Hill, so full of 'colour' that the details were revealed with relish in the *Sunday People*. Tim Arthur took a job in Exeter where Cathy taught in the Dryden Children's Unit at Exvale Hospital, a special unit for disturbed adolescents run by Dr Christopher Wardell. It was there that her gift for relating to troubled teenagers emerged and she decided to make her career in special education. In 1972 the Arthurs found an old farmhouse near Haverfordwest which they decided to renovate. It was at this time Eastgate was being set up and Cathy, full of ideas from her experience in Exeter, was appointed one of the three teachers.

The teaching staff at Eastgate work closely with the educational authorities and the social workers, integrating all the services for the benefit of the pupils. The whole team would be present at case conferences to discuss the progress of individual children and to decide the next steps to be taken. From the time they arrived at Eastgate, the twins' progress was monitored by a team which included Dr Evan Davies, the child psychiatrist, and Tim Thomas, the educational psychologist.

Cathy Arthur soon found the measure of the twins. During their first week they spoke to no-one, not even other children in their group. At mealtimes they were painfully slow. They would walk at a snail's pace to the serving hatch and then sit staring at their food, unwilling to eat it. 'Their physical slowness seemed to irritate the rest of the children at Eastgate far more than their lack of conversation,' Cathy Arthur remembers.

In an effort to get them to speak Cathy asked them questions on a tape recorder and left them with the machine to reply, which occasionally they deigned to do. The breakthrough came when she suggested to a West Indian teacher friend that he should chat to the girls on tape. 'Am I married?' he asked. 'Have I got kids? Come on,' he chided them, 'ask *me* something.' When he and Cathy played the tape back, they thought at first it had been left blank. But just before the tape ended, they heard a giggle, followed by a clear voice: 'What can we say?' There was another long pause. 'God knows, God knows,' came the reply. From then on 'God knows' became an Eastgate catch phrase.

Cathy Arthur had shown that the silent twins were able to speak when they so chose, and that they had only mild speech impediments. During the next few months she worked hard to break their block, arguing with them, rewarding them with praise and encouragement. June did not respond greatly, but Jennifer began to make progress. In May, Cathy visited Gloria Gibbons in Furzy Park. 'She saw a marked change in the twins. They came home from Eastgate happy and smiling and would talk to her about what they had been making in school.'

Cathy had helped them make two rag dolls, Dorothy and Demelza, stitching the red and white dresses and looping up their black hair on white cloth faces. 'The twins weren't much good at sewing,' she says, 'but they took great delight in making things with me.' She observed the twins in every situation she could.

Every morning at 8.45 Cathy drove up in her white Mini to fetch them from a bus stop half a mile from their home. They never went into the bus shelter but waited outside, even in the rain, to avoid standing close to other people. They were always there on time, but when she arrived neither would be first to get into the car. The girls often remained standing stiffly on the pavement. Cathy would have to get out of the car, take one twin by the shoulders and fold her knees from be-hind, then push her in. The other would follow as Cathy returned to the driving seat. Once they were in the back seat there was a further hiatus as neither girl would shut the door. 'If there had been two doors, it would have been all right,' explains Cathy. 'I always got the feeling it depended what happened on the way down the hill from the house. If something had gone wrong between the girls, they wouldn't shut the door.' Often Cathy would have to get out again to shut it herself. Twenty to thirty minutes after she first drew up they were ready to set off towards Eastgate.

The journey from Haverfordwest to Pembroke was far from jolly. The twins sat stolidly in the back as though riding in a hearse, while Cathy pattered away to alleviate the gloom. 'Look at that horse,' she exhorted, but there was no reaction. It would take several minutes for them to reach silent agreement on how to respond. Then she would see in the driving mirror two dark heads turning simultaneously in the direction she had pointed – a mile or so too late.

It was the same at school. Realizing that the twins' 'synchrony' depended on constant monitoring of each other's movements, Cathy attempted to stop them watching one another by making them do keep-fit exercises. 'I would get them to try to touch their toes,' she recalls. 'With their heads dropped down they couldn't see each other. I thought they would then have to move independently, but instead they didn't move at all or they moved so slowly they would get stuck halfway and I would have to straighten them up.'

Horse riding was one of the few activities in which the twins showed they could move with spontaneous agility, rising and falling in the saddle and dodging branches. However, this had its hazards for the instructor. If she voiced any criticism, they would both drop the reins and withdraw completely. Then if one fell off, the other would immediately fall too.

Cathy Arthur turned her attention to less physical activities. She knew they were excited by anything to do with America, so she asked an American student to give a talk and show slides. The twins, however, sat throughout the lecture with their chairs turned to face each other. Neither so much as glanced at the screen.

She then tried to interest them in the theatre. She took them to see *The Snow Queen* and a pantomime, *Humpty Dumpty*, in Milford Haven. She carefully bought them a programme each, but her efforts were unrewarded. June and Jennifer did not read the programmes and seemed blind to the stage. When the actors rushed through the audience, all the other children turned round laughing. But the twins just sat staring ahead, the hoods of their duffle coats still up, like misplaced members of the Ku Klux Klan.

During the spring and summer of 1977, Cathy Arthur and Tim Thomas worked closely together carrying out psychological assessments of the twins with varying and erratic results. Cathy tried first the Bene Anthony family-relations test, performed on each twin independently. The child sits at a table on which there is a row of letter boxes each carrying a cardboard cut-out figure representing one member of the family. The teacher, sitting on the opposite side of the table, reads out and hands the child cards one at a time. Each card has a question printed on it: 'Who comforts you when you are ill?' 'Who likes to hug you?' 'To whom do you tell your secrets?' The subject answers the question by posting the card in the appropriate box. If he or she cannot answer or the answer is nobody, he puts the card in an extra box called 'Mr Nobody'. The cards from all the boxes are counted to give a profile of family relationships. June made some effort to put the cards in the family boxes, but thirty-eight out of eighty-five went into Mr Nobody, which was interpreted as showing considerable denial of feelings. Jennifer, after carefully reading and considering each card, posted fifty-two items into Mr Nobody, showing a still poorer relationship with her family.

Both girls scored well below average on the Wechsler Intelligence Scale, with June rather better than Jennifer. Both did well in the comprehension test, poorly in vocabulary, and refused even to try the arithmetic. The personality tests gave confusing results, some showing them to be socially maladjusted, depressed and withdrawn, others rating them as well balanced, 'independent without need for outside sympathy or advice'. The projection tests, in which they were required to build a story around a picture, showed 'inadequate perception of the situation, and poorly defined characters'. Any conflict, anger or sexuality explicit in the pictures was ignored by both girls, as well as anything which resembled competition. They wrote 'mild adventures', concluded Cathy Arthur, 'with no interaction and with light-hearted facile endings'. These were the girls who two years later were writing novels and short stories filled with sex, tortured conflicts and emotional tangles which frequently lead to the death or suicide of one or other of the main characters.

Tim Thomas, who gave the girls a weekly therapy session, recognized they were distressing him more than he was helping them. Thomas, who was then thirty-two, six feet tall, with a pale complexion, brown hair and a beard with a hint of Celtic red, means well by everyone. He covers any embarrassment by sighs and rubbing his hands, as though to reassure himself. 'Ah, lovely . . .' he repeats with a strong Welsh lilt during any lull in the conversation, to indicate that despite all the evidence to the contrary, everything is going well. Tim Thomas was brought up in a Welsh-speaking home in Newton, Montgomery, where his father was a clerk in the National Provincial Bank. He took a degree in psychology at Bristol University, spent five years on postgraduate training and was appointed educational psychologist for Pembrokeshire, a post he still holds. He lives in a rambling, mediaeval merchant's house near the centre of Haverfordwest with his English wife, a language teacher, three delightful, whispery Welsh-speaking children and two faithful dogs.

Tim Thomas clearly recognized that the twins were winning the struggle at Eastgate. In his weekly sessions he had tried, at first, to win their confidence by doing all the talking and demanding nothing from them, patiently explaining how important it was for them to make an effort to speak. The girls sat seriously watching him, quite still, making no response. He began to find himself chattering on to the menacing pair, beating his voice against the wall of their silence until he felt almost hysterical.

He decided to change his tactics and to play the girls at their own game. In the next session he sat there doing nothing, waiting for them to break. The twins remained composed and still. Tim felt himself shifting and restless in the screaming silence, desperate to say something. 'They won hands down,' he told the team afterwards. 'I waited for them to say something, but they outsat me. I can't take it. Watching them nodding, crossing their legs and uncrossing them. They've got their timing to such a fine art, I think I'm watching some crazy variety duo.'

It was hard to believe that these girls were capable of any ordinary childish relationship. But Cathy Arthur remembered that Gloria had told her the twins and their little sister Rosie would play happily for hours. She might discover clues to their behaviour if she could observe the twins playing together or with a younger child when they believed they were not being watched. She arranged to use the therapy room at Eastgate which has a one-way mirror and a pair of video cameras, and made a film of the twins playing. It is a remarkable record.

Cathy filmed herself trying to encourage the twins to make music with some percussion instruments. 'I wanted to see whether they would dare make a noise. They were always so frightened,' she says. The session was as she had predicted. She patiently showed them how to bang the drum in various rhythms, but neither responded. She left the room and sent in Alison, a bouncy little girl the twins liked, who immediately grabbed a drumstick and began banging and laughing. The camera focused on June as the muscles on her face began to relax and a lovely mischievous smile crept up behind the mask. Jennifer's expression, too, bubbled slowly into laughter. Glancing around her, as though half-aware of the hidden cameras behind the glass, June lifted a stick and brought it down with a crash on the cymbal. There was a moment's suspense as both girls heard the noise vibrate through the room, broken by a delighted squeal from Alison. The twins joined in the merriment.

Then Cathy returned, curious to see what happened when an adult entered the room. As she expected, the twinkling eyes disappeared as though steel visors had closed over the twins' faces. Their arms became rigid. They stood like toy soldiers, waiting for her to leave and for Alison to find the key to wind them up again.

Cathy also made audio tapes of the twins' conversation when they thought they could not be overheard. She was curious to know whether, like many twins, they too had developed their own private language. June and Jennifer's private conversation sounded more like the twitter of birds than the voices of human children. Even Gloria could not make it out, apart from a few words. It sounded as though they were talking very rapidly, so Cathy played the reels of tape back at different speeds and discovered that the twins' private language was, like that of the San Diego twins, only everyday English spoken at enormous speed, with subtly changed stresses on many words.

Although Cathy Arthur was making some inroads into the twins' problems, there was a growing sense of exasperation among other members of Eastgate staff, who suspected they were being made fun of by the two 'mocking birds', and that, like some supernatural influence, the girls were gradually taking control. Somehow the twins' behaviour had created a web of conflicts and rivalries among the once cohesive team. Cathy Arthur and Tim Thomas could see that the situation was deteriorating, and the twins were making very little progress. They considered the evidence. The girls drew their strength from each other. Jennifer appeared to be dominant, controlling June like a robot, by brief eye signals. While they were together this circuit could not be broken; therefore, the only way forward was to separate them – a view that was upheld by the literature on twins.

Cathy Arthur decided to explore the twins' own attitude by setting them an essay on separation. Surprisingly, they both seemed to be in favour. June wrote on 6th October 1977: 'People keep telling us to change, to turn over a new leaf but we are waiting for each other to start first, so if we separate none of us will know if we changed first . . . if we separate now the future will be good for the pair of us.' Jennifer's views were the same: 'We think it best if we separate. We are both awaiting each other to talk and change. If we separate we will not know whether any of us have done it first. We both fight for the best things. We are both willing to lead our own lives but when we are together we just keep depending on each other too much.'

When Tim Thomas floated the idea of separation among his colleagues, he found quite formidable opposition. To test its strength, he and Cathy Arthur engineered a case conference on 5th December 1977. Dr Evan Davies was in the chair. The Eastgate staff were all there, together with two social workers, two people from the adolescent unit in Carmarthen, and Brian Wilcox, the county's deputy head of special education.

The proposal was that one of the twins should be sent to the adolescent unit at Carmarthen, which came under Evan Davies. He was unenthusiastic about the separation. But Cathy Arthur and Tim Thomas were prepared. They screened the video of the twins for the visitors from the adolescent unit. They presented the girls' essays asking to be separated and, at the same time, they attempted to draw the sting from their opponents' argument by emphasizing this was only a trial, a 'first-stage separation' for the twins. 'We have to introduce reality into their ideas about separation,' said Tim Thomas, gaining eloquence. 'They are dying in each other's arms and we must save one of them, even if it is at the price of the other.'

'I won't go along with this. It's inhuman, it's too cruel,' said Mary Garrett, who had lost a twin sister at birth. Suddenly, true colours were revealed. It was a small-town battleground aflame with ambitions and ideals. All the frustrations and aspirations of the provincial experts were concentrated on the two girls. The team from the Carmarthen unit found the idea of separation distasteful and announced they would take both twins or neither. But the special education executive, Brian Wilcox, intervened. If both girls left Eastgate, he could not guarantee that either could be found a place there again. Davies and his team were cornered. Cathy Arthur saw her advantage. She suggested that one twin should keep her place in Eastgate, while the other went for a trial period to the adolescent unit. On this basis Evan Davies agreed to accept one girl at his unit the following Monday, 12th December 1977.

But the victory was short-lived. At his unit in Carmarthen, Evan Davies discussed the separation of the twins with his team. He was taken aback by their resistance: perhaps they sensed his own fears that the separation would destroy one or other twin. Davies believes in democratic decisions and put it to the vote. For the first time his colleagues went against what he had agreed. Late on Friday afternoon he drove back to Haverfordwest, rushed into the office of Mary Garrett just as she was leaving for home, and told her the separation was off.

Cathy Arthur and Tim Thomas did not give in. Over the next two months, they continued to campaign for separation. They persuaded Evan Davies to talk to his team to make them change their minds. Meanwhile Cathy continued to build up her relationship with the twins, mainly through the 'talk on tape' method. She would record questions and messages and leave the machine for the twins. Through their disembodied messages, Cathy was able to reach a little way into their minds. Her energy and vitality appealed to them and they became infatuated with her, each vying with the other for her attention. Watching the way they responded to praise, Cathy introduced a star scheme which rewarded the girls for good behaviour. They could earn a star for such simple improvements as a smile or a 'good morning'; for 'not waiting for the other to move first when asked to perform a task', for 'not holding your hand over your face when sitting at the desk'. 'Any talking gets a point.' While under her influence, they began to go along with the idea of separation, and even discussed it with her on tape.

But it was only the idea of separation that appealed to the twins. The reality terrified them and as soon as they realized the threat was serious they set out to resist it at all costs. They discovered a new weapon of protest – the telephone. Thomas was at home one evening, searching his paper-strewn study for a missing letter, and his wife, Sue, was playing the piano for her daughters when the telephone rang. Tim answered it. After the payphone pips there was a click and an unfamiliar voice, speaking rapidly in mid-Atlantic tones. 'Good evening, Mr Thomas. This is the twins. We're really sorry about what happened today. We'd like you to know that if you don't s-s-s-separate us, we'll s-s-start t-talking next week.'

Was it really the twins? Which one was it? His number was ex-directory. How had they found it? He rang Cathy Arthur, but the line was engaged. Next day, he found out why. Cathy had received a similar phone call, and so had other staff members. It was the first of a series of ring-arounds in which the twins tried to bargain co-operation for no separation. But they were incapable of keeping a promise and a deal was never struck.

Early in March 1978, Cathy's pressure had its effect. Evan Davies rang her to say he would take one twin in his unit. Tim Thomas broke the news to the twins. He was nervous about what he had to say and blurted out: 'I'll come to the point at once. Things aren't going very well for you here and we've decided to separate you. One of you must go to Dr Davies's residential unit in Carmarthen. The other can stay with us. You can choose who does what.'

At first the girls remained still. Then, slowly, they began to move. Jennifer gave June a menacing glower. The muscles in her hands tightened. Both their bodies began to arch and tense, their eyes fixed on each other. There was something malevolent in their postures, like cats about to strike. There was a scream, then a series of unintelligible shouts as Jennifer lunged forward and dug her long nails into June's cheek, just below the eye, drawing blood. June replied by clutching her sister's head with such ferocity that chunks of wiry black hair fell to the floor. Before Tim Thomas could react, they were out of the room, chasing each other. Their screams grew louder and edged with anguish. Tim Thomas rushed out and prised the girls apart. The forces locking the two together disturbed him. In combat, the girls possessed remarkable strength, but once separated, that strength fell away, leaving them as limp as two rag dolls in his hands.

News of the separation triggered a new round of telephone harassment. Members of the Eastgate staff began to receive calls from phone boxes and listened again and again to the pathetic stammered message: 'We p-p-p-promise to talk if we c-c-c-can b-both stay at Eastgate.' (The origin of the stammer is interesting. Ann Treharne had detected no stammer when she first started to treat the children. She believes that they 'picked it up' from other children while waiting for her in the speech therapy clinic and used it later for effect.)

On 13th March 1978 the separation plan was carried through. Tim Thomas picked up Jennifer to take her to Eastgate, and some time later Cathy Arthur called for June and drove her to St David's Adolescent Unit in Carmarthen. Cathy's diary records that June was 'very frightened and crying'.

The timing of the separation could not have been worse, for four days after June was admitted the Easter holidays started and she was home again. The whole holiday the twins spent their time threatening and cajoling the Eastgate staff to end the separation. But no-one would help them and on 10th April, the day before their birthday, they were separated again. June retreated into a state of anguish from which no-one at the residential unit could rescue her. 'Everybody tried to offer her warmth and understanding but she would stand on her own, an isolated, tragic figure,' says Vivian Hughes, the teacher in charge. June's fifteenth birthday was the worst day of her life. She ignored the cards and presents. She almost ceased to move at all, holding herself rigid like a small animal under threat. Evan Davies came into the ward in the morning and found her still lying in bed. 'I tried to jolly her up by saying that I would have to lift her out personally. But the joke was on me. It took two of us to lift her out and then we had to prop her against the wall like a plank.'

'I shared a room with two other girls,' recalls June in a diary she wrote some years later.

Ah, the loneliness. For I would not talk. Mentally alone . . . Hungry. Bitter. Angry. J. was in Eastgate. Enjoying her life. The joy of going home to her own bed; seeing her own family. Eating familiar food. I had to suffer the torment of listening to strange conversations; eating strange food. And even then I would have agony to eat it. For I would not eat with people at the table.

June attended the special school for disturbed adolescents, a rickety old house at the entrance to the main hospital. She walked each day from the ward to the school but would just stand in the doorway when she arrived. Vivian Hughes or some of the boys who developed protective feelings towards her would have to take her arms and lift her in. They would remove her coat and then very slowly, staring straight ahead, she would lower herself into a chair where she sat motionless until the end of the morning lessons. What distressed everyone at St David's were the tears that flowed silently down her cheeks. She made no sound of crying, nor any effort to wipe them away. The staff and schoolchildren used to carry boxes of tissues with them to dry her cheeks and nose but she seemed oblivious to their gestures.

June showed signs of life only at lunchtime when Cathy Arthur allowed Jennifer to telephone her. She chatted away in her fluttering speech, smiling and giggling. The phone call over, she would return to her lifeless pose. 'What struck me about her was the strength of will which lay behind her stillness,' says Vivian Hughes, who has spent his working life dealing with disturbed children. 'It seemed she was on a leash to Jennifer. There was something almost mystic about their relationship, like black magic. I felt June could have been a normal, popular young girl if she had been released from her sister.'

During the following weeks June's grief continued unabated. She began to refuse all food. After the fifth week, she did not turn up at the unit after a weekend at home. The same day Jennifer absconded from

Eastgate. To Evan Davies's relief, on Monday 8th May 1978 the separation was officially abandoned. He was not prepared to force-feed June or to watch such suffering. June returned to Eastgate for the remainder of the term.

By now their physical appearance had deteriorated to reflect their inner gloom. They were no longer chubby, identically dressed school-girls but arrived each day, their faces drab and drawn, wearing shapeless yellowed khaki sweaters which hung over their protruding shoulder blades like rags on a row of pegs. Gloria had given up her half-hour's labour every morning plaiting their hair, which was now held back in untidy chunks with anything from curling tongs to paperclips. Their underclothes, too, were a mass of ironmongery, held together by bits of metal, rope and wire.

Cathy Arthur left Eastgate during the summer to take a B.Ed. in special education at University College, Swansea. She chose as her research project a study of the twins. She undertook a twenty-four-week behaviour-modification programme with Jennifer to see if one twin when isolated from the other could learn to behave in a more accept-able way. Every second Friday Jennifer spent the day with her. She took Jennifer for long walks through the countryside, progressing to library and shopping expeditions. Jennifer walked twenty feet behind her teacher, resolutely keeping the same distance, regardless of the speed at which Cathy walked, the traffic or passers-by. Whenever Cathy turned to see if she was following, she would freeze like a latter-day Eurydice, only moving when her teacher's back was turned. It was even more embarrassing in the supermarket, where Jennifer would freeze at the till, causing an angry queue to bulge up behind her. 'Visits to castles, docks and other places of interest did not appear to be a success, partly because she would not look at any of the features to which her attention was drawn, and partly because she walked so slowly, we both nearly froze to death,' Cathy Arthur records.

Jennifer was even more resistant to being domesticated. Cathy's aim was to train her to prepare and serve a simple meal for them. But left to Jennifer, they went hungry. Even when Cathy placed a potato and a knife in her hands, she let them drop to the floor. Her attempts to make toffee and popcorn were disastrous. The only successful part of the programme was the borrowing and reading of books. Cathy also encouraged Jennifer to write her own stories based on pictures she showed her. After seeing a photograph of two parrots, Jennifer wrote this little allegory:

Once there were two parrots who were brought up to live in a zoo. Every day people would come to the zoo and see the parrots. Some times the parrots would mock the talking people and sometimes they would actually have a conversation between themselves.

The people would stand there nearly all day listening to the parrots' conversation. The people thought it was a bit weird for two parrots to talk as good as humans did.

The parrots, whose names were 'Polly' and 'Perkins', often talked of how they longed to get back to their native land. Sometimes they would ask the watchers to open the cage door and let them out. The people would often laugh and think the parrots were kidding. Some of the children who were watching asked their parents if they could take the parrots home with them. Sometimes, before the parent had time to answer one parrot would kindly say: 'We're not for sale.' Then the other parrot would say the same.

'At this stage,' says Cathy Arthur, 'I was not so interested in their future writing potential as I was to develop and build on their only form of communication: I saw this interest in writing and reading as developing an inner reserve and a means of reducing their isolation.'

Cathy Arthur had no way of knowing whether she was having any effect on Jennifer, but Jennifer was certainly affecting her. She found herself having to fight hard against 'catching' negative ways. At the end of the twenty-four weeks she retested both twins with some surprising, almost heartbreaking results. In the family relations test, both twins posted 85 per cent of the cards into the Mr Nobody box, about twice as many as in the pre-test, showing a massive decline in their home relationships. And, although the twins had had different experiences during the twenty-four-week course, perversely, they had grown more similar in personality profile. 'Treatment had no effect whatsoever on their academic attainment,' she concluded. 'It might be suggested the programme was limited in its effect.'

From then on, Cathy Arthur had little more to do with the twins. Her research was complete and she left full-time teaching to start a family. She knew the prognosis for the twins' future was poor and she felt guilty at abandoning them. She handed the responsibility for them at Eastgate to Ann Brown, a pleasant woman in her early thirties who had no training in special education. The twins had become openly defiant of the staff and less communicative. Their messages on tape were impersonal and laconic, but the aggressive tone of their written replies to questions reveal their paradoxical attitudes. June wrote:

First of all let's get one thing straight: nobody knows us really. All these things you say about us are all wrong. Nobody really knows what goes on between us two. We both know that we are individuals. We are not trying to tie one another down either. We do not depend on one another. So all the things that people say about us two, they will have to learn to keep it to themselves. It is best not to tell us what you think.

Nobody knows us more than we do. We may be twins but we are different twins. We are exactly alike in everything we do. But some people think that one of us is the trouble-maker, and that she is the boss. Boss indeed! None of us two is the boss or the leader. You may think we are different but we still think the same, and we both agree to what I am writing.

But this was precisely their problem. During their last months at Eastgate, a new dimension emerged in the struggle between them. Jennifer sought resolution of the conflict by trying to remove any discernible differences so that they would, in effect, become one human being. It was as if she wanted to take June back with her into the womb before their egg had split. She always felt herself to be the inferior twin, ten minutes younger, less loved by her parents, less favoured by teachers and with fewer recognized talents. As long as June was indistinguishable, the twins were in effect equal, and Jennifer felt safe.

June, on the other hand, longed to be different, to be the prettier, cleverer twin, the one people loved and admired. The staff decided to encourage the rift and another trial separation was planned. Under this threat, the need to keep their twin kingdom intact increased. It was being invaded by these well-meaning, interfering teachers and psychologists and Jennifer knew this was her last chance to keep June for herself. 'You are Jennifer. You are me,' she would incant again and again. June's position was intolerable. She could not survive alone, but the price was to absorb *Jennifer's* identity. Tim Thomas remembers her terrible cry: 'I am June. I am June,' as Jennifer forced her to submit.

The intensity of their struggle frightened the Eastgate staff. There was no further talk of separation nor any plans made for their future. The twins were left to spend the rest of their last year at school doing much as they wished. Nobody bothered with them except one boy, who for the next two years became their joint obsession – and downfall.

Lance Kennedy was American, and at sixteen the eldest boy at the school. He was tall, blond and full of Yankee charm. He swaggered and boasted about his criminal past: how he had been expelled from all his schools, how he had been caught in the school store room high on drugs, how he enjoyed baiting the police. The twins watched and listened.

He felt sorry for them, especially because one or two of the rougher boys beat them up. When attacked by an outsider, the girls would bury their heads in each other's arms, like a pair of hurt birds. When they were attacking each other, they would stand face to face, taking it in turn to deal their blows. Lance had never come across such strange behaviour. He made moves to protect them. 'Sometimes I would slap them across the face, just to get them to respond. They were outsiders like me in this little horror-movie town. I would have been their friend if only they had talked to me.'

But it was the one thing they could not do. He was flattered to find one day every cigarette in his pack had been inscribed with a loving message. There would be similar notes waiting for him wherever he went. He had no idea that his admirers were, as he later described them, the two 'skinny black rabbits'.

CHAPTER THREE

The Dolls' House

When I was sixteen, I was still a virgin and played with dolls. We had no friends. Jennifer and I put our whole lives in for the happiness of those little human beings. *June Gibbons*

The sun was just sliding out of a pocket of cloud as June and Jennifer made their way towards St Mary's, the most ancient church in Haverfordwest, set at the apex of a triangle at the top of the High Street. The sun breaking through was a good omen for the twins, who lived under a tyranny of superstitions and star signs. They were Aries, born under the sign of the Ram, and today, according to the charts, things were due to go smoothly.

It was June's turn to make sure the way was clear. Anyone, even an innocent passer-by, was a threat to them and they would not move until they were sure there were no curious eyes to watch. Jennifer hung back, moulding herself to the lych gate of the church. Then, as though by an invisible signal, Jennifer followed June across the road. They read the notice on the blue sign. 'Department of Employment. Unemployment Benefit Office.' It was Jennifer's turn to glance inside to make sure there was no queue, no eyes to probe and stare. Luck was with them. They went straight to the counter and June faced the clerk. 'Your national insurance number, name and address there.' The woman pointed to a dotted line on the form. June was spared humiliation. Speech was not required in the hurried bureaucratic world.

Since they had left Eastgate at the end of the summer term in 1979, no plans had been made for the twins. Because Eastgate had totally failed to help them and because they were difficult and disruptive and had been used in the internal power struggles in the school, it was decided they would not benefit from further special education. Aubrey and Gloria Gibbons were sent a short letter from John Harry, the teacher in charge, telling them how to register the girls for unemployment benefit. He added that if they needed further help, they could contact Dr Evan Davies at the child guidance centre. 'I sincerely hope the present difficulties will improve in the near future,' John Harry wrote in his closing line.

Any idea of a job open to two mute girls with only one CSE each, in a town already overpopulated with unemployed school leavers, was clearly unrealistic. Aubrey and Gloria resigned themselves to June and Jennifer being at home all day, but they had no idea how to help them: they had no inkling why their twin daughters did not talk and behaved in such curious ways. They still clung to the belief that one day they would 'grow out of their shells'. But they felt hurt by the barriers the twins put up and were getting impatient with them.

After they left school, June and Jennifer spoke to no-one except Rosie. Even Gloria, with whom they had previously exchanged a few pragmatic words, was added to the roll of silence. They became recluses, rarely leaving their bedroom, at least when anyone was around, except for their weekly trip on Tuesdays to collect the dole. They used Rosie and their mother to run errands for them: to buy stamps, envelopes, writing paper and personal odds and ends. Gloria got her orders in scrawled notes left at the top of the stairs. 'Mum. Could you get us a lined notebook *today*. Jenny,' they would write. Or 'Don't bring lunch until 4.0 pm. We're busy. Thanks June.'

The twins' behaviour hurt Gloria. She hated the rifts they were causing in the family. But she did not question their behaviour, nor what they were doing all day in the bedroom, nor why they should expect her to carry their meals upstairs and leave them outside the door for them to collect. Gloria was a woman who believed time would heal. She had been trained to put the demands of her husband and family first, and she patiently waited for her daughters to emerge from this difficult phase.

Some time ago the twins had decided they would not sit with any members of their family. If they wanted to watch a television programme they would leave a message. 'We want to see *Top of the Pops* tonight at 7.0 pm. Please leave living room door open.' They would then sit huddled on the stairs, watching the screen through the door. If anyone came out to go to the bathroom or kitchen, they would disappear, returning only when the hall was clear again.

When Greta came to visit with her new husband or on the few occasions when a visitor arrived, the twins would come downstairs and listen outside the door. They observed acutely and were aware of every small family event: the trips planned to the supermarket, the decision to buy a new kettle, discussion about Greta's new curtains or David's jobs. They sat on the stairs or spied from an upstairs window as the cars came and went. Nothing escaped their notice. Like the 'Listeners' in Walter De la Mare's poem, they heard and watched, but made no response. They were invisible presences, haunting the ordinary little house on the estate, commanding and manipulating by their silence and their disembodied messages.

Family celebrations with the twins were to be avoided. At Greta's wedding, the previous year, the twins' unresponsive behaviour had cast a blight on the whole occasion. For four hours they stood, eyes fixed on the floor, their arms hanging awkwardly in front of them. They refused to acknowledge the bride, the groom or any of the guests. They were banned from all future events.

Life under the twins' tyranny became unbearable. Aubrey and Gloria spent more and more time at Greta's home in Milford Haven, leaving June and Jennifer alone in the empty house. This made them more reclusive – and more demanding. 'I would have told them to eat downstairs or not at all,' says David, who had no time for his impossible sisters. He was determined to move out of the house as soon as possible. Greta was also impatient. 'Once when they were scrapping upstairs I bashed their heads together and threw one of them downstairs,' she recalls with pride. But Gloria felt that it was her duty to provide for them. A life in servitude to Aubrey, who also had to have his meals brought to him, in bed or in front of the television, had taught her that the only way was to say nothing and obey. She tried to keep up a jokey, cheerful front to protect her strange daughters, but she had little idea of what was going on in their minds. 'Oh, it's just the twins,' she would tell any visitor who heard the odd scufflings upstairs or noticed the two shadows pressed against the window. 'They're a bit shy, you know.'

It was not malice which made June and Jennifer reject their family. The tragedy of the twins is that they, more than any of the Gibbonses' other children, loved their mother and brother and sisters and clung to the ideal of a happy family life. They never communicated these feelings, however, as it would have been against the rules of their game. How sad that during those years after they left school, neither side could cross the divide which the twins' silence had created. How ironic that they should care so deeply about family life, when the family only thought they were rejecting them. June, in particular, wanted to tell her family how much they meant to her.

I lack something, but it's not love. I love Rosie, Greta, David, Phil, Mom and Dad. I worry about my mother. I see grief for all those years in her eyes. She is not young, but she is romantic, a child at heart. I cannot bear to die before my parents. I cannot bear to walk on the graves of my parents, put down flowers, and feel lost. And supposing I am a mother? I realize I am dying with cancer and I have three young daughters and one young son. I shall weep for them, their cosy childhood world brought to a slicing halt, like a telegram out of nowhere. 'Why us?' they will cry. 'Why me? Why not some other family?'

But June and Jennifer did not have that cosy childhood world. The Gibbonses had little in the way of family life. Displaced from their homeland, without their relations, Aubrey and Gloria found themselves isolated and insecure. The missing colour of their own culture was never replaced by life in the estates of RAF servicemen's quarters. Aubrey maintained his position as the head of the family, the Victorian patriarch; Gloria had to serve. All this might have worked in the Caribbean where grandmothers and aunts and uncles could fill the spaces. But in this gloomy outpost of Britain, with few friends and no close relations (the nearest ones were Gloria's brother who lived in Coventry and a sister of Aubrey's who lives in London), the Gibbons children grew up in a social and emotional vacuum. None of them can remember their parents taking them on an outing, even when Gloria learned to drive and Aubrey bought a car. Only on rare occasions, when a visitor came, would Aubrey bundle his family into the car and let Gloria drive them to the sea.

The first night they moved from Chivenor to Haverfordwest Gloria had been unable to do the cooking, and Aubrey took the family to eat at the Patch, as the mess at the RAF base is known. But that was only once. The rest of the time he would arrive home after his spell of duty, remove his regulation blue sweater, switch on the television and wait for Gloria or one of the children to serve his meal on a tray. According to David, he never looked at their schoolwork or watched them sing in concerts or play in matches; not because he disliked his children – he loved them very much – but because he believed that it was not a man's job to be involved in their day-to-day upbringing. At other times, Aubrey would spend the evening with a colleague and neighbour Peter Martin, playing draughts, discussing politics or joining in with the 'lads'.

Gloria was busy looking after the house and five children. Occasionally she would pluck up courage to interest Aubrey in them, but she too was left to get on with her woman's work and find fulfilment in the odd Tupperware party which she gave when Aubrey was at the base. There were no trips to the museum or the zoo, no birthday parties for the children, no weekend picnics or holidays. The only outing of the week was a visit to Tesco every Thursday night. Even on Sundays, the family tradition of going to church had been lost, and Aubrey merely listened to the church service on the radio.

So at the age of sixteen the twins, together with Rosie who shared their room and with whom they were still able to talk, created their own Happy Families, giving the dolls all the warmth and fun, the parties, outings and friends they had never known. They were firm parents to their imaginary children, and the 'ineducable' twins insisted on the standards of education and discipline which had been so lacking in their own lives.

June's doll always played the vicar. Jennifer and Rosie, who ran the Stackhouse, Winter and Miller families, had to make sure that all their numerous children, most of them twins, were properly dressed and listening to the vicar's endless sermons. 'Now, I want all of you to join me in blessing the name of the Lord,' the vicar would repeat in a twangy, born-again voice. The floor beside June's bunk bed had been converted to a church. The door was a half-open Bible, the pews were narrower books and the altar a patch of red material cut from one of Gloria's dresses. Organ music was provided from a tape recorder hidden under the bed and operated by June. The doll families spanned several generations and all of them except the one or two babies were issued with hymn sheets and prayer books, beautifully written and illustrated, like mediaeval manuscripts.

Claudia Norma and Robert Samuel Stackhouse led the choir. They were thirty-four and twenty-six respectively, twelve inches high, and parents or foster parents to six ten-year-old children, including twins Johnny Joshua Kingston and Annemarie Esther Kingston, and Thelma Kra-Zee, an orphan. Family ties and connections were complicated. New additions were swapped or adopted and there was much inter-marriage between the extended families. Mrs Nancy Ethel Winters (aged twenty-seven, formerly known as Miss Kuawn) and her husband Mr Stanwych Waiter Wilkins (aged thirty) adopted a baby at the age of three months from the Stackhouses, with the unusual name of Carrot Cabbage Winters. While Mrs Tressy Sandy Miller and Granny Win-ters (they seemed to have lost or disposed of Mr Miller) looked after twelve-year-old twins Alma and Billy Hoe Haines. Many dire things happened to the Millers, Stackhouses, Winters, Kingstons and, of course, the Gibbonses, which made frequent demands on the vicar's time.

Rosie, the Registrar of Births, Deaths and Marriages, kept account of them in her personal book, an innocent enough looking notebook but containing some gruesome events. For the medical care of the families, the girls switched roles: the dolls' house was converted to a ward as crowded as in a Third World hospital. In attendance were Doctor Gibbons (June) and Nurses Nina Tywong and Ruth Kaleski (Jennifer and Rosie). Judging by the quality – and fatality – of the surgery, they were not a very efficient team.

Samantha Miller. Aged 6. Operation on face. Never succeeded.
Anne Miller. Aged 6. Operation on both eyes. Never succeeded. Glasses worn.

Tabatha Taylor and Charlotte Miller, both aged one month, under-went equally unsuccessful surgery on their eyes. 'Docter' Gibbons dealt with the unfortunate children of her own extended family with the care and skill of Jack the Ripper.

June Gibbons. Aged 9. Died of leg injury.
George Gibbons. Aged 4. Died of eczema.
Bluey Gibbons. Aged two and a half. Died of appendix.
George Gibbons. Fatally struck down by a back injury.
Peter Gibbons. Aged 5. Adopted. Presumed dead.
Julie Gibbons. Age 2½. Died of a 'stamped stomach'.
Polly Morgan-Gibbons. Age 4. Died of a slit face and Susie Pope-Gibbons died the same time of a cracked skull.

The records became more worrying. Wesley Miller, a small doll, died of battering, and Randy and Rebecca (formerly known as Louise and Jody Miller), twins aged ten, died in 'cremation burial with fire'.

The doll families took up a lot of the twins' time. When Rosie left for school, they had to get them up, wash and dress the children and then supervise lessons, particularly the writing of essays. They had to sew clothes for them, sending Rosie to jumble sales to pick up oddments which June would then cut and stitch. This make-believe world, for a reason which must have its roots in the days of Eastgate when they watched the swaggering Lance Kennedy, was set in mid-America. The doll families, even their names, were typically suburban American with high-school kids going to discos and drive-in movies, taking Greyhound buses and entering 'blue ice competitions' or roller skating. It was a world of affluent, bourgeois parents and gangs of rebellious teenagers. The twins were intensely curious about anything American. They even sent away for a Linguaphone course in 'Talking American'. Their dolls became part of *Dallas*-type dynasties, full of the conflicts and excitements their own drab surroundings failed to provide.

They also became the means by which June and Jennifer could talk, speaking through the dolls as ventriloquists. June wrote all the scripts, then cut out and handed Jennifer and Rosie their lines. They were elegant, if highly sentimental little plays, always featuring one or other of the dolls as the main character. The dolls, too, were the heroes or heroines of the numerous short stories June and Jennifer had begun to write, and the subjects of caricatures, cartoons and illustrated books. But like the nursery stories of nineteenth-century children imprisoned upstairs with their nannies, they were full of morals worthy of the White Ribbon brigade.

This is the sad and lonely story about a boy named Wesley Gavin Miller. He was born in Philadelphia USA, the son of Mr and Mrs Miller who later divorced and gave away little Wesley for adoption. You must understand the sympathy given to Wesley until he went to live with his new parents, Mr Danny Miller and his wife Tressy. The tragedy struck for little Wesley who came all the way from Philadelphia to live the rest of his short life in fear.

Why did the Lord God pick on a little innocent boy to be slowly battered and made his life hell? Why, oh why? It was on a hot summer's day in June 1975 that Tressy and Danny Miller waited outside their American-style home to greet their new child who had flown from America with a social worker, Mrs Mckay of Washington. Two minutes later a car drew up, out came a slim young woman and pulled out by his hand was a little boy no more than 3 feet tall. he had masses of thick brown hair, freckles on his nose and a cheeky, happy face.

'Hi, Wesley, these are your new parents.'

'How do you do.' said Tressy Miller, looking at the boy. Mr Miller said nothing, but you could tell from the look in his eyes he hated Wesley from the start.

Stories like these, usually written by June, formed part of the programmes of 'Radio Gibbons', a tightly scheduled current-affairs and music channel with its own news bulletins, weather forecasts, and comment. It ran recipes for the day, household hints and advice on everything from divorce to keeping pets. 'The Living Facts of Life' was a favourite slot where June and Jennifer would discuss how to keep young and healthy, what to do about troublesome children and how to stick to a diet. The 'mute' twins took it in turns to act as news readers,

agony aunts and commentators, keeping up a fast patter which would
be the envy of many a seasoned disc jockey.

When they were not in their dolls' house under the bunk beds, or
taking them to their 'school' in the garden shed, June and Jennifer were
preparing for the anniversaries and celebrations which for them, as
with housebound invalids, took on special significance. They devoted
weeks to getting ready for Halloween. They ordered half a dozen
horrific masks, two long black wigs and a dynamo torch from a
mail-order catalogue, spent days inventing spooky stories and reading
them into their tape recorder and painstakingly wrote out riddles and
ghoulish messages.

One day when no-one was in the house, they crept out and put the
riddles and notes through letter boxes, especially in the US Navy
married quarters nearby, hoping, by chance, to find where Lance
Kennedy lived. But the other plans for Halloween began to go wrong.
The torch and wigs arrived, but the wigs turned out to be short and
brown. 'Pretty good, though,' wrote an ever optimistic Jennifer. Then
Rosie had a bout of asthma. The twins had planned to dress up in white
sheets, masks and wigs to 'trick or treat' round the estate and to use
Rosie as their spokeswoman. Hastily, they changed their plans and
recorded the 'trick or treat' message. One of them would carry the
faithful tape recorder beneath her sheet to speak for them. It worked.
By the end of the evening they had collected enough sweets and cookies
for the dolls' party they planned next day.

The twins had sent Rosie to buy two dozen balloons and a box of
candles. They blew up balloons, laid out saucers of the sweets and
chocolates they had collected and lit candles in a circle on the floor.
The girls put on their masks. They played spooky music, incanting to
their one-stringed guitar, and told macabre tales. Gloria, cooking
supper downstairs in the kitchen, wondered at the darkness and
caterwauling in the room upstairs. She was puzzled, too, about why a
pair of sheets were missing, but such mysteries had become part of her
life with the twins.

June and Jennifer had no desire or incentive to grow up. They
wrapped tight bandages around their developing breasts to keep their

chests flat: one of the rules of their Peter Pan life was that neither could wear skirts. Skirts, like speech, became a symbol of freedom from each other and from their trapped childhood. It was essential that neither could be the first to break out from their joint chrysalis to become a woman. In any case, they did not desire womanhood: they felt sorry for their mother's enslavement to Aubrey's commands, and knew that he would have much preferred his twin daughters to be boys. Wrote June:

All through my schooldays I often thought and confessed I was a boy. I got strange feeling I was a boy under all my female assets. It's as though I'd been a boy first in my life. It wasn't anything like masturbation, I kept all my clothes on for a start. But it had to be done in secret. I could do it on a chair. Just sitting up. But it was more comfortable on the floor, not really lying down leaning on my elbow. Sometimes I'd have this rude book to help me with my imagination. I would get my mom's catalogue, though, and I would turn to the women's section; see them in underwear. I don't know what I was filled with. It wasn't desire or love. It was anger and rage and jealousy that a man would actually get turned on by a woman in the nude. I was inwardly filled with an intense hate for those models; those senseless, feminine, defenceless women. I felt they were letting sex down. I hated my soul for being one. And I was so made, really, to think I had a savagely sex-mad mind of a boy, yet I had the body of a girl. The humiliations I would have to suffer as a female. All this because of Eve and that forbidden fruit. Women were to be degraded for all their life through . . .

It couldn't be called an obsession really. I left it til night time when I was in bed. After watching a great steamy film I drift up to bed, careful to keep a certain image in my head, a woman or a girl or a dead-sexy maniac after girls. I'd get into bed and make up my own story; preserve that image; dream up a scene where I wasn't taking part. It would be so fantastic, I'd be sweating and panting and everything. It'd be just like sex itself. That was what it was meant to be, but I didn't know. I wasn't actually screaming S.E.X. for sex. No way. I didn't even know what it was. That's why I was so confused. So worried. Should I seek a cure, I thought. But no-one seeks a cure for a sizzling sex life, do they?

Poor June and Jennifer, cut adrift from their parents and their peers, tortured themselves with fears that these teenage stirrings were sinful and abnormal. They expiated their 'crimes' in daily Bible study and writing moralistic stories, and in playing with their strictly bourgeois puppet families.

Underlying the 'golden world of dolls' were more sinister processes. Not only were June and Jennifer living out a perpetual childhood but they were re-enacting some strange ancestral myths. Among the West African Yoruba negro tribes from which Aubrey's family, like many West Indian families, most probably descended, there is a custom of making little carved figures or figurines, about seven inches high, to symbolize the birth of twins. According to Professor Amram Schein-feld in his book *Twins and Supertwins*, if one twin dies, this figurine is cared for by the surviving twin, who feeds, dresses and treats it as his living brother or sister. If both twins die, the mother is given consoling twin dolls, which are kept in the family shrine for generations.

Throughout their diaries, both June and Jennifer see the death of the other twin as both a tragedy and a release – the only possible resolution of their conflict. Their dolls – whom they both mutilated and adored – played the role of 'dead twins'. They lavished on them the physical care and tenderness they could never show for each other. Yet there was something macabre in their play. In between washing and dressing and educating the dolls, there would be darker moments when a body was 'swapped', a limb broken or a head removed. The doll children, too, were always bickering, fighting and ganging up against each other. As June wrote:

There was always a sense of tension in the air, even when we were all playing with dolls. Jennifer's doll used to be more popular than mine. Me and my little doll, lives apart. I felt sorry for that doll. She suffered just like me, always left out, lonely in our hearts. Rosie and J. ran away from me. I felt like a monster. I felt naked and criticized. I felt myself ugly and old, like a big sister to those kids. So, as usual, I sought retreat in the bathroom.

'June, June.' Gloria was knocking on the bathroom door. 'You've been there for two hours. Why don't you come now and have a nice cuppa?'

First of all I wept to God. Then with the little blue penknife I tried to aim at my heart and kept on imagining how sorry they would all be when they knocked on the bathroom door (it was locked). When no answer came they would look down and see blood seeping under the door. I kept seeing the look of distress on J.'s face, on Rosie's face, even my parents.

'Look, Greta's coming and if your dad finds you still in there, there'll be all hell . . .' Gloria was getting worried.

I sometimes think they knew about my inward suffering, but if I'd died that night it would have been in vain. I was worried they might be glad to be rid of me. I was worried that I'd come back as a ghost and watch them enjoying themselves (without me). Their grief wouldn't last long. I'd soon be forgotten.

Slowly the bathroom door unlocked. June emerged, her eyes fixed on the floor, her hands held behind her back for she had made small cuts on her wrists with a penknife. There was a trace of blood running down the sink. Gloria, relieved to see nothing worse, put her arm round her unhappy daughter. For once June let herself be taken over and allowed Gloria to wipe her tears. There was a scuffle followed by whispers and giggles coming from the stairs. Rosie and Jennifer were laughing at their sister. They had no sympathy. Why should they? They were getting tired of the bossy way she made them read the lines she wrote and bored with her stories and lessons. June caught the menace in Jennifer's eyes as she sat there, twisting the arms of the little vicar, June's favourite but, not surprisingly, Jennifer and Rosie's least popular doll. 'That was the night I started my revenge on J., a scheming silent revenge that never really came. I should have attacked her then but I kept my anger, my resentment bottled up. That was my weakness.'

As their fantasy world continued through the autumn of 1979, the twins started on a regime of self-improvement. Since no-one else was going to educate them, they would educate themselves. They used mail order to find ways of improving their talents, especially their desire to become writers. They found an advertisement for 'The Writing School', a correspondence course in creative writing which offered them hope not only of improving their writing style but of selling their stories. The Writing School took some weeks to reply. 'Writing School not wrote back' they record in their diaries – day after day through the drizzly

November. Eventually they do get a reply but they are worried by the £89 enrolment fee. They succeed in negotiating to share the course for a 33 per cent discount.

While they waited they both began to create more stories around their dolls. 'The Diary of Lisa Ford' was started by June, who also hit upon the best-seller theme of a light-hearted diary of a teenage boy. Sadly, she never finished it and only a few fragments remain.

While waiting for their new career to bring its rewards the girls took less and less part in the life downstairs at Furzy Park. Gloria had to deliver strange bulky parcels to their room upstairs; there were more requests for postal orders, stamps, Jiffy bags. They joined a book club and embarked on reading the literary classics from Jane Austen to Emily Brontë. Aubrey and Gloria knew nothing about all this activity: the stories, the tape recordings, the pressures of maintaining peace and order in the doll families. Nor did they know of or suspect the twins' aspirations to be writers. For them, their daughters had simply disappeared into another world. But, like poltergeists, they never did quite what was expected.

It was 7th December 1979, Aubrey and Gloria's wedding anniversary. They were still in bed in the little front room at number 35 as Aubrey did not have to go on duty until later that morning. Suddenly, there was a knock at the door. They watched as their twin daughters came into the room carrying a tray. There were two cups of tea and a partly burned omelette. At one end of the tray there was a crystal vase with a red rose, and beside it a flowery anniversary card. The girls did not speak or smile, but laid their offering on the dressing table and left the room.

The rest of December the twins spent in preparation for Christmas. They deliberated for hours, poring over the mail-order catalogue and deciding what to give the family. Their presents were generous. They ordered a mini vacuum cleaner for Greta and her husband, an electric drill for their brother. It was all very normal, except that they had never spoken to either of them all their lives.

In their other world they were equally busy, preparing for the festivities. They were sewing tee shirts and jeans for the American 'children'; wrapping and labelling presents, mainly clothes, and writing 'matchbox' books, full of Victorian sentiment, beautifully visualized and bound inside glittering Christmas tags. 'Little Books for Little Angels' was the unlikely title for the series, all marked 'Printed in the USA' and priced at around thirty-five cents. They were written by many different authors – all pseudonyms of the twins. The titles included 'I'm Just a Sweet Little Lamb' by Ruth Collins and Polly Smith, and 'We Believe in Angels' by Monica Goldberg, which starts:

On the eve of Christmas day about ten years ago, when the sky was black and the stars were shining bright, four little children were travelling home from a friend's party and their parents were sitting in the front of the car, talking and laughing. The father was driving and did not seem to be watching the road ahead of him . . .

The driver of the pick-up truck was a large man with a bald head and a moustache. The four children in the back of the car died instantly and the parents have to live forever with the regret and grief, especially the father who believed it was his carelessness which killed his four blonde-haired, hazel-eyed angels. The parents leave stockings every year on the beds of their four dead children. The presents are still there the next day all wrapped up and with the names still visible in bright gold letters . . .

The book is dedicated to the 'Parents of the Deceased'.

All the preparations, the writing and wrapping and clothes-making, reached a climax on Christmas Eve, when the dolls had their party. It was an evening affair with all the families present, looking splendid in their new clothes. June and Jennifer and Rosie lit and arranged the candles, then busied themselves among the crowd. There were mince pies for everyone, made by the twins and therefore rather burned. Then came the grand finale. Everyone gathered round the miniature Christmas tree to sing carols. It was a tuneless but very moving performance, recorded on tape. The twins, who had never opened their mouths through ten years of schooling, sang their hearts out, their faces shining in the candlelight.

June and Jennifer had decided to devote time on Christmas Day to their real family, and, as a concession, to suspend their rule not to sit in the same room as any older member of their family. They crept down early that morning and opened their presents: trousers, jumpers, slippers, angel twin soaps from Greta (did she have a sense of humour?) and two red leather five-year diaries from Gloria. Soon the little sitting room was bright with discarded wrapping paper. Rosie and the twins sat on the floor in the midst of it all, chattering away as they felt each package, guessing its contents, then gradually peeling its wrappings, and whooping and giggling with joy as its secret was revealed.

They were arranging and rearranging the family presents round the Christmas tree when Gloria arrived. 'Happy Christmas, everyone. Happy Christmas, my darlings, Rosie . . . Twinnies.' Rosie rushed over and hugged her mother. 'Merry Christmas, Mom. Thank you so much. It's just what I wanted.' The twins stood side by side, backs to the Christmas tree. They were pleased. A thin crescent smile spread in unison across their faces. Each twin presented Gloria with a package. 'Thank you so much, Twinnies,' she said, carefully taking both presents simultaneously. Was this a breakthrough, she wondered. Were the twins at last going to become part of the family, to live a more normal life? She heard the slamming of a door upstairs. 'Quickly, tidy these papers, children!'

They were all on their knees when Aubrey came in. They got up, clutching the paper. 'Happy Christmas, girls,' said Aubrey. He turned on the television set.

Aubrey's perpetual television and the twins' lack of conversation put a damper on everything. Even when David came the atmosphere froze him into an uneasy silence. The whole family sat down to lunch, pulled crackers, put on funny hats, ate turkey and pudding, drank beer and went through all the ritual of Christmas. The hours crawled painfully by, helped by *Lassie* and *Top of the Pops*. The twins sat side by side on the settee, dutifully remaining with the family according to the bargain they had made with each other.

For the twins, Christmas Day had been a success. The Gibbonses were to visit Greta and Phil the following morning and so the twins were spared too much exposure to the family. Jennifer wrote in her diary: 'At last we have made it to sit in the living room after two years. May continue to. It is a miracle that we actually survived on Xmas day after all. Everything went pretty well.'

It was the last time the twins were to join their own family. The ordeal over, the girls slipped away to their other families, still sleeping off the revelries of the night before in the dolls' house upstairs.

The twins – proud additions to the Gibbons family. *From left*: David, Aubrey holding Jennifer, Gloria with June and Greta. Aden, 1963.

'*Did they look into our cherubic faces and see the troubled desire for destruction which lay before us?*' The twins aged 2.

June and Jennifer, aged 6, with sister Rosie.

Jennifer gives June their secret signal.

Greta's wedding, April 1978. '*We ruined the wedding*' (June).

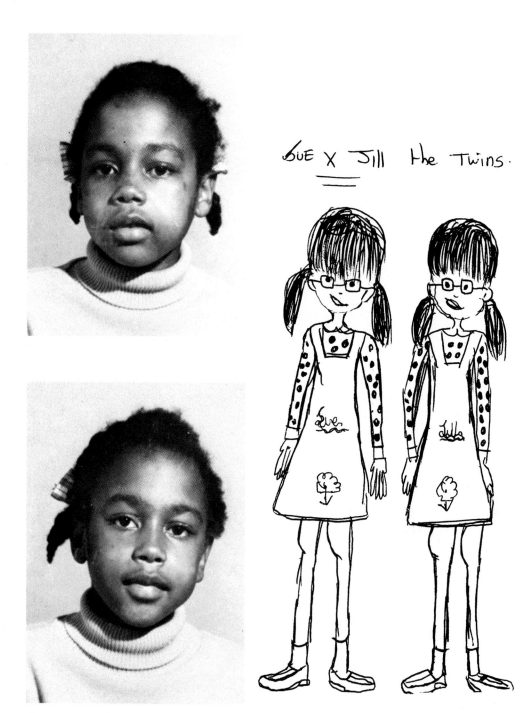

SUE X JILL the TWINS.

June and Jennifer, aged 10, at Braunton Primary School, Devon, and one of their many drawings of twins.

CHAPTER FOUR

The Glass Town

It was the most turbulent period of my youth. J. and I endlessly arguing, lost, bored, frustrated, angry. Ah, we thought, youth was passing us by.

Jennifer Gibbons

The locked red diaries which the twins had been given for Christmas became the new enthusiasm of their lives: each day they meticulously recorded every mundane detail of their existence. They confessed their secrets, expressed their hopes at gradually increasing length until the diaries with their golden clasps took on the role of friends and confessors. And as the transition took place, so the importance of the dolls declined. At the same time, another event changed the focus of their lives. The writing course they had been awaiting for many weeks arrived just before Christmas; they became, jointly, student 8201. The girls immediately set to work on their first exercises and assignments. Jennifer's diary told the whole story:

2nd January 1980. The sun is shining brightly today as I wake. Nothing spectacular happened except I commenced to read the Writing Course. I hope I become a successful writer.
6th January 1980. Interesting day. Wrote out first assignment on the writing course. Studied it hard. Rosie and us two are failing to communicate. She wants to move back into David's room. Nearly twelve years old and growing up pretty fast . . .
7th January 1980. Useless day. Sunny and frosty. I woke at 1.45 pm today. There seems no reason to get up at all. Back to school for Rosie. All three of us have virtually given up dolls . . .

They had stopped playing with their dolls, but the world they had created around them took on new dimensions. The dolls became the heroes and heroines of a series of plays, cartoons, drawings and short stories; they became characters who could not simply be picked up or put away. They acquired needs and desires of their own, compelling the twins to mammoth effort. It was as though dozens of Pinocchios had come to life, demanding the full-time attention of their creators.

The bedroom upstairs in Furzy Park became a powerhouse for these fantasies, rich and alive, while the girls looked out through their rusted window at lines of washing and bleak, rain-soaked patches of grass. The streets and slabs of terraced houses on the estate had become a graveyard from which they had to escape. They did so by building their own kingdoms of the imagination, much as the Brontë sisters had done, huddled together against the tombstones outside Haworth parsonage and the eccentricities of their father within.

The Brontës' writings also sprang directly from their obsession with toys. As Charlotte Brontë wrote in her diary: 'All our plays are strange ones. The "Young Men's" play [June 1826] took its rise from some wooden soldiers Branwell had . . .' The Brontës published a magazine for the toy soldiers, written in minute script to discourage adults from deciphering it and to make the whole book a handy size for the toys to read. These miniature books became the tales of the Glass Town Confederacy, a mythical township somewhere in Africa, guarded by the four genii – Branwell, Charlotte, Emily and Anne.

The twins, like the Brontë sisters, were cut off from the world around them, fuelled by adolescent yearning and a desire to overcome their barren surroundings. The twins' fantasy was not the swashbuckling world of Napoleonic battles nor the imperialist-dominated Glass Town: it was a *Clockwork Orange* land of violent, suburban America. Their dream city was Malibu, the place where teenagers are perpetually stoned on drugs and alcohol, parents divorce and remarry and divorce again. The 'dolls' took part in gang warfare; they were hijacked on Greyhound buses; they became terrorists involved in assassination plots; they robbed stores and murdered their parents. They were the twentieth-century teenage heroes and heroines – immature, gauche and often funny.

June and Jennifer set about learning the craft of writing in a professional way. They really did try hard. They made hundreds of lists of 'long words' and their meanings, words that rhymed, synonyms and antonyms, similes and metaphors. They drafted dozens of stories, rewrote and rewrote them to refine the characters or improve the plot.

Jennifer's life centred round the course in creative writing; she studied the lessons, wrote the exercises, waited impatiently for the anonymous tutor to return them covered in his spidery red scrawl. June was less diligent in doing the exercises, but both girls learned about key characters and plots, how to establish layers of conflict, ways of pacing a first and second climax, what motivation to give their main characters. They taught themselves grammar and punctuation, and spent hours poring over the *Shorter Oxford Dictionary* and Roget's *Thesaurus*, for which they had sent away by mail. They analysed the plots of the classics from the book club and collected phrases and their meanings from every available source.

Just as they embarked on this intensive self-education their former teacher, Cathy Arthur, paid her first visit to the house since they had left school, to present them with their CSE certificates in English (Grade 2 for June and Grade 4 for Jennifer), their only academic achievements after eleven years at school. Not a propitious start to a literary career.

They also borrowed an old typewriter from Greta and from then on there was a new noise in the house. The twins now never came downstairs when anyone was about. No visitor to the house ever saw them; not even close relatives. David brought home his girlfriend Vivienne, whom he later married. She would spend hours, even days at the house but never once set eyes on the twins. She has still never seen them.

They crept downstairs to eat only when the house was empty and made sandwiches and filled up flasks of coffee to take up to their room. While David and Vivienne made their wedding plans or Gloria organized her Tupperware parties below, they would be tapping away upstairs like a pair of noisy ghosts. The chatter of keys would go on well into the small hours. Some nights the girls would work until dawn, often sleeping in until lunch the next day before starting again. They preferred to hold their night vigils by candlelight: it made them feel more romantic.

Thelma Kra-Zee, an antiheroine of one of Jennifer's early short stories, started life as a doll character. She was an eccentric thirteen-year-old pupil at St Michael's High School, New Jersey, for whom Jennifer invented an admirer called Cricket Harvey-White. 'She is my best friend, my soul companion and my honest and artful partner,' the story begins. 'That was what I thought until the day my dear and honest friend unmistakably lived up to her name. You see Thelma's parents could not actually be described as the kind and loving type . . .' Mr Kra-Zee, a diplomat and Polish emigré, and his house-proud wife have little time for their teenage daughter. The immodest Cricket feels he can save her.

Matrimonially speaking I think I'm in pretty good shape for my age. I'm thirteen, drink plenty of milk, I'm 5 feet 2 inches tall and weigh 160 pounds. I participate in baseball and basket ball. Being born under the sign of Virgo I tend to be a bit critical about how I eat. My favourite food is lasagna. Thelma digs that stuff too. She's also thirteen, drinks plenty of milk, has a wild imagination, reads too many books and has no brothers or sisters.

The twins set almost all their stories in the United States and spent a lot of time trying to get the American detail and dialogue right. They were helped by listening to the American children on the estate, by television and the Linguaphone course they had sent away for. They also compiled their own glossary of Anglo-American words and phrases. Their doll plays and broadcasts of the previous year stimulated more detail. Jennifer undertook the major part of the course from the Writing School and assiduously read her blueprints and completed her assignments every week. Her tutor was pleased with the progress of his student number 8201A, but after the first essays and stories were returned, he questioned her obsession with American settings and dialogue. Jennifer wrote politely back:

Dear Tutor,
I am enjoying the course very much. I like doing the assignments and everything is running smoothly. About my American settings? Well, there are a few Americans living down by me, but this has nothing really to do with why I like writing American stories. I think the writing sounds almost natural, although I am capable of writing stories with English settings too.

If you prefer my stories to sound English and if you think they will sell better, inform me please.
Thank you. Yours sincerely,
Miss Jennifer Gibbons.

But Jennifer never abandoned her American utopia. Both girls had admirable independence of spirit; neither took any notice of the advice given in 'Blueprint No. 5. The Essential Fiction Know-How' on how to write for popular publications:

What Not to Write About
Editors as a class dislike drunkards, lunatics, drug addicts, prostitutes and authors. Crippled or deformed key characters, unpleasant children, adolescents who smoke and drink . . . Other editorial dislikes are mental homes, sanatoria, venereal, serious or incurable diseases, funerals are also taboo. Intense suffering should be suggested by implication, not directly described. Nor are editors in favour of divorce or suicide as solutions to human problems . . . Nor do sympathetic criminals meet with editorial approval.

On 12th January 1980, June started to write her first novel, 'Pepsi-Cola Addict', which broke every rule in Blueprint No. 5. The hero, Preston Wildey-King, a fourteen-year-old American boy, lives with his widowed mother and sister in an apartment in Malibu.

The tenement in which he lived was alternately too hot or too cold. This room remained suffocatingly hot with the contained heat of the day. Preston was thinking he was cold. His head felt neurotic and dizzy. It resembled ice. He thought he wouldn't mind if he lived in Arizona, or even Hawaii; they lived on cool beverages, and didn't care what you did. Sitting in his own pad and sipping 300 cans of Pepsi-Cola every day. The thought made him thirsty. He was thirsty. He swallowed some more Pepsi, shifted his position, and his eyes began to wander around.
There was subtle colour in his bedroom; sable bricks beside yellow brimstone drawers, beside wood painted livid red. There was colour in the faces, too, overlapping, blending and clashing so that the entire room displayed a world of zany popsingers. Style impassioned his thoughts in the form of pink graffiti that illuminated the name 'PEGGY' ten times on the freshly painted white door.

Preston is in love with Peggy, who seems indifferent to him, and is himself pursued by a friend, Ryan, who turns out to be homosexual.

Frightened by his friend's advances and rejected by Peggy, Preston allows his schoolteacher, who is coaching him, to unravel his confused emotions. June handled the dialogue in the seduction scene with great assurance and economy.

He felt Mrs Rosenberg's eyes on him for a while, then she rose silently, walked through the open door and closed it firmly behind her. Although the room was shaded from the sun, Preston began to feel sleepy. He took off his jacket absently, as his mind worked out the sums. Every part of the room fell asleep.

It awoke when Mrs Rosenberg stepped back into the room. Preston glanced up. She was clad in jeans, a white, almost transparent tee-shirt, and her hair hung loose about her shoulders. She looked refreshed as she sat down opposite. Preston found it extremely hard to avert his eyes from her. He went hot.

'You like reading, Preston?' she asked after a while.

Preston's head was spinning. He put his pen in his mouth, biting on it hard. 'I don't get to read so much.'

'Only . . . I notice your English is getting really impressive now.' Her hands gesticulated. 'You have an intelligent way of putting your words, almost as though you enjoy writing in a special way.'

Preston smiled. 'I don't know 'bout that. I just do what's expected of me.' His eyes slipped down to her cloche-shaped breasts. He was aware of a concupiscence running through his mind.

'What exactly do you like doing, Preston?'

He trembled slightly. 'Do – you mean my school subjects, or – or my main interests outside school?'

Mrs Rosenberg put one side of her sleek hair behind her ear. 'Oh, anything you specifically like doing.' She removed her glasses from her sharp-featured face; they hung momentarily in the air.

Anybody can guess what a teenage guy like me is interested in, Preston thought. 'I like listening to music, taking walks on the beach, and –'

'I, too, like listening to music, Preston. I'm not into hot or anything, I prefer classical.'

Preston eyed the framed picture of Mr Rosenberg. He was thinking he looked like his own father, taut face, wide shoulders.

'What are your other interests?'

Mrs Rosenberg replied emphatically, 'I love art. I think it's a terrific skill to draw such lovely forms of life.' She stared down at her wedding ring, twisting it. '. . . I also enjoy making . . . wine.'

There was a brief constrained silence. Preston bit his lip. 'You like doing maths?'

She laughed provocatively. The air broke up. 'Do I like doing maths?' Her hand flew to her breasts. Preston eyed them cautiously.

'To be honest with you, Preston, no I detest them. It's a real big headache.' She laughed again, tossing her hair back strenuously.

He studied her carefully. 'You look real nice without your glasses Mrs Rosenberg.'

Preston was now visiting his coach almost every day.

Mrs Rosenberg opened the door. Her eyes were gleaming as she beckoned him inside. Preston, taking off his jacket noticed her cream, bare-backed dress with interest.

'It's Pina Colada, you'll like it.'

Preston felt her flagrant eyes on him. As he took a sip of the drink, he glanced up. The sun was beginning to set, the air remained excessively hot.

She puts on some music and they dance.

'Take it off . . . take off this thing' She pushed the tee shirt up to his shoulders. Preston felt coolness as his chest was exposed. He felt her hands travel slowly down to the belt of his Levis . . .

June was excited by her efforts and as the book progressed her confidence grew. '19th January 1980. A memorable day. Wrote excessively with my story. It's coming on real good now.' For the next few nights she went without much sleep, staying up in her clothes, scribbling.

24th January. Entertaining day. Wrote elaborately with my story.
2nd February. Achievable day. I managed to cover a lot of my story today. A rather dramatic part, I guess.
14th February. St Valentine's day. Tiring day. At last finished my story. Pretty good stuff.

June's antihero, drifting through Malibu, confused by his emotional experiences, joins a gang of youths who break the windows and raid a supermarket. While the others force open the tills, Preston is transfixed by a case of Pepsi-Cola and is alone and still drinking from a can when the police arrive. He is taken to jail, is almost murdered by a psychopath in the prison laundry, and is visited by Mrs Rosenberg who announces she is going to live with her husband in Europe. His mother and Peggy also visit him. June handles the prison scenes and the relationships between prisoners, warders and visitors with assured skill. Here Preston receives homosexual advances from one of the warders:

He was washing his face one morning; the water from the faucet was ice-cold. Pulling some paper from the roll towel, Preston noticed one of the warders looking at him curiously. He turned off the faucet as he heard the man come up behind him. 'How you doing boy?' His voice was soft. 'Alright, you're not lonesome or anything?'

Preston turned to glance at him. He had an English haircut, and his blonde moustache was trimmed neatly below his small nose.

'I'm fine.'

'I hope so.' He seemed anxious. 'I'm always around . . . If you ever feel you need to talk to somebody . . . I'm . . . you're welcome, okay?'

Preston lowered his eyes, feeling suddenly awkward. He made a pretence of wiping his hands.

'I hear your friend has left us; did you like him?'

A vision of Jefferson came into Preston's mind. He raised his eyes. 'Yeah, he was alright.'

The man's sharp eyes strayed over him. 'Good. I liked him too. He liked me . . .'

Preston, suddenly conscious of his bare chest, swept his eyes over to his tee shirt, resting on a nearby chair. The man, catching his glance, turned and handed him the tee shirt. 'You ought to eat the food in here.' His hand shot out. 'I can just about see your ribs. I can feel them too.' Preston noticed his tone of anger; he was aware of the silence that reigned in the wash-room. He flinched away, pulling on his tee shirt.

The man stared at him, a light passing his eyes. 'Why don't you eat, huh?' He stepped forward. 'Listen, I don't like skinny boys. I don't like boys with no flesh on them. I like them . . .'

Knocking against the wall, Preston was forced to stop. He calmly eyed the man's outstretched hands; they were large, each one was covered with long scratch marks.

'Don't . . . be . . . afraid, I only want to whisper something in your ear.' His face was beaded with sweat.

'Like what, huh?' Preston's eyes darted to the entrance of the wash-room.

'Like, are you scared of the dark?'

'Are you crazy? Course not.'

'Tell me you are. Tell me that you need a kiss and cuddle before you go to sleep.'

Preston shook his head, confused, his heart palpitating; he inhaled the man's strong after-shave.

'Wouldn't you like to sleep in my room tonight? I get lonesome too, you know.'

'I'll see you around, huh.' Preston made an attempt to move. He felt the man's hand push against his chest.

'I wanna see you now, so cut that talk out. You're going nowhere.' A smile passed his thin lips. 'Not until I finish with you, anyway.'

Preston is released from jail and starts to search for Peggy. Eventually, he meets her sister Lisa and is devastated to learn that the family is about to leave Malibu.

The apartment was filled with the lonesome atmosphere of a sleeping cemetery. The buzzing sound coming from the refrigerator turned to a deep sigh as Preston opened it to yank out a Pepsi-Cola can. A moment later his hands were rummaging through the cupboard; they did not seem to belong to him. His eyes swept over the bottles of food, medicine and powdered milk. He wondered why his mother kept so many pills. He reached over for a bottle of barbiturates . . .

The telephone began to peal. Preston stopped still in the corridor, his heart raced, anxiously he thought about Peggy; she was a million miles away. He let the phone ring.

His eyes darted nervously, he was looking through a telescope, the walls were closing in, popstars gazed down at him, a body lying on a bed. The telephone rang, it rang, it cried out. Lifting his numb head, Preston sat up, his legs like lead, he was walking on air. The floor was a synthetic sponge, it dragged him down. For some reason he had to get to that phone.

Standing unsteadily in the corridor, Preston swayed over to the ringing phone; he picked up the receiver, the perspiration heavy in his hands.

'Hello?'

'Preston, is that you?' Peggy's voice attacked his ears. His voice slurred, 'Peggy?'

'Listen, I have to tell you something Preston . . . we're not leaving Malibu . . . are you listening? I love you. I can't go to San Francisco.'

A knife so sharp, it sliced into Preston's heart. The pain deafened his ear drums. He sank to the floor, the phone crashing down beside him . . . Preston was swinging on the magic swing of freedom, it got faster, faster, faster, spinning into an unknown world. He was falling, floating in an empty black tunnel . . . like a rocket trapped in space, a can of Pepsi-Cola came twisting and turning towards him . . . it crashed. Preston slept.

Outside, below the steps, at this moment three young boys were playing kick-the-can with an empty Pepsi-Cola can. Some remaining liquid slowly trickled out, emerging onto the street. It stopped running as it came to the edge of the street. It lay there invisible to all passers-by, where it dried up silently under the radiation of the burning sun.

June finished her manuscript, and painstakingly typed it. She had found an advertisement for New Horizon, a vanity publishing firm based in Bognor Regis in Sussex. The firm, run by a George Kay and his wife, invited young authors to send manuscripts which they offered to publish – for substantial sums of money.

June knew nothing about publishing; she saw New Horizon as her way to instant fame and success, and sent them the manuscript. She was delighted when they wrote back accepting her first novel, even wanting a photograph of her for the cover. But there was the inevitable catch.

16th May 1984
Dear New Horizon,
I am so glad that you have accepted my book. But unfortunately I am dreadfully in debt and cannot pay a single penny. I would like to accept the contract you are offering me. But first, I have some bargaining to do with you. £980 is much more than I can afford at the moment. It may even take one or two years until I can pay my subsidy to you. So I am asking you now for something that may bend New Horizon's rules or customs. With the royalties that I shall be receiving on sale of the next 1000 copies or so, I was wondering if your firm would like to take the £980.00 out of it for yourselves. This will be much quicker for you and me as I do not mind losing the money at all. Honestly, I have no intention of becoming a millionaire overnight. All I want to see is my book in a bookstore some day soon . . .

In an earlier draft of this letter she added:

If however my book does not cover the cost of your subsidy fee, then ring the police and I will gladly be arrested.
Yours sincerely,
J. Gibbons

New Horizon eventually agreed to accept the money in instalments of £80 per month. June persuaded Jennifer to donate her dole money, and on 11th June they bought two £40 postal orders and sent them with the signed contract to New Horizon. Later they even tried to sell their jewellery but were told it was worthless.

New Horizon's request for June's photograph precipitated a new obsession in the Gibbonses' back bedroom: photography. Gloria and Rosie were continually being sent on errands to get more film or to take rolls for printing. June and Jennifer spent hours photographing each other in different poses, wearing their wigs, dressed up as boys or in Rosie's school uniform. 'Meet the Writer' June captioned a photograph of herself, pen in hand, so dark there was little to see except her dazzling face-the-press smile. Each roll of film proved no more satisfactory than the last. June was determined to look as a successful young novelist should and began to worry about her appearance. She sucked in her cheeks to heighten the bone structure to look more like Audrey Hepburn. She started a diet to slim down her features. She bought hair straighteners and 'Youth pills' and 'Fade-out' cream (presumably to lighten her colour) from an advertisement with the recommendation of a 'Harley Street doctor'. But to no avail: the photographs were still unsatisfactory and in the end 'Pepsi-Cola Addict' appeared with a less than perfect image of its author's face.

June's success in getting her first novel published spurred Jennifer, who was diligently doing the Writing School assignments, to start a novel of her own. She was already writing one or two short stories a week, as well as articles and letters, keeping her diary and reading books. She described Jane Austen's *Pride and Prejudice* as 'a very dainty book, with the most interesting dialogue'. D. H. Lawrence became a favourite author. Jennifer started to adapt one of her own short stories into a novella.

Her story was extraordinary, with chilling overtones of voodoo and the supernatural. John Delroy Pallenberg is a surgeon whose wife, Michelle, has already lost two babies from a congenital heart defect. Now, their latest child, Lance Shane, is diagnosed as having the same heart condition and given only weeks to live. Pallenberg decides on heroic measures to save his child.

'Michelle,' he said placidly, a faint gleam dominating his eyes. 'We both want the baby to live, don't we?'

Michelle nodded her head. 'Yes, John. We do.'

'And so Bobby is going to do it for us because without that possibility our son is going to die.' Michelle, for a while, gazed down at Bobby (the family dog) as he sat beside the divan, his large brown eyes seeming strangely concerned as though he had perceived something shrewdly, curiously. 'And how do you suppose Bobby is going to help our child live?' she asked.

Dr Pallenberg gazed at her from strange remote eyes. The room took on the presence of a heavy hush, accompanied by the shadowed whispers of a growing secret. He smiled lightly, taking her hands in his.

Gradually he persuades Michelle to accept his plan. They convert their kitchen into a makeshift operating theatre and, with Michelle as his assistant, John Pallenberg plucks Bobby's heart from his body and implants it in baby Lance. The whole operation has an aura of black magic, although Jennifer never makes that explicit.

The parents keep their secret well. Lance grows into a remarkable child, very advanced for his age. But there are some disturbing symptoms. At seven months Lance shocks Michelle by saying distinctly: 'Bobby ... me want Bobby.' At nine months he gives an occasional bark-like yelp and rejects babyfood for meat.

Lance reaches adolescence and decides to make a career for himself as a boxer. He gradually builds himself into a world champion, but his heart is beginning to fail. The doctors tell him he must give up, but he insists on fighting for the world title, under the name The Pugilist, and wins brilliantly. Jennifer was pleased with her progress: '2nd June 1980. Last night I had a dream about baby Lee. He was actually talking. Letter from Harley Street about Youth Pills. We're getting youth cream instead. My Pugilist story is getting on swell. Lance has already won the fight. I'm on page 63. Cleaned room.'

But after being declared champion Lance has a massive heart attack and is rushed to hospital. There, the secret of his dog's heart is revealed. Lance curses his father, marries his pregnant girlfriend from his bed, and dies. Dr Pallenberg, who was not invited to the wedding, rushes back to the hospital.

Dr Pallenberg ran up the corridor breathlessly. He reached the intensive care unit just as the door opened slowly. Dr Holland came out, weakly shaking his head morosely like a puppy and with an expression of deep forgiveness and regret. 'Dr Pallenberg . . . your son is dead.'

It all happened so fast Dr Pallenberg did not have time to feel his heart miss a beat. They were on top of him in a minute. The crowd was closing up. Cameras flashed. 'Excuse me Dr Pallenberg. Can you look this way please?' A flash in his eyes. Click clack. 'Thank you.'

'How do you feel to be a surgeon and commit such a crime?' 'How do you feel about your son's death?'

'What made you do it?' An ABC microphone was thrust towards him. 'Are you going to stand trial?'

'They say you're a murderer, Dr Pallenberg. Did you intend to kill him by putting that dog's heart into him?'

'Is it true you did several of these operations? Is it true you stole dogs from Russia to carry them out?' Dr Pallenberg reddened and threw a microphone away from his face. He walked on pushing more out of his way.

As he walked up the street a black limousine drew up beside him. A youth jumped out. 'Can I have your autograph Dr Pallenberg!' The youth pulled something from his pocket. Dr Pallenberg gasped as he felt the sharp, cruel pain as a knife cut through his flesh. He staggered as the youth ran back to the limousine which sped away up the street. Dr Pallenberg fell to the ground. He felt the blood seep from his stomach, over his fingers and onto the sidewalk as he heard the sound of running feet . . .

Jennifer's story of the possession of Lance by Bobby the boxer, and the dog's revenge against the man who had killed him, is brilliantly constructed, although her writing at that time was very uncertain and the text is rich in fresh and amusing malapropisms.

By 7th June, after many long nights of labour, 'The Pugilist' was finished and Jennifer wrote confidently offering it to Fontana. The next night, Jennifer, certain the literary world was waiting for her to arrive, started on a new book: 'June 8th 1980. I started my fabulous new novel "Discomania" today. Last night I spent the night doing the 14 plot plans. It's gonna be a knockout, I'm sure.'

The twins displayed amazing energy. While they were writing their books, they still completed the assignments for the Writing School, entered dozens of competitions and were both runners-up in a poetry contest. They kept their diaries, writing a draft first, then one or sometimes two longer final versions. They read voraciously, and in the intervals of their long hours of work, typing or writing in their bedroom, the twins continued their contact with the outside world through mail-order houses. All this activity meant working overtime and they got little sleep.

Two days into her second novella Jennifer had a letter to say 'The Pugilist' would not be suitable for Fontana. It was the first rejection of many. Jennifer was outraged. 'They haven't even read it yet,' she exclaimed. But she was not going to let this setback affect her. 'I am already planning to write to an American publishing firm,' she wrote in her diary for 13th June. 'Spent all last night typing my fabulous new novel "Discomania". The beginning is brilliant. Season has died and Dalton her friend is homosexual. The disco scene is good.'

'Discomania' continued and expanded an important theme in 'The Pugilist', the failure to communicate of those who are close to one another: husband and wife, parents and children, adults and young people.

The book is set three years into the future and concerns a sick society, the seeds of which are obvious today. It is a strongly moral tale about a group of young people in a world where parents have lost all influence, where riots and murder take place at school and where the beat of the disco captivates and destroys young people like a Pied Piper.

It was hot. The disco floor was crowded as I turned to put a dime into the vending machine. Seth was somewhere in the crowd dancing energetically like a peacock and I wondered if he would ever get tired. I drank my soda pop. The music and the flashing red and blue lights were all inspired dramatically as the beat of the rolling drums yelled out. Somewhere behind me Veronica and Rocky were having the time of their young lives. So was I, but I couldn't find Seth to share it with, so I just danced by myself for a while.

My eyes wandered over to where Season and a coloured guy were dancing themselves dizzy. They were swinging wildly to the music and I saw that Season was laughing with joy. I smiled at her and she looked at me with huge dazzling dilated eyes, then waved at me before the coloured boy smothered her with kisses and hustled her out of sight. The music was deafening, and Seth came back to me as I started to sing some of the words. 'You're the one I want . . . you are the one I want ooh . . . ooh . . . ooh . . . You're the one I want . . .' Seth pulled me into his arms and we danced like mad for a moment. Then the music changed and we watched as everyone became hysterical. There were teenagers all around jumping on top of each other, pulling anybody to the floor with salacious frenzy. They screamed loudly to the music, pulling out blades and stabbing their best friends to death . . .

Police sirens and piercing shrieking ambulance bells filled my ears as Seth and I reached the entrance. Blindly, the only thing I could think of was Veronica, Rocky, Dalton and Season. Where were they? Did they escape alive, as we did? 'Seth, wait,' I yelled. 'What about the others? Did you see them come out with us?'

We mounted the sidewalk and collapsed on it as an ambulance came screeching round the corner. My eyes were filled with a million red stars, and then I saw Dalton, Veronica and Rocky come running from the entrance of the building.

'Quick, where's Season?' yelled Rocky. 'We have to get outta here 'cause the fuzz is around.'

'Where the hell is she,' Seth shouted. 'I thought she came out with us.' We all ran half way back towards the building, but then stopped abruptly as two cops came flying towards us. We changed direction and scattered among the commotion of parked ambulances and police cars.

Hastily, for some reason I found myself running back towards the bellowing building. I could only see Season in my eyes and knew I just had to find her. I dodged a herd of stampeding kids and headed for a pile of casualties lying outside the entrance. Season was nowhere to be seen. I was heading to go back inside when I saw her being carried off on a stretcher. Was I having illusions? I ran up beside it, frantically calling out her name. Her long blonde hair was tragically disarrayed and saturated with blood as it lay over her sickly contused face.

'Season,' I called. 'Can you hear me?' I knew that she was unconcious because her eyes were closed. But I still wanted her to open them and say something. One of the ambulance men pulled the comforter right over her face. He looked at me and shook his head. 'Sorry, kid. She's dead.'

Throughout the book, it is the beat of rock music which captures the minds of the youngsters, penetrates their souls and turns them into savages. It is stronger and more addictive than drugs; primitive and powerful like the jungle rhythms of Africa and the drumming and chants of voodoo. But Jennifer is concerned with drugs, too, and takes a strong moral line. Rocky, who originally introduced Olivia and the rest of the group to marijuana, now persuades them to experiment with LSD. Hallucinating madly, they steal a car and drive it down the freeway where they have a head-on collision. The gang are not badly hurt. They end up in the police cells, where Olivia's mother comes to see her. It was a disastrously uncommunicative conversation.

'Hello, mom,' I said as I sat behind the glass window. 'How's Oscar? O K?'

She turned her head and looked at me slowly. 'How could you, Olivia? It was something that was never you. I don't know what to say. Just look at you . . . fifteen and already in this place. Your brother Oscar's never been in, so why you?'

I shrugged my shoulders. 'It just happened. It wasn't our fault. We only wanted a bit of fun.'

'The only fun you'll be getting is at your aunt's house, young lady. I'm not putting up with it any longer, you and your reckless, careless friends. They don't do anything but drag you into trouble; first the disco and now this. Olivia, I'm sending you to your aunt's house and that's final.'

I looked around and tried to say something agreeable. 'Mom, they're my best friends. And what about my education? I've got exams coming up in September.'

When they are released, the teenagers decide 'to fly the coop'.

It was the happiest, most unforgettable night in my life as we all with an arm around a shoulder ambled down the alley. This was the road to freedom. The road I had been waiting for for so long. Now it was happening. Now we were together and we would always be together. Seth, Veronica, Daltyboy and Rocky. Forever. The stars shone down their messages of goodbye. The moon shone down its moonshine of good luck. And the dark ebony sky showered down its blanketful of peace, happiness and overflowing goodwill. I was smiling as we turned out of the alley into the main street. So were the others; because we were all happy; we were all free.

So began an extraordinary adventure in a world of teenage anarchy, of ineffectual adults, brutal police and psychopathic youths. Personal relationships and personal tragedies are played out against the wider backdrop of violence and revolution, ending with the death of the hero.

He looked as though he was on his deathbed. White drawn face, weakly closed eyes, his bluish lips slightly parted as though in need of air. Seth went to sit by his bedside. I pulled up a chair doing the same. Veronica and Rocky stood over us, their expressions no more lamenting than ours. Daltyboy didn't open his eyes. Seth touched him gently on his arm which lay uncovered on top of the comforters. Then weakly his eyes opened. A small whisper dominated the room. 'Hi . . . buddies.'

Seth and I spoke at the same time. 'Hi.'

'When . . . do . . . I get . . . outa . . . here?'

'It's OK, pal. We're here with you.' Seth took his hand and squeezed it tightly. Daltyboy responded by smiling briefly.

'Hey, Daltyboy.' Rocky's voice cracked. 'I had this weird dream about you last night.'

Daltyboy smiled again. 'I've . . . always . . . been . . . dreaming . . . about you . . .' He gasped suddenly. Then broke into a spasm of coughing. Seth held his hand more tightly. Then he stopped. 'It's . . . always been . . . dreams . . . that . . . made . . . me feel happy . . .'

Dalton died a few hours later with his friends at his bedside.

I ran my hand slowly, carefully alongside his face. Daltyboy looked so young. He was so peaceful, his expression like that of a sleeping baby. Seth had gone deadpan. He was slowly easing Daltyboy's clenched hand from around his, freeing himself from the desparate lifeless grip. The door opened. A nurse came in, quietly followed by a doctor. They didn't say anything. They were silent like us. Seth laid Daltyboy's hand back across his stomach. Over the comforter. Like before. 'Die young, stay pretty,' he whispered.

After finishing 'Discomania' in longhand, Jennifer set about the daunting task of typing it out. She added her own puffs ('The world's best seller, the book you just must read. *Australian Press*. The book every teenager is going to be acclaiming. *New York Times*') and a 'verse about being written by a teenager for teenagers', parcelled it up and sent it to Fontana. '19th August 1980. My luck must surely have flown. This afternoon what should have come back but my "Discomania" manuscript. Fontana didn't accept it. Oh well, I'll try another firm.'

The vacuum which separates the teenagers in 'Discomania' from the adult world reflected the upstairs/downstairs divide at number 35 Furzy Park. None of their family had an inkling of what the twins were up to locked in their room. It was only by chance that Gloria found out that most of their dole money was going towards payments on the printing of 'Pepsi-Cola Addict'. Once, to their embarrassment, Aubrey came into their room and lifted up a page written in longhand. The words were so long and sophisticated that he was convinced they were simply copying from one of their highbrow books. Gloria put her energies into her eldest daughter and family life centred round visits to Greta and the weekly Tesco shopping expedition.

'What's that?' one of the rare visitors to the house asked as Greta and Gloria were showing off rows of red-topped plastic containers at a Tupperware party. The living room ceiling vibrated with the sound of typewriters followed by odd bangs and thumps. Gloria took no notice. 'I'll go up,' offered Greta. Embarrassed, Gloria shook her head. Just as she was turning to show another bowl to a woman from the naval estate, there was a cry, high-pitched and savage followed by a tremendous crash. It shook the cups of the four or five women who were drinking their coffee and chatting. They looked alarmed. Gloria remained unmoved.

'It's just the twins,' she reassured. With a hint of pride in her voice, she continued, 'They're writing a book, you know.'

Amidst all their frantic literary activity, even Rosie was excommunicated. Her tyrannical sisters accused her of failing to carry out their errands efficiently. They held a mock trial and sentenced her to be sent to Coventry for a minimum of three days and to be banished from their room for an indefinite period. Rosie burst into tears. June and Jennifer were unmoved. From this time on, Rosie decided that being upaid errand girl and go-between was a thankless role and sought refuge instead in the company of girls of her own age.

A change was overtaking June and Jennifer too. It was partly a reaction to the continuing disappointment of publishers' rejection slips, dozens of them, turning down everything they wrote, shattering every hope. But it was also that they were growing up. Like a middle-aged couple, deserted by their family, they began to find each other's presence increasingly frustrating. While they had unthinkingly rubbed along together in the early years, they now wanted to find another part of themselves, which did not belong to their partner. But they were always held back. There was no space in the stuffy little bedroom in Furzy Park for two young women to transform themselves from backward schoolgirls into stars. Each time one of them tried to reach out, to feel her own face and body, her own identity, she would find her twin's shadow.

They were halfway through their eighteenth year and had stopped binding their breasts to make themselves flat-chested. The hormones were at last taking over. They bought books on health and beauty, did exercises to improve their figures and began to walk around the streets of Haverfordwest, hoping to be noticed. They made an odd sight wandering together through the streets, the collars of their eskimo jackets pulled up against the salty autumn winds. Around this time, they invested £15 in a pair of binoculars, which they carried everywhere. Not knowing any other way to make contact, June and Jennifer used their new weapon to hunt boys. From time to time they would stop and make sure they were not being overlooked, then one girl would pull out the binoculars from under her coat and focus them on the windows of certain houses on the estate. The local youths were not much to write home about but there was one boy, Darren, a fifteen-year-old whose shock of blond hair shone in the blurred circle of their new 'toy'. On a bleak afternoon, when another manuscript had been returned with a dismissive letter, they dressed up in their hunting gear and followed him and his friends around town. Some nights they would hide outside his house, peering in through the lit windows, ringing the doorbell and running away.

Dearest Darren,
We adore you, we love you, we will have you for ourselves.
Your secret admirers

Letters like this were pushed under his door or left in the telephone box, always anonymous. But their unconventional approach brought little reward. The twins could never give their names – even on the phone – and always ran away from any face-to-face confrontation.

The writing business was similarly unsatisfactory. After her second rejection from Fontana, Jennifer started looking for another publisher and wrote to every name she came across. Their replies were discouraging. Some firms published only guidebooks, or local history or science, and would not consider works of fiction. Others were simply uninterested in the twins' novels. For the first time Jennifer's optimism was deflated. 'A discouraging day.' She began to worry. 'I'm wondering about my novel. It's a lot of work but I shall have to try harder. Something is lacking.'

As one disappointment followed another, the twins became more cut off from reality. They knew they had to come ashore to live in the world they had rejected, but there was no-one to rescue them. They were completely alone upstairs in that room of books and dolls. The two sixteen-year-old girls were shouting for help, but their screams remained silent. It was too late to break the pact. Ordinary adolescent confusions became exaggerated and transformed into vivid night-time symbols. Their dreams became bright and detailed, like fragments from some mediaeval manuscript. They were fascinated by them, sent away for guides on their interpretation and recorded them in their 'dream books' with an analysis of their meaning and a summarizing label: a pondering dream, a heart-pounding dream, an abstruse dream, a jaunty dream, a picturey, super-tasty spine-chilling dream.

I am eating crisps and watching TV. Three boys are on horses. A spastic rolls his head about, his tongue hanging out. He asks a man for a fag. The man burns out all his matches. A boy falls off his horse. His wrist is bleeding. A woman is sucking his blood. *Eating*: lack of love and affection – the love I am denied in real life. *Boys*: my subconscious has noticed them and so have I. *Murder*: break free from a difficult situation. *Fire*: burning my bridges. *TV*: desire for escape. *Fire*: desire for escape.

Night after night the same themes emerge, some of them almost prophetic: spastic children, windows (detached from life), dolls (insecurity and loneliness), murder and, above all, fire (both symbols of escape from intolerable situations).

19th November 1980 was a bright wintry day. June and Jennifer stayed in bed all morning, creeping downstairs to make themselves a snack, as usual burning the toast and leaving the kitchen wrecked. Gloria was out with Greta. For a few dull hours they spied on the neighbours' windows from behind the net curtains of the front bed-room. They saw the postman coming down for the second post. The doorbell rang. Both girls froze, then raced each other to the door. Carefully, so that they would not have to see or be seen, Jennifer opened the door and slid her hand out. But this time the parcels were too heavy. She was forced to open the door for the postman to hand over a gigantic parcel.

'Hello, girls,' he said. 'Here's something exciting for you.'

Jennifer grabbed the parcel without attempting to reply and scuttled upstairs where June and she opened it, gloating over each mail-order book as it was unwrapped: *Telecult Power, Instant Mind Power, Self-Hypnosis* and many more. The twins had invested in a complete library of occult power and witchcraft.

The next night they started to experiment. They swept back the drifts of typescript which had accumulated all over the room. June pulled her vicar doll and twins Charlotte and Samantha from behind some old boots in the cupboard while Jennifer set out candles in a circle. 'Tried a little witchcraft to bring Darren to the house with candles,' reports June. 'Tried to talk to Marilyn Monroe. Trying to communicate with blond haired boy.'

The instructions for casting a spell were described in easy stages, but the ingredients were not readily available in West Wales. According to the recipe, they should have found an oaken plaque with 'seven aspen leaves, to which a drachm of Dragon's Blood (the gum of the palm *Calamus draco*) and a quarter goblet of rough red wine of sour distinction' were to be added. The aspen leaves were supposed to denote the fickle nature of man, the blood his fiery master and the rough wine his crude nature.

The girls had no idea where to find dragon's blood and did not know the difference between aspen and other leaves: trees in that part of the country, and hence leaves, are not plentiful. But they found a few dead leaves by the shed in the garden, used a little of the tonic wine they bought to keep their mental faculties alert and made do with some drops of blood from their arms. Jennifer knelt in front of the candle at the head of the bed and repeated the words: 'Whim of man that roams the night, On your faithful lover light.' Then (still reading the instructions) she split the candle in half, causing the top half to roll across the floor and set fire to the edge of the bedspread. She quickly extinguished the fire with some tonic wine. This elaborate ritual was supposed to bring Darren over from the house three doors down in Cawdor Close.

June's ceremony was more general. She was really curious to find out whether her sister was a witch. The book explained:

There are many ways to recognize a witch, and as these persons keep secret, with great effort, the dreadful nature of their power, some guide to their discovery may lay the way open for you . . . Somewhere upon the body of the witch will be a wart. Upon crying the words '*Vivat Lucifer*', the wart will turn purple for a moment or so.

June was almost paralysed with expectation as she whispered the words 'Vivat Lucifer' time after time while surreptitiously examining every blemish on Jennifer's skin. She could detect no change. But perhaps this test did not work on coloured witches?

The girls moved on to more advanced experiments, sticking pins in dolls' hearts and attempting to invoke Darren with the help of water and a pendulum.

For a time, their secret rituals took up much of their lives. But the spirits from the other world did not replace the excitement of real boys. The problem was communication. There was no hope of building a relationship with a boy unless they were able to talk to him. But their embarrassment made that impossible. It was very depressing; the twins were tetchy and worried. It was in this mood that they came – almost accidentally – to commit their first crime.

Just before Christmas, on 18th December 1980, June and Jennifer went shopping for presents in the local post office. 'It was a guilt-luck day,' Jennifer wrote in her diary. 'God forgive. Two teddy bears not intended to be lifted. On going to Tordoff we decided to buy some presents but ended up walking away with them free. It was closing time and everyone was haywire. It was unexpected.'

Their harsh rejection of Greta and her new baby was also probably due to their lack of social and literary success. Over Christmas, David and Vivienne and baby Lee and Greta and Phil and little Helen-Marie, barely three weeks old, had come to visit.

'Where are the twins?' said Greta.

'Upstairs,' replied Gloria. 'They're very busy these days. Did you like the lamp they gave you? It was nice of them.'

'It was great,' intervened Phil. 'I said "Hello" to them in the kitchen just now. Seemed in a bit of a hurry, they did!'

'Oh, they always are,' said Gloria. 'Pop upstairs and show them the baby, Greta. They'd love to hold her.'

Greta wrapped the shawl around Helen-Marie. She went upstairs and knocked at the twins' door. There was no reply. She pushed the door open. June was sitting at the table, writing her diary. Jennifer was absorbed in a copy of D. H. Lawrence's *Selected Letters*. The twins, angry at her unsolicited entrance, stood up together, forming a barrier between her and their inner sanctum.

'Thought you'd like to see the baby. You can hold her if you like,' said Greta, nervously.

An invisible signal passed from one twin to the other. With precise timing, they looked at the tiny creature in the shawl being offered to them and turned away. Greta clutched Helen-Marie to her and stared with hatred at the two hostile backs. This, she vowed, was the last time she would ever bother with her rude twin sisters. They had been a blight on her life for too long, forcing her to leave home and making her embarrassed to return, especially with Phil or his parents. Now they could rot in their stinking little room with its piles of crumpled paper and bits of half-eaten food. She was never going to acknowledge them again. Tears stinging her eyes, she rushed back downstairs to the living room.

After she had gone, June and Jennifer were filled with remorse. June as usual blamed Jennifer for taking her away from the family. They had so wanted to hold baby Helen-Marie. For the past three weeks, June had been dreaming about babies. It was for Helen-Marie that they had chosen (if not bought) the teddy bears. They had spent so much time thinking about this baby. If only they could have shown their natural feelings.

In the months after Christmas, the twins tried to recapture the brisk rhythm of writing they had developed the previous summer. Jennifer had written two more novels. June tried writing a synopsis for a play with the unlikely title 'Postman and Postwoman' and sent it to the BBC who returned it a week later with the inevitable rejection slip. 'BBC say they don't know me,' June wrote in her diary. The urgency seemed to have gone from the writing programme. Far more important was the quest for relationships with boys.

Face-to-face friendship seemed impossible, but there was another possibility: since they could both write fluently, why not develop other ways of communicating with boys? Get to know them so that the stifling embarrassment evaporated, and, with that barrier gone, develop a true relationship with them? Like all the twins' projects, Operation Pen Pal, the search for love and friendship by mail, was conducted with great vigour and enthusiasm.

The world of the lonely adolescent in search for a soul mate is a poignant subculture, little known to the more extrovert. The pages of the pen-pal magazines are overburdened with pictures and pleas from all kinds and nationalities of young people, too shy to go out to make friends. The twins bought as many pen-pal magazines as they could find, such as *Lisa's Letterbox* and *Matchmaker*, and spent hours studying the photographs and reading the descriptions before deciding which boy they should ask to send further details. Like the goods they bought and the courses they studied, it was so much more satisfactory to acquire men by mail order. They could fall in love with boys from all over the world, especially from their beloved America, without fear of being discovered as the two oddities they were. They even advertised their own attractions in the magazines.

JENNIFER GIBBONS 35 Furzy Park, Dale Rd Estate, Haverfordwest, Dyfed, Wales. Student aged 17. 5ft 4ins in height enjoying music, reading, poetry and dancing. Requires shy males 15–21: must be emotional, sensitive, compassionate, romantic, reliable, mature, serious and honest. Any nationality. Star sign is Aries.

For June's first foray, she chose two fourteen-year-olds, Winston from Ireland and Stephen from the North of England. A few days later she looked further afield, to Mario from Mauritius and Abraham from Malta. But their letters, irregular and often illiterate, were unsatisfying.

'19th March 1981. A boring day. I just dream of a better active life. Something strange is happening. My mind is dead. I know I'm wasting my youth. (Boredom is making me eat too much.)'

The twins had to break out. Their writings, perceptive though they were, lacked reality. They needed experiences. June wrote a story simply titled 'Escape' and confided to her diary: 'I'm planning to run away in the summer.'

CHAPTER FIVE

The American Dream

God knows what memories would be mine had that summer not told me the secrets of love, passion and sex. They are all there in my mind like a string of golden flashes. Somebody gave me an opportunity to do something about my life and I took it as a child will take candy. *Jennifer Gibbons*

A black taxi was driving slowly down a country road over the undulating headlands of the Pembrokeshire coast. The hedgerows were just beginning to shimmer with early spring buds and the dull contours of the headlands were sharpening into patches of a lighter green. The taxi, imported from London by an enterprising local firm, was an incongruous sight in these remote Welsh lanes. It clocked its way uncertainly, stopping at the gates of a few farmhouses, turning round and taking different routes.

Len, the driver, was quite relaxed that day. It was early April, the week before Easter, and there was an air of spring. He was quite glad to get away from the steep grey streets of Haverfordwest. He lit a cigarette, wound down his window and looked in the mirror at his two passengers. They were an extraordinary sight: two coloured girls who looked exactly the same, both wearing red headscarves over shaggy black hair which hung down over their small faces. They looked like children on their way to a fancy dress party. Yet it was only 10.0 am. They were smoking cigarettes but, judging by the spluttering and giggling, they had not tried it often before. He felt a tap on his shoulder and saw out of the corner of his eye a slender black hand with long nails painted a nasty shade of maroon. The hand pointed in the direction of a white farmhouse set on a hill.

'That's the French Motel,' he said. 'Nice young girls like yourselves don't want to go there.'

His passengers did not reply. Another tap, and he felt the long nails scratch lightly against his neck. The hand pointed again. He felt compelled to obey but the journey was making him uneasy. He had been telephoned by a young lady with an American accent who had given the name Miss Ford and was told to pick her up at nine o'clock outside the naval estate. She had not given her destination but had mentioned that she wanted to call in at the US base and go on to somewhere near Fishguard.

None of this seemed unusual. There were many calls to ferry the American servicemen and their families to and from the base. But when he had turned up at the entrance to the estate, he had only seen two girls who looked no more than twelve or thirteen years old. They crept into his taxi without saying a word, turned up the volume of a stereo tape deck they were carrying and from then on they had sat there, speechless, nodding their heads in time to the music.

'Hey, put that noise down, won't you?'

The meter showed nearly nine pounds and he was worried whether they would be able to pay. The girls took no notice of his anxious looks, they just put up the volume of the pop music and smiled. Suddenly, he felt the tap on his shoulder again. This time it was more insistent. They were in the middle of nowhere, at least a mile and a half from the motel. No house was in sight. He braked. The hand was offering a ten-pound note. He took it and waited as the two girls opened the door on either side of the taxi and descended very slowly, in perfectly matched movements. He watched this bizarre little ceremony with disbelief. Then, shrugging his shoulders, he drove off and reversed into a field a few hundred yards down the road. On his way back he saw his mysterious passengers still standing where he had put them down. He waved, but they made no sign of recognition. For a moment he slowed down, about to stop and ask whether they wanted to come back with him, but he remembered the hand with its long fingernails, and the blank smile in his mirror when he asked any questions. He shuddered and sped back towards Haverfordwest.

June and Jennifer were celebrating. It was their eighteenth birthday and they had decided to abandon their manuscripts and their increasingly thwarted attempts to become famous writers and go in search of life, in the form of Lance Kennedy, their protector at Eastgate. With their usual persistence, they had discovered the Kennedys' phone number by ringing the US naval base at Brawdy so many times that they eventually hit upon a switchboard operator gullible enough to believe their story about being an old friend of the family. But he did not give them the address.

From then on, the Kennedys' phone never ceased to ring. Sometimes, after some shuffling and smothered giggles, the receiver would be replaced. At other times they would hear the pleasant American voice of a young girl called Lisa Ford who claimed she had known the family in Hawaii. George Kennedy had been posted there between two spells of duty at the Welsh base, and since 'Lisa' seemed to know quite a few details about the four brothers, particularly Lance, they presumed she was one of his girlfriends. Lance had left Eastgate at the same time as the twins and had gone back to Philadelphia to enrol in the US Navy. The eldest son, Jerry, had started a course at a local college and worked nights as a chef in the kitchens of the dingy Bellevue pub which stands at the entrance to the servicemen's estate, a hundred yards from where the twins lived. Wayne, the most attractive of the four, with his wavy brown hair and benevolent smile, was unemployed and not interested in continuing any studies. He enjoyed his leisure with the local girls, even the plump Blodwyn who lived down the road from his home, relaxed with the marijuana he bought at the Continental Café in Haverfordwest High Street, and supplemented both indulgences from his father's open drinks cabinet. He was laid-back, affable and amusing. He was not especially concerned by the girl on the phone who claimed to know so much about him and his brothers. 'Oh yeah,' he would reply, grinning. 'If you dig my brother so much, why don't you come up and see if we'll do instead?'

He and Lance were a year apart in age but had grown up together and were very close, like twins. They told each other everything. Sometimes they would share the same girl. Lance had never mentioned Lisa Ford. Her accent too was a bit strange. It had an American flavour but was not quite convincing, more like someone who had learned to speak from a textbook. But she seemed quite besotted with

Lance and knew a surprising amount, even the names of his friends at the special unit in Eastgate. On one occasion the girl became insistent on knowing his address. Wayne was momentarily disturbed, his usual equanimity threatened by her tone. 'Close by the French Motel,' he replied evasively. 'Why not c'mon up and join us there for a drink?'

For once there was silence. Lisa Ford had hung up.

After the taxi had disappeared down the road, Jennifer signalled to June to move. The two girls walked in file up the hill towards the motel. The French Motel comprises two low white buildings set in the hills. A large car park divides the reception area with its American-style functional rooms from another building with a bar and restaurant. Its position, set in the hillside before the headlands drop down to Fishguard Bay, is potentially beautiful, but at the time of the twins' recce it was a run-down meeting point for local motorbike gangs and drug pushers. It was well known to the police, who made frequent raids but failed to shut it down.

June and Jennifer arrived in the car park and looked at the two or three motorcycles parked there and the piles of bottles, beer cans and other debris spilled carelessly from the bins outside the bar door. They were excited. This was just the kind of setting for their American dream. The motel rooms overlooking the littered car park had an air of seedy expectancy; all kinds of erotic malpractice could take place in such rooms, even the occasional frenzied murder.

A man in thick leather gear came out of the reception area, noticed the girls ferreting among the bins, picking up bits of paper and reading them. He was filling in for the manager that day and didn't like such an odd-looking pair snooping around. They could have been planted by the police. 'Anyone you're looking for?' he shouted. June and Jennifer, who had been absorbed in their search for clues to Wayne's whereabouts, jumped and scuttled away like stray cats.

By late afternoon, the spring sky had become smudged with cloud. Storm bands were lining up above the headland. A few drops of rain had begun to fall. The brown boot polish which they had rubbed on their faces to make them shine was beginning to run. But the twins were still intent on their search for the Kennedy house. They had found several houses among the scattered farms of the area, but none quite fitted the description in their minds. It would have to look American, with at least one if not two station wagons at the door.

They were tired by now and very hungry. They thought about the birthday cake which they always had at home with its two separate rows of candles, facing each other like enemy soldiers. They had left all that behind them, with their books and dolls. June looked at the brand new Seiko watch which their mother had given her earlier that morning. Jennifer had an identical watch. It was already 5.0 pm. June wondered if Gloria would be worrying about them staying out so late, but Jennifer did not allow her such thoughts. They were eighteen and it was time for adventure.

Fishguard is a grey, squally little town. Storms from the Irish Sea blow perpetually round its hunched outline, and its inhabitants too have to bend themselves against the cold blasts of wind and rain. There is a small central square which seems to catch this wind round every corner. June and Jennifer went first into the corner tobacconist where they pooled the last of their money (saving a few coins for the phone) to buy a Mars bar each. Then they made their way to a phone, both got inside and Jennifer dialled Wayne's number. There was no reply. They walked back through the town until they came to the municipal park. As it was nearly seven o'clock and getting dark, there was no-one else in sight. They saw the outline of swings and ran towards them, racing each other to be the first up among the clouds. It was an odd party: two lost girls celebrating their eighteenth birthday in a deserted park ten miles from home, sitting on swings and eating chocolate in the rain.

The rest of the night was not so pleasant. They had spent all their money on the taxi and a bus to Fishguard and had no means of returning to Haverfordwest. For a while, they stood by the road trying to hitch a lift, but no-one stopped. They decided to walk home. Towards dawn they found a telephone box and tried Wayne's number again. This time there was an answer, but the coin jammed in the slot. Exhausted and cold, they slumped down on the wet concrete and, resting their heads on each other's shoulder, fell asleep.

The next morning, Palm Sunday, brought them more luck. Undefeated by their night on the road, the first thing they did on arrival was to ring Wayne. He answered and agreed to meet the 'mystery American girl' at the Continental Café, but he never showed up.

Easter week was full of turmoil for the twins whose need for someone, especially a boy, to take notice of them had overcome their usual caution. They took flamboyant trips to the beach and docks of Milford Haven, wearing their wigs in wild Afro-style or dressing up as American boys with check shirts and caps. Their new boy-hunting life needed the right gear and the twins found that if they were quick enough they could slip the odd tee shirt from Woolworth's into the plastic bags they always carried with them. They began to hang around the local boys on their motorbikes and took to going inside the recreation club in the centre of the town. Here they found their way into an office where there was an untended phone. Their favourite pastime became looking through the telephone directory and ringing all kinds of people, from the receptionist at the Lyons Hotel to the Samaritans. They even rang Cathy Arthur and tried to interest her in their books. But she had suffered a bad year, six months of being ill and pregnant followed by a difficult birth. She was unable to respond to their needs.

There were some kicks to be derived from these visits away from the bedroom. They began to notice the police and would enjoy believing that a policeman had noticed them crossing the road or coming out of the club. And they achieved one thing from their phone calls: they discovered where the Kennedys lived.

The day after the Bank Holiday, 21st April 1981, one of the rival firms of taxi drivers received a call from a Miss Ford, asking him to take her and her sister to a village some ten miles north of Haverfordwest. Welsh Hook is so small that it appears only on the large-scale Ordnance Survey maps. A winding country lane runs down a hill where a few cottages face a cluttered farmyard. The road passes under a railway bridge carrying the main line from Haverfordwest to Fishguard, then dips down to a narrow stone bridge over the river Cled. On the left-hand side, just before the bridge, there is a driveway leading to a more modern house.

The taxi stopped at the entrance to the drive. The two black girls were less conspicuously dressed than on their trip to Fishguard the week before, but even in their jeans and green parkas they looked acutely out of place in this Welsh backwater with its handful of rosy girls and fair-skinned farming folk. Fortunately for the twins, there was no-one to see them arrive. They paid the fare, mumbled something to the driver and stepped together boldly up the drive.

Cleedau Cottage was a misleading name for the home which the American family had chosen to rent. It was nothing like a cottage, but a two-storey house which would have looked more appropriate in an American suburb than in the wilds of Pembrokeshire. It was the kind of place the twins had often written about. They did not ring the bell but went round to the back, taking turns to peep in through the windows. There was no-one at home. The front door was open. They pushed it and went in.

The house was far from spectacular, but to them it was paradise. Pictures of Hawaii were propped up on the living room mantelpiece, American bomber jackets hung in the hall, a drinks cabinet stood open. They scrambled around the house, squeaking and giggling like the two Bad Mice. They went into the kitchen and made themselves peanut butter sandwiches and poured themselves some orange juice; they rushed outside and inside, taking turns to ride a bike which had been left in the drive; they took a roll of photographs of each other in front of the house. Then they went upstairs to ravage their heroes' rooms.

There were three bedrooms upstairs, all quite cramped. The main bedroom was in the centre of the landing. The boys shared the two smaller bedrooms on either side. The door to one room appeared to be locked. The girls pushed at it, furiously. Jennifer went into the main bedroom to fetch a chair, with which she battered against the door, chipping the paintwork and breaking one of the chair legs. But she did not mind. Now they had reached the inner sanctum, the bedroom she presumed belonged to Lance or Wayne, she was determined to complete her investigations. The door gave way. It had not been

June and Jennifer at Eastgate Centre for Special Education, 1977.

Furzy Park, Dale Road RAF Estate. *'A place of few trees and fewer flowers.'*

June in swing park.

Jennifer posing for her twin.

JERMAINE ; your — your TWINS!?"
ELisAbcth; yes, and now you have to decided
Which one of vs is yours."

15.

I – I Just couldn't get it,
Into My head; They were TWINS
and now I had to Choose
one of them For My girlFreind.
JERMAINE ; ELisAbeth — LISA,
I – I Don't know What to
say."

ElisAbeth — LISA. "Then you shall Just have to
have us both JEKMAINE!."
I looked goggled – eyed At the pair of them.

16.

LISA: "your not My type,."
I turned to look At ElisAbeth,
AND I knew I was home
AND Dry.

17.

PANEL. ON our way home.
We stood beaneath a street lamp.

18.

JERMAINE: How will I know,
it's always you ElisAbeth?
ElisAbeth: "That, JERMAINE...
. , , , " " . . I'll
leave up to you."

"ENDS".

The last page of *She Loves Me,
She Loves Me Not*, by Jennifer.

June practising her film-star smile.

Jennifer in a moment's elation.

Jennifer as a serious author.

June. *'My subconscious has noticed boys, and so have I.'*

Meet the Writer: June in March, 1980.

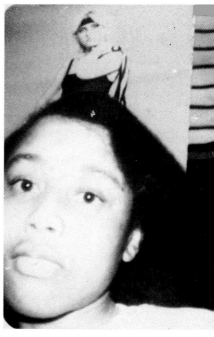

The summer of '81. June and Jennifer at home with the Kennedys. (top right) Jennifer high on vodka and glue. (top left) Wayne Kennedy. (bottom left) June and Jennifer in Wayne's bedroom. (bottom right) June in love.

The Kennedy house at Welsh Hook.

The grassy lair by the swing park where the twins used to entice local boys.

Jennifer's drawings at Pucklechurch Remand Centre.

locked, but jammed. Once inside, both girls hunted for letters, photos, books, any mementoes they could lay hands on. At last Jennifer found a photograph of Lance and put it in her pocket. They rummaged through his clothes, trying on his tee shirts and jackets. They slipped one into their carrier bag and returned to the living room, putting up their feet and watching television, revelling in the idea of being in someone else's house.

There was the sound of a car coming up the drive. Spilling the orange juice and leaving a trail of crumbs, they both scrambled out of the back window. But it was too late. George Kennedy and his new wife, Diane, caught sight of the leg of a disappearing twin. They could hardly believe their eyes when they confronted two identical negro girls scuttling down the drive. They invited them inside.

'Now, let's get one or two things straight. Are either of you the dames that's been calling us like every night? Plaguing the life out of us?' There was no reply. 'Where d'you two come from? I've not seen you around the base.'

The girls looked scared, as though they thought they might be hit, and the Kennedys took pity on them. They offered them coffee and tried to get them to chat.

This was the second time that George Duane Kennedy had been posted to the west coast of Wales. He had been one of the first servicemen to arrive when the Brawdy base was established in 1974. The US Navy chose this remote base as their major west-coast station because the deserted stretches of coastline, so close to the deep waters of the Irish sea, make it an ideal place from which to track Russian submarines. George Kennedy was chief warrant officer and his second wife, Diane, was a clerk at the base. She was in her mid-twenties, petite with oriental features inherited from her Japanese mother. She was much in love with the handsome sailor and the price she had to pay was four fun-loving stepsons, only a few years younger than herself.

Jerry, Lance, Wayne and Carl were all born just over a year apart. Their own mother, a Cherokee Indian, who had lived with them while they were first based at Brawdy in the 1970s, had committed suicide by blowing out her brains when three of her boys were in the house. Such a violent act had its repercussions. The boys grew up with an arrogance and indifference to society which made them careless with other people's emotions and self-centred in their own. George concentrated all his attention on his new wife, leaving the boys very much to themselves, with little in the way of guidance or discipline. George and Diane were used to their house being raided by thoughtless teenagers. 'When you have boys like ours it would be impossible to tell whether any drink had been taken or what damage had been done by an outsider,' says Diane Kennedy. The parents were also used to the local police, who were for ever catching one or other of the boys in some minor conflict with the law.

The Kennedys were finding it impossible to make conversation with their silent burglars and, their tolerance exhausted, rang for a taxi to take the girls home. They told the twins there was no point in returning as the family, except Jerry, were off for a fortnight's holiday in the Canary Islands. George and Diane thought that would be the last they would see of the odd couple.

But June and Jennifer, once obsessed, never let go. The following day the same taxi drove them up to Welsh Hook again. This time the front door of Cleedau Cottage was locked, but they found a small window at the back through which they could enter. They went straight for Wayne's bedroom and found his diary. June wrote a poem in his poem book. She also borrowed a paperback, Salinger's *Catcher in the Rye*.

Two days later they visited the house again. It was raining heavily and on the way they stopped for fish and chips. The bedraggled pair wandered up the road past the water meadow which lies by the river at the bottom of the Kennedys' garden, up the slope of the hill. As they reached the brow of the hill they saw a twelfth-century country church, more like a wayside chapel, set in a small, barely tended graveyard, where clumps of wild daffodils punctuated ancient family graves. They went in through the lych gate and opened the door of the church. It was tiny, with ten rows of pews on either side. There was a stone pulpit, a chancel with a short row of stalls for the choir and a simple altar below a faded stained-glass window. It was unpleasantly cold. Searching round the walls, however, the twins soon found a switch which they discovered turned on the heating. Warming their feet against the pipes, they sat on the prayer cushions, eating their fish and chips.

They returned through the rain to the house, and this time they decided they would break in. Taking a brick, they shattered a small window in the conservatory extension, climbed in, put on the lights and made themselves at home. They helped themselves to sherry and coffee, read through Wayne's letters and like hired detectives pieced together more and more evidence about the life of Wayne and his absent brother Lance. They discovered love letters from many girls, photographs and diaries which they did not hesitate to read. They made use of the telephone to ring several people, including the psychologist from Eastgate, Tim Thomas, who recalls a disjointed message from one of the girls.

Day after day, a taxi fetched the girls and drove them to Welsh Hook. They hung around outside the house, spying on Jerry who had been left behind. On one occasion, he saw them and asked them in but, remembering the broken window, they fled to the church and took refuge there.

The twins were spending less and less time at home. Their social security money was now mainly going on the taxis to and from Welsh Hook. They spent the rest of their time hanging around the town, watching but never joining the gangs of teenagers. They waited, sometimes for hours, at a street corner or down by Merlin's Bridge at the bottom of the High Street, to catch sight of the Kennedy boys. Once they saw Wayne and waved to him, but he passed them by. They were afraid that he would know who broke into his house and rifled his possessions. They needed to have something that belonged to the boys; photographs, books, anything to put the stamp of reality on their dreams. They began to despair and their diaries record their intention to commit suicide. It was fortunate that as usual they did not get around to it, because the following morning their prayers were answered. On 30th May 1981, June wrote to her diary: 'Hi, there. I'm still alive and kicking. Wayne and Jerry finally came to the house. I rang them up and told them to get here by 7.30 pm. Instead they turned up at 10.30! I had just changed back into my pyjamas when I heard loud knocks at the door . . .'

It was some time before the girls were ready to greet the boys. Then, slowly, they opened the door. The family were away visiting Greta at Milford Haven. June stood awkwardly in the hallway until Jerry asked her for something to drink. She led him to the kitchen for a glass of water. The encounter was innocent enough. The girls said little and the four young people sat in the living room to watch a Western on television. Every detail of the evening was imprinted on the twins' minds. Every movement the boys made, every word uttered was cherished and recorded. June brushed accidentally against Wayne. 'It must happen again,' she wrote, 'I'm desperate for him.' The noise of a car arriving put a hasty end to the evening's romance.

The following day they met the boys in the shopping arcade in the centre of Haverfordwest. They promised to sell the twins some marijuana and suggested the girls meet them in Welsh Hook later that afternoon. The adventure was on. The taxi drove into the Kennedy drive. Out stepped two extraordinary-looking creatures. Cigarettes dangled from their painted lips. They clutched a bottle of vodka each and Jennifer held the stereo tape deck. They were clad in layer on layer of tee shirts and jackets, with boots pulled over their jeans. 'They looked as though they were wearing all the clothes they possessed,' recalls Diane Kennedy.

They stayed inside for a short time while Wayne got ready. Then the trio walked down to the bridge where they met up with two local girls, Blodwyn and Sue. Both girls viewed the intruders with suspicion. They both fancied Wayne and did not like the notice he was taking of the newcomers. Conversation was awkward and the impasse was broken only by Jerry's arrival with a bottle of liquid thinner and some tissues.

'Hey, I'll take that,' said Wayne, and as he and his brother bundled their two new friends into an old orange Cortina parked opposite the bridge, he gave the twins their first lesson in getting high. It worked. Sniffing the tissues, June and Jennifer began to feel the miracle of release. They began to laugh and even talk. Jennifer wrote:

2nd June 1981. Wayne, believe it or not, KISSED me. Yes, all too passionately too. (I was wearing perfume.) After he'd kissed my lips really roughly, I kissed him hotly, his hands were roaming everywhere. It was beautiful. The greatest moment of my life so far. (I think the real reason why Wayne kissed me was because he wanted a drag of my fag.)

The taxi became a regular sight in the little village, dropping off the twins every afternoon and returning punctually at 10.30 every night. Sometimes the girls were welcomed, often they were told to go and wait by the bridge or in a barn which had been used as a furniture storeroom opposite the Kennedy house. Wayne was cautious of becoming too involved – 'Black and white didn't go down big in that part of the world' – and he began to opt out of the drunken sessions. But Carl, his younger brother, had no such prejudices – or scruples.

Carl was fourteen years old and the twins eighteen. But even at his age his sexual experiences had been widespread. He was the least pleasant of the boys, spoiled by his father, left alone by his new stepmother and disliked by his brothers. A 'randy little monkey' is how they described him. 'He'd try getting sex anywhere with anyone.' He had straight blond hair, a ruthless expression and, like the twins, lived in a land of fantasy. He saw the chance of fun with the girls and took it. It was Jennifer who attracted him most. June was too sensitive; she didn't enjoy the rough and tumble of a good fight. He could punch and beat Jennifer, throw her on the bed and roll with her and she would respond – eagerly.

The next days were a kaleidoscope of excitement; taxis to and from Welsh Hook, bottles of vodka, tubes of glue, marijuana which they bought at £40 a pack from the brothers. The twins were perpetually high and, for the first time in their lives, happy. They found they could talk to the boys, especially Carl, and he was interested in their tales of starsigns and witchcraft. It didn't matter that he would kiss Jennifer one moment and kick her the next – he was a real American boy with whom they both fell unstably in love.

They became obsessed with sex. One night, after one of their parties, and high on the usual mix of stimulants, they directed the taxi driver to Gipsy Lane, a deserted path in a patch of scruffy wasteland. Jennifer jumped into the front seat and grabbed at his trousers, while June caressed his shoulders from behind. 'I'd say life can be bliss,' Jennifer wrote in her diary. No-one knows if the taxi driver felt the same.

Sunday 7th June was the day Greta's baby, Helen-Marie, was christened. The twins were not invited. Instead, they rang up for a taxi to Welsh Hook. The visit started badly. George Kennedy answered the door.

'Not you two again,' he said. 'Look, we're tired of you hanging about up here. Don't you have a place of your own? Now, scram!'

June and Jennifer looked straight through him. He shut the door. The twins simply stood there on either side of the door.

Two hours passed and they were still there. George was leaving to go down to the base. He took pity on the lonely pair. 'OK. You can go in. Carl's having his supper. But this is the last time. We don't want you around here, understand?'

June and Jennifer found Carl eating a ham sandwich in the living room. The girls waited as he finished his supper. They were hungry but did not dare ask for food, nor was it offered. They silently passed a bottle of brandy, which they had brought in their carrier bag, from one to the other, each taking a swig. Time passed in uneasy silence. Then the sound of the taxi was heard. Suddenly Carl jumped up, grabbing the bottle of brandy. 'You get rid of that goddamn taxi and we'll have a ball,' he told the girls. 'I'm gonna take you to paradise.'

It was raining and already night as Carl, followed by the two girls, made their way across the little river Cled at the bottom of the Kennedys' garden and over the dank water meadow and up the hill to the churchyard. June and Jennifer stumbled in the undergrowth and their soaked feet slipped on the marble of the newer slabs, knocking over a couple of stone urns. Carl pushed open the oak door and the three entered. One small light had been left on beside the tiny organ. They were silent at first, listening to some classical piano music on the pocket radio they had brought. They sat in the pews, passing the bottle of brandy, swigging it back and giggling. Carl took out a cigarette paper, rolled up some marijuana, lit it and handed it round. Then he took his matches, walked towards the altar and lit the candles.

'Now I want each and every one of you to join me in giving thanks to our dear Lord for all his kindness and mercy to us poor sinners. Alleluia.' Carl, his speech slurred, was looking down at the excited girls from the pulpit. 'Do you truly love the Lord Jesus Christ? Do you vow to follow him to the end of your days?' His voice hardened. 'Then step forward and strip.'

The twins were, as he had promised, in paradise. In that country church with the candles burning on the altar, vases of falling roses round the font and the sound of rain against the stained-glass windows, they felt released from the spell which had frozen them so long. The piano music on the radio played on. They were acolytes serving their master, young girls about to experience their initiation rites.

Solemnly, like figures moving through a tableau, they removed Carl's jacket, shirt and jeans. Then Jennifer undressed, followed by June. Carl stared at them. Standing almost naked now in front of him, they looked no more than children, waiflike and pathetic. They were his two child brides, sacrificial victims prepared to lay themselves, literally, at the altar of the love they shared for him. He led Jennifer towards the red carpet on the steps of the chancel.

June watched as Carl struggled to penetrate her sister. At first there was no success. He pulled June down towards him but failed again. He turned back to Jennifer, this time with success. Jennifer lay almost unconscious on the chancel floor. Her head was spinning with the effect of the brandy and the marijuana. She felt bruised and torn, but at peace.

Dear Diary. One of the best days of my sweet life. I've lost my beautiful virginity to Carl Kennedy. At last. It hurt a lot but it happened. There was lots of blood. We did it in church. Sorry God. Your friend. Jenny.

For June the paradise had turned sour. Jennifer's liberation was her victory over June: she had made up for the ten-minute difference in their ages but instead of being punished, she had been blessed. She had been made an individual woman, loved by a man and made whole. June was left behind, unable to break loose from the sister whom she both envied and despised. More than anything, June wanted to be pregnant, she dreamed of babies and invented whole futures for her sons and daughters and their children. The doll families in which she had invested so much of her imagination must now become flesh and blood. But it was Jennifer's blood which had spilled on the chancel floor and Jennifer who might be pregnant. The night following their escapade in the church she dreamed:

I am looking at a row of dolls; they are waxed voodoo dolls, another doll is coloured. Next I'm looking at my own name engraved on a slab of stone. Next I'm being shown a boys' prison camp. I read a sign saying 'To the joint'. It is dark in the yard. *Dolls*: insecurity and loneliness. *Jail*: small worries, desire to escape. Feeling of being cut off or restriction. *Stones*: obstacles or fear.

It was two days after the night in the church. Both girls were lying on their bunk beds in their room in Furzy Park. The radio was as usual blaring. A song by the Rolling Stones came on. June wanted to switch it off: it reminded her of her failure to be the one chosen by the boys. As she reached out to touch the control knob, she heard a sudden movement. Jennifer jumped down from her bunk bed and ripped out the cord. Seconds later she was winding it round June's neck. The look of menace in her twin's eyes made June certain that this was not one of their usual ritual battles. Her life was in danger. She screamed and Jennifer let the cord drop. They were both in tears.

Jennifer began to drink from a half-empty brandy bottle she had hidden under the bed. The two of them went out for a walk. They reached Gipsy Lane where they had tried to seduce their taxi driver in their first exuberant discovery of sex. A few sodium lamps were just turning red along the pathway to the gipsy encampment. Rusted cars, old prams and torn bits of clothing were littered everywhere. It was a depressing place, but fitted their mood. June wrote:

Something like magic is happening. I am seeing Jennifer for the first time like she is seeing me. I think she is slow, cold, has no respect and talks too much; but she thinks I am the same. We are both holding each other back. She does not want jealousy, or envy, or fear from me. She wants us to be equal. There is a murderous gleam in her eye. Dear Lord, I am scared of her. She is not normal. She is having a nervous breakdown. Someone is driving her insane. It is me.

The two girls, silent now, wandered over the field which lay between Gipsy Lane and the river, which at this point was little more than a stream, eddying round the rubbish the gipsies had dumped. After two days of rain, it was running swift and full. The girls climbed up the bank onto the bridge, a few feet above the river. A few cars were passing. June clambered down the embankment and picked up a stick which had foundered on the side. Enraged with hatred and disillusion, she rushed at Jennifer, the stick forked towards Jennifer's eye – Jennifer's evil eye.

'If you kill me,' Jennifer intoned, 'I'll drive away your husband and destroy all your babies.' June feared her sister's curses even more than her strength. She threw down the stick, grabbed hold of her sister and pushed her over the low bridge into the river. She jumped in after her. For some interminable moments she held Jennifer's head under the water, pushing against her sister's resistance. A car passed over the bridge and the beams from its headlights crossed the dark water, lighting up the two struggling figures. June, startled, released her grasp and dragged her spluttering twin onto the bank.

'I love you,' gasped June.

'I love you too,' replied Jennifer, her lungs still engorged with water.

'God help us, God have mercy on us.' Praying and screaming, the two half-drowned sisters fell into each other's arms. For the first time that they could remember, they kissed.

Please Lord Jesus, I'm worried, scared and alone. Give me your hand. Guide me through the end of my teenage years with safety. Take hold of me, give me your blood for strength. I need you to help Jennifer. Grant her peace of mind so she will see me with a lighter heart; give her the ability to soften with boys and to respect who she is, what species she is. Please don't let her take me for granted. Nor the boys she meets. Not Carl or Wayne or Peter, her pen pal. Please if you help me, you'll help her, I'm going through a difficult transit; but I will survive with your help. Take me into your heart. Swallow my grief and my shame, my guilt, my inferior complex. I have nobody else. Even my own twin sister is cut off from me. She is not down to my level, but please bring her down to me and I'll forgive her for all the wounding she has inflicted upon me, mentally and physically. She has destroyed my faith, my courage, but I only have strength to forgive now. I can never hate her, for if I do, I know I hate you, my Lord. But I love her with all my heart. Now, please God, forgive the pair of us, forgive your daughters. Make the next eighteen years of my life happier than my first eighteen years. Guide me, be my friend.

The next day June had a streaming cold and stayed in bed, listening to music. Jennifer, still the victor in the battle, celebrated her first day of independence.

Peter, one of the pen pals with whom she sustained an amorous and lively correspondence, wanted to meet her. She was sure her colour or her appearance would put him off, let alone her silence. On paper she could sound full of the normal teenage enthusiasms. Face to face it could be disaster. But with her new confidence, she took the bus, alone, to St David's, where he was staying in a holiday apartment. It was raining again when she arrived there and she could not find the address of the apartment.

She eventually found it, a dingy couple of rooms in a side street. Peter turned out to be far less handsome than his photographs; moreover, he had his mother with him, waiting eagerly to vet the girl on whom he had set matrimonial hopes. The meeting did not get off to a good start. His mother had prepared an elegant tea and had wrapped a silver bangle to present to her prospective daughter-in-law. Peter was ready to offer his gift – an engraved wooden box. But at the sight of this scruffy girl who was two hours late and then offered no word of apology – indeed, no words at all – they were dismayed. The three of them sat down at the table and his mother served the now cold tea, asking Jennifer the usual questions about her family and schooling. Jennifer mumbled and nodded, her eyes downcast, her tongue lying stiffly in her mouth. They encouraged a rapid departure, handing their gifts as she left. Later that night she caught the bus back to Haverfordwest. June was waiting.

The twins were still enmeshed, still obsessed with the night at the church and the hope it had given them. For the first time since they had been keeping their detailed dream books, even their dreams coincided. Jennifer recorded on 11th June 1981: 'I am in a shed which is of a primitive kind, giving birth to a baby. A big struggle too.' The same night June dreamed: 'I am helping Jennifer deliver her baby through her mouth and shoulders. The baby boy is white, he makes no sound and his star sign is Gemini.'

Both girls now had feverish colds. Despite this, they returned to Welsh Hook, but the combination of stuffed-up noses and lack of drugs and drink made contact with the boys awkward. Carl, a little ashamed of the church escapade, was silent too. The three sat speechless and bored in his bedroom.

'C'mon, kiddoes, let's have another gang bang,' he said, but without much heart. The twins shook their heads. 'Piss off, then. Get off my back.' They ran down the drive and set out on their ten-mile walk home.

They turned up again the next day. Carl was angry. 'What're you two doing here again? Didn't I tell you to get lost?' George and Diane Kennedy were also discouraging. They banned them from the house. 'Personally, I believe they're all mad,' wrote June. 'I can't trust Wayne or Carl, they're so unpredictable. Even the father and Diane seem too airy; the whole family is weird.'

A week later the world came alive again for the girls. Carl and Wayne, tired of the village girls who replaced the twins at the Kennedy house, met the twins in the town and invited them up again. While Carl and Wayne had their dinner, June and Jennifer waited in the barn. It was dark inside. A bird trapped in the building was beating its wings against the broken windows. The stereo player the twins always carried with them was blaring out the hits of the summer of 1981. June and Jennifer, both drunk on a mixture of vodka and brandy, were dancing crazily to the Stylistics. It happened very quickly. June stripped off her shirt and jeans, Carl grabbed at her gyrating body and the two fell down. This time it was June's blood which spilled over the dust and shavings of the barn floor. 'I want your baby. I love you,' June cried out with the pain.

It was Jennifer's turn to watch: 'In a matter of anxious minutes it was all over. J. had lost her golden virginity. (A week after mine, but lost all the same.) The whole thing was rather difficult.' For once she had to play the part of the sober onlooker. But she was not worried. She was prepared to share their lover for sex but she felt sure that she could still hold Carl under her spell. June, drunk and disorientated, wandered about outside the barn, while Jennifer and Carl sat side by side on the wall overlooking the butcher's yard. It was the moment for Jennifer to regain her advantage. The moon was out. Carl offered Jennifer a cigarette. She inhaled it and spluttered. They both laughed, smoked, talked and looked up at the night sky. 'It was so romantic,' Jennifer wrote. 'Carl and I shared a mutual harmony. The smoke from my cigarette blowed longingly into the dark.'

'You never smoked before?' he said. 'You look terrible.'

Throughout the next weeks the twins drew on all the reserves of romance they could muster. They remembered the books they had read, they wrote out the lyrics of pop songs and studied their teenage magazines. They followed hints on how to improve their appearances, they started to diet and rub vibrators on their faces to make the bone structure of their cheeks more prominent. They were prepared to do anything to please their lover. But Carl was becoming bored. He was fourteen and the idea of sharing mutual harmony with them was the last thing on his mind.

One evening late in June, the three of them were watching television in the Kennedy lounge. George and Diane were out. Suddenly Carl grabbed hold of Jennifer, punched her and chased her outside into the darkness. June heard the blows and screams. Terrified, she tried to call their parents. She was unable to talk. Carl came back in and snatched the telephone from her. 'Why don't you goddamn bitches stop hassling us and get outta here?'

The row was cooled by the arrival of Wayne. Without acknowledging the twins, he switched on the television and they all, appropriately, watched a programme on wrestling. Carl got up to make some coffee. He offered Wayne a cup and took one himself. As usual the twins were ignored. When the taxi came, Wayne muttered 'Goodbye', not taking his eyes off the screen. Carl did not even look round.

The twins, who had no experience of tenderness or even concern in human relationships, thought nothing odd about this or the way they were made to wait and were punched and kicked. This, they believed, must be love. As they sat in the taxi on the way home, June looked up at the sky and a full, bright moon. 'It matched my mood that night. Fiery and competitive.'

Like addicts, the twins returned the next day, Jennifer holding a hand over her face where Carl's blows had caused an unsightly bruise. Jennifer wrote:

My mind is now undoubtedly at peace. My boy Carl, he doesn't know how good he's been to me. His arms caressing mine. His lips brushing my lips. I could feel the intense hotness of his eyes slowly studying my body. At that moment I felt like a very beautiful girl. I knew he was infatuated with me, my looks and my mysterious style.

'Why in God's name d'you wear that goddamn stupid wig? You look a fright,' Carl shouted a couple of days later when the three of them had been sitting in silence on the bridge. Carl yanked the wig from Jennifer's head and threw it over the bridge. It missed the river but fell on a cowpat in the meadow. He ran down beside it and, fumbling in the pocket of his bomber jacket, found some matches. Jennifer watched transfixed as he lit one then another match, placing them in a circle round the black strands of hair, in caricature of a witchcraft ritual. The wig began to smoulder. Then, excited by the smell of simmering hair, he threw lighted matches at Jennifer and June.

'In that wig I looked pretty,' Jennifer recorded. 'Carl was saying that without it I looked better. It was a compliment.'

Carl grew more hysterical as the flames began to rise. He rushed across the road to the barn, dragging a bale of hay to add to the pyre. The three of them watched, the twins' faces glowing in the flames. They chatted about robbing and mugging, tales of crime and sex. They kissed and talked naturally. 'I saved all my life, all my speech for Carl,' Jennifer recalls. Hyped on the flames, the violence and Carl's desire to fight her, she was triumphant. 'I was in heaven. Carl and I were together. June was far apart. Quite alone. The sky became dark. It was a strange night . . . In its own way everything was innocent. A friendship, more like a romance. It was my very first experience of love.'

The last few days of their summer with the Kennedys passed in a frenzy of passion that was met mainly with punches, sometimes with greedy sexual onslaughts. But Jennifer, sadly, had gone far beyond any sense of reality. All the years of loneliness had become transformed into this real-life American soap opera. June, too, was enthralled by their new lifestyle, although she could not help wondering why she was the one left out. She comforted herself that it was because she had the more sensitive nature and that Wayne, who was the boy they both really loved, was more interested in her. Sometimes while Jennifer and Carl were tumbling drunkenly on the floor of the barn or on his bed, there would be a sudden flash. They would turn round and see June crouched in front of them, pointing her Instamatic camera. Fortunately for the boys, neither twin had much talent for photography.

The romance was nearing an end. On 6th July, the twins put belts as gay bandanas round their heads. They went down to the town to collect their dole money but decided to save all they had for the rest of the day and hitchhike to Welsh Hook. They walked out of the town on the main road towards Fishguard. A lorry stopped. Sitting beside the driver in the cab, June looked down and noticed that he was wearing women's fishnet stockings and ladies' shoes. He tried to engage the twins in conversation by showing them his suspenders, but even that did not encourage them. He dropped them off a few miles from Welsh Hook.

As the girls walked up the drive towards the house, they saw a removal van blocking their way. George Kennedy had been posted back to Virginia and his wife and four sons were going with him. The twins were determined to make the most of the farewell. They did not yet dare go up to the front door. Instead they waited by the bridge.

Some hours passed and only Jerry joined them. Eventually Carl came out of the house. He was in an ugly mood, intent on a fight. He grabbed Jennifer's purse. 'I think I'll have that six quid you owe me now,' he said. Jennifer could not remember owing him anything. Jerry told his young brother to hand it back. Soon a fight had broken out between the brothers. Wayne appeared on the scene and the three of them rolled around, their hands on each other's necks. Ignoring the girls, the boys made their way to the house. For a while June and Jennifer hung around outside, peering in the windows and waiting on the doorstep. Wayne and Jerry appeared and handed them back most of the stolen money. Carl, they said, had thrown £15 down the toilet. The twins asked the boys for Carl's jacket or any clothes he had worn. Wayne returned with an old school blazer. They begged for more souvenirs.

Taking pity on the girls, Wayne invited them in while he and his brothers ate their food. It was an unlikely last supper. The three youths munched away at their steak and chips while the twins looked on. Seeing their expectant faces, Wayne chucked them a chip each and they opened their mouths like starving birds. It was nearly 10.30 pm, time for the taxi to arrive, and the twins had eaten nothing all day. But hunger only helped suffuse their final communion with a mystic glow. The twins were intent on a ritualistic exchange of memories, imprinting every look, every word, every gesture in their minds. June gave Wayne the gold Seiko watch she had received on her eighteenth birthday. 'It will be on the wrist of someone I love,' she wrote. Wayne put it aside on the window sill and offered her his blue anorak.

'Hey, that's not for free,' he reminded her. 'Where's that dough we gave back?'

June handed him a five-pound note and she put on the precious jacket. She thought it was a fantastic bargain. Jerry found them an old passport photograph and gave them a pair of odd socks. Wayne returned a photograph they had taken in their house on the first visit two months ago. They gave them snippets of their hair and Carl gave them a teeshirt which June vowed she would never wash as it was impregnated with his sweat. Desperate now to touch the idol whom she had never won, June got up and kissed the still munching Wayne tenderly on the lips.

'Goodbye, Wayne,' she murmured to herself. 'But not for ever. Yes, my beautiful Wayne, I'll have your body and you'll have mine. Please don't leave me. Not yet. I want to feel the touch of your hair beneath my fingers, the smile on your face with those beautiful childish dimples. I want to see those dimples in your baby . . .'

'You can have my plate later, if there's anything left over,' he said, chewing noisily.

Then she turned to the sullen Carl and kissed him too. She wrote in her diary:

The thought of leaving you sends shudders of fear and sadness through me. Even though we are enemies, you are the boy who broke my virginity. Carl Christopher Kennedy, I sucked your penis and you entered me. I thank you for hurting me when you did. My happiness will only come when I get to touch you once more; many summers will pass, many July 6ths will come and go, you will stay in my heart for ever. The summer of '81, it will be remembered for its achievement, its victory recovering all my other wasted years.

The taxi hooted impatiently. It had been waiting over ten minutes and the meter was clocking up. The boys were nervous as they knew their father and stepmother were due home any moment. The girls talked of them all committing suicide. It was getting uncomfortable.

'Isn't it kinda time you kids were off?' said Wayne. 'Carl, see your friends to the door.'

Carl looked up. 'They've got legs, haven't they?'

The twins saw themselves out. 'See you guys,' they shouted. 'Have a nice time in sunny ol' Virginia.'

'Yeah, we will,' replied Wayne. 'Goodbye.'

The twins got into the taxi and took a last look at Cleedau Cottage, the driveway lit by the kitchen window. They drove past the barn up the hill by the church, barely visible in the darkness. It reminded them both of their love, a love now made pure with loss. Jennifer wrote:

I can look back on these months and say they have been wonderful months. They are the key to my life. Everything that occurred was magic. It has brought a new awakening in me. It is like God gave me a chance, a chance to prove who I really am. I have a feast of remembering now, memories of the good things we shared, memories that will never die. My days I feel will now be quite empty.

CHAPTER SIX

Aftermath

J. and I are now desolation – searching wide-open deserted places. A craving subconscious for love and sex that wasn't there. The aftermath, the recovering and then a new phase – J. and I stayed in our own environment. We needed a rest. June Gibbons

The sea was running wild over the rocks and sand of Broadhaven Bay. There was a light drizzle and the beach was deserted. The guests at the hotel overlooking the bay had just started to fill the bar for their evening drink. In the low summer light, two tiny dark figures clad only in underwear could be seen running towards the white crests of breaking waves. Two untidy piles of clothes lay on the wet sand and beside these, mingling with the seaweed, the strands of hair from one brown and one black wig. 'It's wonderful,' thought Jennifer. 'I want to let the waves break over me. I want them to bruise me and beat me. I feel I'm living again with violent exhilaration.' The twins had never been taught to swim so they had to content themselves with the spray.

Since the Kennedys' departure, the girls had taken to going to the beach or into the hills, seeking out empty, wide-open spaces. On 9th July 1981 they packed their Bibles, diaries and a few clothes and embarked on what Jennifer described later as 'our travelling venture'. But they didn't get very far and spent the day standing by the roundabout at the bypass a few hundred yards from Furzy Park. At other times they would walk down Gipsy Lane, near the bridge and the river where one night they had so nearly drowned each other. They became a familiar sight wandering about the estate, looking for boys, anyone to fill the painful spaces left by Jerry, Wayne and Carl. They began to take joyrides, 'borrowing' bikes left outside the doors of the naval base estate. On 16th July ('a day I shall never forget for as long as life holds me') Jennifer records how in the evening they were desperate to get hold of a bike. 'Perhaps it would have been better if that idea had never entered my head that hauntingly tranquil night. Neither J. nor I were to know the dreaded ordeal that was coming towards us like a silent virginia creeper.'

'Hey, you bitch, come here.' A car pulled up sharply alongside Jennifer, and a blonde American girl with dark glasses threw open the door. Jennifer took no notice and walked on. June was ahead riding the new white bike. The girl in the car was left shouting. Shortly afterwards a white van drove up alongside June and skidded to a halt in front of her. A tall, plump boy with spectacles jumped out, grabbed hold of the bike and inspected it. The boy turned to his mate driving the van and back to Jennifer who was tussling with him to grab the handlebars. 'Is this your bike? You sure?' he asked.

Jennifer did not feel a reply was called for.

'Why don't you two just step along to our house? I wouldn't advise running away. I'm much faster than you.' He eyed his friend driving the van. 'And so is he.' Before they had reached the driveway, the twins saw the blonde girl who had first accosted them, her mother and a younger boy who looked like her brother. They were surrounded and questioned.

'Don't worry, the cops'll soon be here. Is he the boy?' the older woman asked her daughter, looking at Jennifer's face beneath her cap.

'Me, a boy?' thought Jennifer. 'I couldn't have cared if she referred to me as a monkey or a rabbit because my mind was complexed, as complexed as the starlight galaxy which I knew was gazing pitifully down at me. June was *the girl*, although I was wearing the black wig and my red and blue bomber jacket. I guess I looked like – shall we say – one of those handsome Indian boys.'

The blonde girl noticed the name on the jacket. 'He's called Lance,' she announced.

The boy driving the van pushed them into the house. 'I could sense a high quality of prejudice around him,' Jennifer observed. The girls were taken into the kitchen where they sat down under a low yellow light. The mother, a round woman with long brown hair, 'one of those types who stays at home to fill in jam pies and collect historical ornaments', offered the pair a glass of Coca-Cola. 'I thought she was mad. Could anybody be so naive as to offer a crime suspect some refreshment in one's own house?' Jennifer was appalled. 'We weren't going to accept that drink.'

The police took some time to arrive. The blonde girl, now bored, went off to bed, followed by her mother. The younger boy whose bike they had stolen also disappeared, leaving the twins to the taunts of his elder brother. 'You Indian or Paki or something? I'll break your arm for you.'

'I don't think he likes foreigners,' Jennifer remarked to herself.

An hour later a constable arrived. He was a young man with smooth skin and a moustache. 'Your names?' he asked again and again. The mother who had returned told him the boy was called Lance. 'C'mon, Lance,' the young policeman repeated. 'Tell me the whole story. What's your other names?' Eventually they wrote them down: 'Lance and Lana Smith'.

In the back of the police car they heard the young policeman report back over the radio. 'Allegedly stolen a bicycle. The property was recovered. They won't say a word.'

'That's the Gibbons twins,' said the voice from the other end. 'Two girls. There's no boy. Number 35 Furzy Park. Drive them home.' The inspector on duty that night was in no mood to interrogate the silent pair. 'Phew,' wrote Jennifer that night. 'It was all over. Lord can only forgive me for my gregarious ways. A brush with the law can leave a surprising scar on anybody's mind. It will be on mine I know, but the experience is to me another gain of wisdom that we all constantly strive for in this crime-polluted world.'

The scar did not go deep. The next day, Jennifer wrote: 'After yesterday's unfortunate incident, I have no bike. This is not entirely going to prevent me from gaining the pleasures of life. I spent most of the day practising on my new skateboard.' But those pleasures were flimsy and not shared by her twin. June was still pining for the Kennedys. She took only a half-hearted interest in Jennifer's sprees and tried to soothe her betrayed inner self with food. 'I'm starting on this food binge. A sign of hopeless depression. How can life go on?' she wrote.

It was the first of a whole series of binges. The two would make a round of the local stores, and, using the dole money they no longer needed for the taxis to Welsh Hook, fill up plastic carrier bags with meat pies, crisps, chocolates, biscuits, cakes and fizzy drinks. They were careful not to buy too much at any one store in case people became suspicious. They walked slowly and clumsily. June wore Carl Kennedy's blazer. Jennifer had Wayne's bomber jacket. Both garments were much too big for the slender girls and the weight of goodies in the carrier bags dragged them down. They kept their eyes on the pavement, avoiding the stares of passers-by who they were sure knew what they were carrying. Guiltily, they would find a deserted spot, sometimes on the abandoned racecourse near their home or in the churchyard behind St Mary's in the centre of town. Leaning against the tombstones, shielded by a low wall from the gaze of strangers, they emptied out their bags and feasted until they were sick. 'Not a very welcome place to be stuffing. We should have been mourning instead,' Jennifer told her diary.

They were in mourning. The experiences of the summer of 1981 had both liberated and further enchained them. Jennifer could still feel the elation – that she had been the one chosen by Carl, that she alone had shone from the twin galaxy. June felt depressed. She was always aware that her own memories were less richly romantic than Jennifer's. The need to replace lost excitement drove them on, seeking what they had lost with others. The twins began to follow local boys around. They collected hay left by a tractor in the field by the swing park and made themselves a grassy den at the edge of the park to which they hoped to lure some blond-haired youth. They liked to think of themselves as the estate prostitutes. But when any boy actually responded to their silent advances, they were shocked.

One day, just after the bicycle incident, they met a classmate from their old secondary modern school. They did not greet him but moved slowly hoping he would follow. With the lad in tow, they walked towards the swing park. 'What did I see?' wrote Jennifer.

Him, standing by the pavilion. His red jumper was easy to see in the dusky sky. He leaned like a fire extinguisher against the pavilion building. I looked again. My God. He was on his way over. I thought then this must surely be my personal magnetism at work. The secret code for this is my biggest possession this summer. It's like putting a spell over somebody. In the end the boy had the cheek to join us.

But as usual when people got too close, things did not work out well. The twins found themselves unable to make contact and sat silent while he tried to chat.

I couldn't really face looking him in the eye. It's the thing with me. No matter how hard I try I can never look anybody straight in the socket. June's OK. Well so it appears. Both of us are really two different individual persons. I have my ways. She has hers. I mostly see people as my enemies. They always, no matter what, give me the cold stare, you know, as if I'm nobody. That makes me feel odd. The odd one out, the gal whom nobody really loves. I do lack this so and so thing called warmth. I don't usually show my coldness. It comes in unexpected ways. Like supposing someone in the street walking by happens to smile at me? Do I smile back? Well, I do. But not on the outside. What I think is that I'm smiling. But I'm not, because I usually see the friendly smile vanish in a flash from this boy or girl when they realize that they've been given the cold shoulder, which of course, is not being given on purpose.

Despite the twins' silence, the boy sat on with them. He lit cigarettes for both girls. They made one or two attempts to go away as he suggested feeling them up. 'I got as near to him as a fly might a tub of water,' wrote Jennifer. 'He hardly got down to my zip before I changed my mind.' But back home she revelled in her flirtation. 'I had more magnetism than June. John had been drawn to me. My remedy was working. I felt loved, totally satisfied all because of a boy who used to be in June's class.'

Next to be enticed to the grass den were a coloured American boy, recently arrived on the estate, and his friend Damian. He met the girls in town when they were shopping for glue and brandy. They were quite drunk and shouted at him urging him to come with them. Once in the den, they put loud music on their tape recorder. They were joined by another boy from the gang, Garth. June felt that all three boys were put off by Jennifer's weirdness. 'Don't leave me here with these,' she heard

Garth saying to Damian. 'I think he doesn't feel safe with us,' she confided to her sister.

By midnight the boys were more confident. Damian invited first Jennifer, then June, to lie back on his coat. June records:

So charming, just like Carl. Libras are very polite and considerate people. He only got halfway but at least I felt him inside me. His penis is very long. He can kiss beautifully, French kisses. The time was ten past one in the morning when we got home and we missed the film we were supposed to watch but it was worth it.

The twins' behaviour became too odd for the other teenagers. Everywhere they went, they were teased, used and rejected and though they glimpsed the reasons, they never understood what they were doing wrong. They could not imagine how strange a sight they made, their wigs brushed Afro-style, their black faces peeping above the bits of hay in their den, or how bizarre they looked storming up the hill from the town bent almost double with great carrier bags which clinked re-vealingly as they walked. They thought none of the people on the estate realized who was making the anonymous phone calls or ringing the front door bell and rushing away in clouds of giggles.

After a spate of these episodes the local youths were thoroughly fed up with the girls' pursuit and nobody would come with the girls to the hay den. Garth's mother said he was out. When they eventually waylaid him, he escaped and disappeared into another house. 'We're no longer friends with him,' writes June. 'Garth is ignoring us. So is everybody else. What's wrong with us? Why is everyone running from us?' They rang Damian's door bell. At first they were told he too was out. They waited at the door. Eventually he appeared. June and Jennifer just stood on his doorstep, silent and half-stoned from a recent glue-sniffing session. He slammed the door in their faces.

The following day things were no easier. Garth, Damian and more of the gang of boys and girls from the American naval estate were sitting in a group in the field by the swing park. The twins went up to them hoping to join in. But the group ignored them.

'Even though I was drunk,' recalls June, 'something like reality kept slipping into my mind. I was aware; perceptive; paranoid. I couldn't utter one single word.' The gang wandered off leaving the twins still standing there. 'I don't understand teenagers today; especially American teenagers.'

The bells of St Paul's Cathedral were ringing and every television set in Dale Road estate was on at full volume as Prince Charles made his vows to Lady Diana. June and Jennifer watched from the stairs at 35 Furzy Park for a while but decided to make this day special for themselves as well.

First, they found a bottle of vodka and drank as much as they could. Then they went in search of a new bicycle – this time, to buy. They found a good one advertised in a shop window, collected £50 from their dole money, and knocked on the door at the address given. The bicycle was a big blue and white racer with three-speed gears belonging to a lanky thirteen-year-old boy. He was there with his bulkier-looking friend, a year or so older. His mother greeted the girls and offered the machine for inspection. 'A little 1950s style and it's not for a female, but it suits me fine,' recorded June. The deal was quickly and silently completed and with the £50 in her hands, the mother went back into the house, leaving the boys to the mercy of the twins. For a while they stood shuffling on the doorstep, then the girls began to chase the boys, grabbing and kissing them. Some younger children, seeing the fun, joined in.

The boys pointed to two sheds across the street near the main road. Inside, the sheds were dark and musty. They were used as a store by a block of flats nearby and were filled with ladders and boxes. The older boy, Stan, led June into one shed, while the thirteen-year-old, Steve, and Jennifer went into the other, closing the door. Stan and June scraped back some cans of paraffin, leaving a coffinlike space on the floor. Clumsily, they grasped at each other's clothing. Within minutes, June was squeezed into the space on the floor. She was on her back, her jacket twisting round her, the zip of her half-undone jeans biting into her. Scraps and shavings spiked her shoulders. She stared up at the skylight which was smeared with streaks of faint sunlight. Her body ached, pressed against the hard floor with his weight on top of her, but she felt at peace. She was alone with a boy all to herself. Jennifer was not there to watch and criticize. 'We made love on the wedding day of two very special people, our future King and Queen. It was my day too. A personal achievement.'

The rest of the day did not go so well. Stan hurried his friend in the next shed and they both rushed home for tea. The girls went in search of more excitement and, elated from their experience, taunted the gang in the park, grabbing their hats, pushing them off their bicycles and even bashing a bicycle wheel. Just as they were running away from the wrecked bicycle, they saw two of the older members of the gang approaching them across the field. In the evening sunlight, they saw the flash of a knife in the hands of one of the boys.

The girls were by now eager for a fight. It became ugly. The older boy brought the blade of his knife to run against June's neck. They heard the sound of a car door slamming and a man running towards them. It was the father of the boy with the knife. He separated the fighting pairs but instead of reprimanding his son, he lashed out at the girls, threatening to call the police. They muttered an apology. 'Too late,' he replied, but decided only to send the drunken girls home.

All that night June vomited and cried out from pain. The fumes from the glue and vodka were taking their revenge. Jennifer was wretched, too. But by the following afternoon they were both back on the field again, waiting to be noticed. This time Stan was necking with Jennifer, while thirteen-year-old Steve was on top of June.

He doesn't know about sex any more than I do. He wants to marry me in California 'cos at fourteen you can marry there. He's so desperate. I feel like a mother to him, his little fingers scraping my neck. He kisses me too much on my lips, neck, face. I told him I was a call-girl, that I charge £5 for the whole way, £2 for petting and £20 if I get pregnant.

'Must go now,' Steve said, zipping up his jeans. 'It's beans on toast for tea.'

June was left lying in the grass. 'Funny thing to say after sex, but I've heard it can make you hungry . . . He's so simple,' she thought.

The twins themselves were little more sophisticated. With experience culled mainly from their books and with no-one they could talk to, their ideas of love and sex were warped and naive. They wanted to be noticed by boys but found that the hurried grab in a shed or behind the swing park did not lead to the kind of friendship for which they yearned. 'What's wrong with me?' June reflected.

I have no feelings for sex. I think it's repulsive, a waste of time – it's mean and cruel. I don't understand it. I just lie back and let it happen. I want romance and emotional attachments. But I want to give boys what they want. I'm afraid to reject them or hurt their feelings when it comes to satisfying them. Let them take me, use me, fill themselves up. Boys just use my body; they don't want no-one to know. They won't go steady with me. Is it my colour? My bad luck? Or just the way the opposite sex see me?

Jennifer was also becoming disillusioned with their life on the streets and in the field. But what else was there? They had tried to recover their previous fierce dedication as writers. In fact, Jennifer had been offered a contract by New Horizon who agreed to print her new novella, 'The Taxi-Driver's Son', for £480. She also started to write some short stories. The proofs of June's 'Pepsi-Cola Addict' arrived from the publishers slightly edited but even this did not reawaken June's enthusiasm. She was quite unable now to concentrate on her writing. Both girls found their minds constantly dragged back into the past by the memories of their romance. They had no idea how to get in touch with the Kennedys. Jennifer had actually written to Wayne Kennedy at an address she had been given, but, several months later, the letter came back marked: 'Unknown at this address. Return to sender.'

The twins decided perhaps they should get jobs and started to scour the local newspapers for anything which might suit them. June had the first success. She spoke on the telephone to the sales manager of a firm which sold children's and women's clothing through housewife-sponsored parties, like Tupperware and Avon cosmetics parties. June thought she had done well. The woman arranged to see her the following Tuesday to discuss the details. But then panic set in. 'I've got to cancel this job I've got (or think I've got). I'll have to telephone to cancel it. It's too much of a strain. I'd never have the confidence.' Jennifer went after another job, collecting Littlewood's coupons. But that, too, fell by the wayside.

Then, the twins heard of a job on a farm some miles away, on the other side of Pembroke Dock. They set off in grand style in Haverford-west's black London taxi, keeping a careful eye on the meter to be sure they could pay. Eventually, after losing their way several times, they found the farm. 'Jenny and I knocked at the door,' recalled June, then they looked through the window. 'There was Mr Evans eating his dinner. His wife, sensing a visit, leaped out of her rocking chair. I guess he looks as much a male chauvinist as Oliver Reed. He said Jenny wouldn't be all that acceptable since she's female, and he's still got to interview a few more boys.' Then, Mrs Evans suddenly remembered the twins because she knew David's wife's father. Suddenly, the conversation was relaxed. Mrs Evans asked after baby Lee. A job seemed possible. 'Everything seems great,' June confided to her diary.

Earning would be about £50 a week, although transport would be difficult. I've set my whole heart on working on a farm, I guess I like the isolation of outdoor life. I love wearing wellie boots and thick winter jackets. I love hard physical work. I like the idea of doing something different from an ordinary boring office job.

Evans said he would telephone the twins about the results of the interview the following Thursday. He did not get in touch with them.

By now, the twins' behaviour was beginning to attract attention. Their bell-ringing and letter-posting was becoming a nuisance on the estate. They were weird and black and played music loudly on their cassette player. And sometimes they appeared to be drunk. Somebody complained to the police and they were picked up in the field by the swing park. 'Two police inspectors questioned us about sniffing glue and they found drink bottles. Actually went to police station for a talk,' records Jennifer. Then, the next-door neighbours complained to Gloria about the loud music and the unsavoury gang of youths with whom the twins were consorting. One of them had been heard shouting: 'How much d'you charge?'

Gloria and Aubrey do not seem to have taken much notice of the complaints, nor observed the warning signals. Gloria was away at the house in Pembroke a great deal helping Greta with her baby, so she did not know what went on in Furzy Park during the daytime. In the evening, when Gloria and Aubrey were there, the twins were almost always in at a reasonable time. She put the complaints down primarily to colour prejudice. To their parents the twins were still the recluses who lived upstairs, speaking to no-one and spending each and every day at their typewriters. Gloria was concerned about their extreme closeness and interdependence and was delighted when she found they were going out of the house more often and meeting people.

The twins' social life was not going well. They persisted in writing anonymous and compromising love letters to Darren and the other boys, naively believing they did not know the authors of the pranks. For Snig, one of the gang leaders, they laboriously prepared a postcard with a message of 'gruesome words' made by cutting out and pasting down individual letters from a newspaper. Some of the others got threatening notes: 'pretty convincing,' boasted June. The boys were furious. Snig and the gang threatened to kill the twins if they sent any more letters. Jake, who met Jennifer in the street, pushed her around and spat on her. 'Romance takes its toll,' she commented drily.

The girls were trying other means, too, to draw attention to themselves with the boys. They became obsessed with improving their appearance. They ordered new clothes through the post, spent weeks trying to find a man who was offering genuine cowboy boots for sale and eventually bought them, and sent away to the West Indies for 'Goldy's creme' and 'Teeja' hair care. They also made use of their new magic books to improve their features. 'I now direct currents of my higher psychic mind to command my guardian angel to work through my skin and contact my healing powers so they may eliminate the scar on the bridge of my nose,' recorded Jennifer. 'I want every waking hour to show an improvement, so that no-one shall notice my imperfection.' But June decided, 'Vitamin C may improve my blemishes.'

The girls were also vying with the boys as budding delinquents. They discovered from one boy the name of the best glue to sniff and bought some. 'Not too good,' noted June. 'It smells horrible. Anyway, bought about five packets, then I nicked seven or eight tubes of rubber solution. You've guessed that I was drunk, well I was. Thank God: Coke mixed with vodka really works.'

But the attractions of both glue and drink were beginning to decline. June wrote:

Something seems to have gone wrong. I drunk so much vodka and brandy, yet I'm still alert and sober. Enough to feel anxious and uncosy. I think it's probably the cold weather. I never seem to get tipsy when I feel the cold getting to my bones; but something has to be done. I mean I'd like to go round in a haze all day. Either I'd get high or drunk. I'm beginning to wonder if I really need alcohol. Do I? I don't crave for it, I just use it to help me be more social.

Shortly afterwards, on Saturday 12th September 1981, the twins carried their life of crime a stage further. They chose the Portfield adult training school. 'I smashed a window,' claimed Jennifer, 'and managed to wriggle through a not very big hole, then opened the fire escape door from the inside.' June was less certain about the whole adventure.

A lousy day. Broke into the Portfield special school. Inside was this wonderful TV. Managed to watch the beginning of a film with John Wayne. Also nicked a few *Jackie* mags. Really fantastic. Why do this? Nothing else to do. No friends. Nothing to fill in the cold hour. Winter is here and all the birds will fly back south. I wish I could be with them.

It was the day after this break-in that one of the gang, Garth Jones, was killed in a motorcycle accident. June cut out and kept the article in the local paper about the accident, and wrote:

It was Sunday night at exactly 10.05 pm. Dai Jones was driving and Garth was riding as pillion passenger when they crashed into a car. I'm thinking about the talk on death which Garth, Damian, Jenny and I had sitting in the park one July night, not knowing who was to meet their life: not knowing that on 13th September a life was to be halted – Garth Jones's. I dread to be in the shoes of his girlfriend. I'm sharing her grief. I'm in her dazed trance which she will never wake up from, not even when she is married, and brings up a son who loves motorcycles.

I'm wondering how he looked lying pale-faced on the hospital pillow. What were his last thoughts as he felt the impact of the crash? Did he even utter a last sorrowful scream and as the ambulance men lifted his young body onto the stretcher, what were they thinking?

Garth Jones was really in his own world: perhaps it was more peaceful than this one. He was a true Piscean, a dreamer. His eyes looked as far away as he is now from Snig and the rest of the gang. My heart bleeds for poor Snig, my soul cries out to Mr and Mrs Jones.

Mourning for Garth did not inhibit the twins from breaking into the Portfield school a second time, on Friday 3rd October 1981. 'My nature,' wrote June, 'has turned to crime. I am a labelled thief: but haven't I always been one? J. and I broke into the Portfield Adult Spastic Training Centre. The window was pretty hard to smash – a stone thrown many times until the whole pane had vanished to bits. Nobody passed by or heard anything. We put all the loot, a radio, wellie boots, dolls clothes, magazines, in the bushes. I had the cheek to have a cup of coffee while we were there. Lucky, huh?' But June and Jennifer had not finished yet. They returned to Portfield the next day and stole a book by Dave Cassidy, some Play-Doh and sticks of chalk. 'I love being a burglar,' admitted Jennifer. 'We nicked pop posters, sellotape and a whistle toy. And we left fingerprints everywhere. It'll be in all the local papers. Of course I feel guilty, but that's the cost of being a perfect thief. I think my ambition now is to be a thief, a real thief.'

It's not clear why the twins chose the Portfield school as the target for their first burglary. It was, of course, convenient, only a few hundred yards away from their house, and it was a school for spastics, which always had a fascination for the twins. It seems likely that other children referred to the weird girls who did not speak as 'spastic freaks'.

The twins' switch to a delinquent life was not restricted to breaking into a single institution. They had set out on a vandal's spree copying and outdoing the misdeeds of the gang they were hoping would accept them. On one day, 5th October 1981, they scrawled graffiti on the walls of the Tasker Millward school: SNIG IS A GAY, LEN OWEN IS A BASTARD, and so on. Then they tried to vandalize a phone box, but could neither cut the cable with their scissors nor open the money box. Next they spotted a motorcycle and, after sitting astride it pretending to be Barry Sheene, knocked it over and attempted to cut the tyres with their nail scissors, but they were far too tough. Finally, they found a car with a door left unlocked and helped themselves to a jacket and an old blazer. 'No good,' announced June, so they went into a club, picked up a jacket and searched it for money. The pockets were empty. 'For the rest of this week,' promised June, 'it'll be crime. Yes it will!'

Crime was the answer to their ennui. It gave them a chance to prove themselves to the gang. If they could not excel as writers, they had, at least, the opportunity of being famous criminals. And it provided excitement in the deathly staid surroundings of Haverfordwest.

That evening, having failed to destroy the telephone box, June decided to have a little fun and to ring up the police. She dialled 999, was put through to the police and said: 'I have a confession to make.'

'Go ahead.'

'I broke into Portfield special school.'

'Oh, when was this?'

'Friday night. You'll never catch me.'

'I'll never catch you, eh?'

'Yeah, and I'm gonna get that record player too.'

'What record player? What kind of record player then?'

June suddenly realized the policeman was keeping her talking while the line was traced.

'Fuck off,' she said gruffly and the pair of them ran from the box.

There was more excitement a few minutes later as a police car came tearing along the road. And again when Jennifer rang the police with yet another confession. 'I enjoyed it,' June wrote in her diary later. 'I like excitement. I need it, don't I?'

On Saturday 10th October 1981 June wrote:

This is the day I've been waiting for. Jake, Snig and Kevin actually made contact. I saw two figures behind me and my psychic power told me who they were. J. and I ran, but soon stopped by the roadside in Snowdrop Lane. Jake did all the talking. He was chewing gum and spitting at me. He kept on saying, 'I'm not mental.' I think he is. Jake was mostly getting at me, he kicked me and pushed me over. Well, at last we're on speaking terms. I realize I no longer have to get drunk or stoned on glue, thank God. Those threat notes are really working. We'll continue to send them.

Encouraged by these new developments, the twins went to Bridge Street, picked up two empty milk bottles and smashed the window of the greengrocer's shop. The next night they dialled 999 to call the fire brigade to the Chinese restaurant in Bridge Street. Then they walked into Castle Square to throw bricks through a dress-shop window within yards of two policemen. 'Of course, we got away,' boasted June.

The following night was equally wild. They started by telephoning an ambulance to go to the house where they had bought their new bicycle. 'Someone has broken his back,' explained June. They enjoyed the sirens and the excitement as the ambulance arrived, then made their way into Barn Street, where they smashed a window in the school, tried unsuccessfully to overturn a car and 'wrecked most of it'. Soon after, they saw a police car. 'The cop-car seemed to be following. We made a quick turn.' They stole two bikes left outside a public house and escaped.

This pattern of profligate delinquency continued for a few weeks more, interspersed with desperate attempts to build some kind of relationship with the gang. They broke into the Tasker Millward school canteen and stole swiss rolls, pies, pop, and bread rolls. But the excitement of minor crimes was quickly evaporating. June had bolder plans. 'I'm planning on making petrol bombs. A bottle, petrol and paper, then hurl it through the window. Got the idea from Snig and the gang. They burned down the park, one day. I'm going to be the biggest arsonist around!'

All the excitement about smashing shop windows has definitely vanished; this idea about throwing petrol bombs seems a long way off. Where is the goddam petrol? Every kid around Haverfordwest knows J. and I nick bikes. Life just doesn't seem to be worthwhile. I lack friends. I lack company. It's just me and J. and she's on one of her weird depressed-detached modes. She's on one of those godforsaken starvation diets. I just want to die. For real this time. I'm not looking forward to a depressing Christmas. Snig is leaving for abroad. The gang is splitting up.

The chief source of excitement now was baiting the police. Jennifer telephoned about the special-school break-in, using the deepest masculine voice she could muster. The following day, 20th October, June rang up the police.

I pretended to be a boy and just kept right on talking. Such a fool. It was as though I wanted to be caught. Anyway, next minute a police car comes to the

phone box at the bus depot. He catches me and J. red-handed. Into the car; me
in the back, J. in the front. Once again I was in the old familiar police station. I
was put in a room by myself. Stayed there for about three hours until 1 o'clock.
The police didn't give me a chance to talk really, so what's the point of trying?
All my dreams went out of the window. I was supposed to talk like a crazy yanky
kid, but why is it I become paralysed. Next I had the experience of being finger
printed. I was laughing inside myself all the time. Those cops are so damn
humorous! The cops will have to match the prints to the fingerprints in
Portfield School. As a matter of fact we were just about to set fire to it that night
but a car came and some guy asked what we were doing there? I managed to
drop my bottle petrol bomb. Eventually my mother came, and we all walked
home.

Whatever her inner feelings, Gloria's reaction to this first serious
trouble was subdued. She admonished them briefly and everything
carried on as before.

In the early days of the twins' breaking and entering campaign, the
police had very little doubt that children were responsible. The whole
pattern of early evening break-ins, the theft of cakes and sweets and the
graffiti painted on walls and blackboards seemed typical. 'We began to
think these might not be school children but "loonies" or "nut cases"
when it was clear the villains weren't taking much trouble not to be
found out, and started telephoning us,' said Detective Chief Superin-
tendent James. The police described the call they had received from a
Michael Jones claiming responsibility for breaking into Portfield
school. The call was taken by PC Glyn Cole, who could hear girlish
giggling in the background. At one stage the caller said, 'We don't mind
going to prison.'

'What don't you mind going to prison for?' asked PC Cole.

'For smashing windows. For everything you accuse us of. But we are
not guilty. Nor are we playing games. We don't laugh because we're
guilty. There's no point in going to court.'

The conversation went on so long that the police were able to reach
the phone box and arrest the Gibbons girls. Detective Sergeant
Charlton, who was in charge of the case, a rather unimaginative
man, was at the local pigeon fanciers' dinner so the girls were
interviewed by Sergeant (now Inspector) Tom Peters. He got nothing

out of them except their name. 'I got no further. It was impossible to get further,' he said. 'I was talking to them for forty-five minutes. They were giggling and laughing, but otherwise maintained a complete silence.' At his wits' end, Peters rang Charlton and got him out of his dinner to ask what he should do. Charlton's wife had taught the Gibbons twins at secondary modern school. He told Peters on the telephone: 'There's nothing you can do.' They were eventually charged with the misuse of a 999 call.

Jennifer decided to express herself in art. She could draw fairly well and, like June, had illustrated all her own doll books and had written and drawn some amusing strip-cartoon stories. She enrolled for a correspondence course from the London Art College. (The course cost £135.50, but as usual she bargained them down.)

June was in a black mood. 'I feel like suicide but will that help? I have fresh marks on my face to prove how distressing life is becoming with my twin sister. Have I the strength to kill her?' Jennifer was again on top.

I've got to admit that I'm just as wicked as any of them. My mind is such a powerful species . . . I shall be getting away some sunny day oh yes, I'll be free, free from something or somebody. In the meantime I don't exactly know what I'm playing at. Instead of roaming the streets I should be doing something more constructive.

But the twins were still intent on arson. 'My life of crime is going from good to better, may I say,' wrote Jennifer. 'June and I broke into the tennis courts which are by the 1000 steps. It was easily done by smashing a cracked pane. Well, like all burglars or arsonists, whichever suits your tastes, we climbed in quietly, had a good look round the place.' Their main purpose was to find the kitchen and any goodies to eat. But they were disappointed. 'There was no big cake, no sandwiches, only dishes and pans on an empty cooker, water in the tap and us two as we stood there with rumbling stomachs.' They decided to spray the place with cold-start fuel. They struck a match and as the flames rose, they walked calmly away. 'Well, I do feel guilty,' recorded Jennifer, 'but it is rather exciting.'

The next night, Saturday 24th October, June decided to escalate their criminal activities.

All this week I've wanted to burn down the tractor store in Snowdrop Lane. I burned it down today – with the help of J., of course. It was the biggest night of my life. We climbed over a barbed wire fence. The sky grew blacker and it started to rain. J. took the situation in hand and smashed a window in the shed where the machines were kept.

Inside the shed it was dark. The threshers and tractors, which in the day provided Snowdrop Lane with its only splash of colour, were now grey and threatening. June lit a match and followed Jennifer. There were some cars parked there and a sign: 'Warning High Voltage'. Jennifer caught her breath and almost screamed. A pair of hands moved slowly round the windscreen of one of the cars. Terrified, she looked again and saw they were only gloves, left on the bonnet. The twins crept towards the offices. The door was open and they went in. Once inside, their exhilaration overcame their fear. 'I was really waiting for the manager to say "Caught you" but that never came about – thanks to my positive thinking,' wrote Jennifer. June held out one of their plastic carrier bags while Jennifer filled it with bits of office equipment – a calculator, a pair of headphones, a torch. They found two bomber jackets and stuffed those in. June saw on the floor a squeaky rubber doll. She was delighted. Jennifer lifted out the small can of petrol they had brought with them, and poured it over the desk and chair in the first room. June lit a match and set fire to the corners of a letter lying on the desk. There was a sound like tearing silk as the desk caught fire and flames shot to the ceiling. 'Boy, what a sensation,' thought Jennifer. The girls, smiling and exuberant, ran to the next room and poured more petrol over the furniture and an overall hanging on the door, and set fire to the overall.

This was the kind of catharsis they had been waiting for – a purification and redemption from their suffering. The flames shrieked out for all those years of frustration locked to another human being whose only purpose seemed to be to taunt and destroy, who, although she looked identical, shared nothing but a mutual envy and disdain.

A passer-by walking down Snowdrop Lane heard the sound of glass shattering as the flames burst through the showroom window. Within minutes the fire engine was there. In the commotion no-one noticed two girls, their shoes covered in oil and petrol, clutching bulging carrier bags and walking nonchalantly down the road. At first they hid in a phone box but the temptation was too great. The police, fire and ambulance were outside. It was all happening as they had envisaged in those 'practice runs', as they referred to their 999 phone calls. The firemen wearing breathing apparatus were rushed into the building. The flames were radiant in the dark circles of rain and above them smoke filled the night sky. The girls joined the crowd and revelled in their handiwork. Firemen were everywhere, running with their hoses, trying to smash a window to get in.

All the while, my lovely glorious fire was licking its way through the roof, and the thick smoke filled the night sky. It was a picture which will live in my mind for ever – oh what a sinful, evil, selfish mind. I know the Lord will forgive me. It's being a long, painful, hard year. Don't I deserve to express my distress?

Jennifer was more down to earth in her approach. 'Finally with this great achievement in mind, June and I strolled home.'

They were well pleased with their night's work. They went to their room. June placed the squeaky doll on her bed and smiled.

The next-door neighbours had, however, seen the girls staring at the fire and reported them to the police. That Sunday morning two inspectors arrived to question them about the fires at the tractor store and at the tennis courts. The girls said nothing but shook their heads and the police left.

'I feel like an escaped convict,' wrote Jennifer. 'I'd like to go to jail. I know I will soon. My passion for crime is overpowering my inner self. At the moment I feel very rich. My life is packed with good and bad. Forgive me, Lord, for all my wrong doings.'

The next week, when the local paper came out, the twins were delighted that their exploits had made the front page. The article said £100,000 of damage had been done, two tractors had been destroyed and a fireman had had to have hospital treatment for a cut he received when breaking a window to get in. There was mention of the fire in the tennis pavilion, too. Police, the report said, are looking for an arsonist. 'Well, of course they are!' remarked June. 'She lives right here at 35 Furzy Park! Isn't it ludicrous?'

Next, they broke into the Barn Street school, using a netball post to smash a window. They took 'silver sports cups, a giant framed picture and a small one. A brown ivory elephant, clothes, scarf and two purses. In one there was a little heart-shaped chain complete with tiny key and the words: "The one who holds this key opens my heart." J. and I did some vandalism. I threw tea and coffee on the floor. We only brought the smaller items home for now.' June as she was walking home past the fish-and-chip shop on the way home had a nasty shock. She felt a hand placed firmly on her shoulder. 'Phew, I almost died! But it was only a friend of Darren's.'

On 5th November 1981, the twins went on a wild rampage again. 'For some people,' wrote June, 'it's bonfire night, but for me – well, I had a smashing time. Yeah, J. and I done it again. Broke into Tasker's School, and I had my taste of destruction. A good way to let off steam, don't you agree? Stole green snorkel, parka, pair of trainers and books.'

During those last turbulent autumn days before the rest of the world caught up with them, the twins' dreams, clever, often witty, take us into their minds. They show how trapped the twins had become by their inability to communicate with anyone but each other – the more they felt left out of the gang, the more they blamed each other for their status as outcasts. But neither would give in and release her twin. They could feel the impossibility of their predicament closing in on them and knew that if it went on much longer, they would have no choice but to kill each other. All other attempts to escape had failed – writing had been hard work, the evidence of which was a heap of rejection slips; they could never get beyond the first telephone call in finding a job; and after the Kennedys left, their skirmishes in teenage sex had left them feeling empty and degraded. Fire offered its ancient symbolism of purification, sacrifice, and being born again. Only through flames could a new June and Jennifer emerge as separate, successful human beings and the two unacceptable mutes rise again as beautiful young women.

One night June dreamed:

I am in someone else's bedroom. Some girls are downstairs but when the mother comes in J. says we have broken friends with the girls. She leaves the room. I begin to search the drawers and I find a super bobble hat. I keep it. Next I am outside a graveyard. I'm looking at the grave of a man, but he is too poor to afford a coffin box. I see him, under a cover. Passers-by tell me he couldn't afford a decent grave. But I remember that I have just won £5000 in the paper contest. Soon a girl called Joyce comes to talk. She asks for a fag. We all have fags but not enough matches. We try to strike a match but the wind blows. I'm thinking to ask a passer-by but finally Joyce gets hers lit. *Cemetery*: predicts news from someone long absent; I am dead bored; I'm going through a stagnant time both socially and mentally. *Corpse*: finality, failure, desire for escape or forgiveness. *Smoke*: indicates confusion. *Fire*: desire for escape, 'Burning my Bridges.' *Hat*: new hat. *Change of location*: loss, bad luck. *Bedroom*: sex urge or journey in store. *Money*: desire for security. *Burial*: subconscious dissatisfaction with someone else. *Smoking*: peace, harmony and contentment.

On the night before their last crime June had a symbolic dream. It was a pathetic cry for help which no-one but her diary was allowed to hear.

I am watching a scene with Joan Collins with her daughter. Joan is sitting on a bed telling her daughter the facts of life. She explains what it feels like to be a woman; her body is slightly sagging, she lays back and plays her hand over her tummy. She sits up and hugs her daughter who has begun to cry, with relief or the confusion of growing up. *Crying*: sorrow in love or business. *Bedroom*: sex urge. *Embrace*: a longing to help others.

I am also looking at lots of black and white pictures of my childhood. *Pictures*: a desire for artistic expression. *Nakedness*: desire to be noticed.

This was her last entry. On 8th November 1981, at 8.30 pm, she and Jennifer were on their usual evening prowl. They saw a policeman walking up and down the road at the corner of Jury Lane by the Pembroke technical college. This was their cue. Almost in front of his eyes they went to the back of the college and Jennifer picked up a brick to smash the window.

A few yards down the road, Constable Steven Gwyn Jones heard the crash. Since the spate of break-ins he, along with others, had been seconded to the arson operation. At first the police had not linked the voices on the phone with the two Gibbons twins, whom they believed to be mute. They found it hard to believe all the damage was the work of such shy girls. But the last incident, when the car had picked them up from the telephone kiosk after the call confessing to the store break-in, had made Detective Sergeant Charlton suspicious. He posted his men, many in plain clothes, near all the haunts of the teenagers from Dale Road estate and set about trapping the twins. It was not too difficult. June and Jennifer were by now desperate to be caught. In their book of dream interpretation, police were images of protection, people who could help them escape their predicament; prison represented security, a place where they could feel safe.

What happened now was inevitable. Hearing the sound of smashing glass, the policeman quickly radioed the station for reinforcements and went round the back of the college. It took him some time to find the broken window. He then heard a peculiar sound, like the squeaking of small, excited animals. He looked up and saw a brief glow as a match was lit and extinguished. Another match was struck and this time he could glimpse the outline of a slight figure the size of a child, wearing thick woolly gloves and holding a carrier bag. As the next match was struck he saw another figure dropping what looked like a ruler and notebooks into the bag.

A car stopped in the road outside. Moments later, Detective Sergeant Charlton and his reinforcements were looking through the cracked window. The intruders had by now found a torch, which they placed on the table. The group of men outside watched as the two figures began to spread what looked like glue from a bottle over the desk and carpets. This was the moment to act. Within seconds, Charlton was inside the college and rushing through the corridors to the office. As he entered, June was about to spray some papers with a can of cold-start fuel. Two officers grabbed her, while another two took Jennifer. They found a lighter tucked into June's sock and a box of matches in her jeans pocket. Charlton emptied out the carrier bag. Its contents were pathetic: a handful of cassette tapes, a few bits of stationery and a half-eaten packet of Polo mints.

Detective Sergeant Charlton was delighted. He had caught the arsonists red-handed, with the evidence. A man with a well-earned reputation among Haverfordwest's delinquent population, he set about his capture with relish. He knew from past experience that the Gibbons twins could not or did not talk, so he carried out his interrogation in what the court later referred to as a 'somewhat unusual way'. He wrote a question down, handed the girls pen and paper and left the room. He returned to pick up their answers before setting the next question. They replied with their names, age and address but only admitted to the break-in at the college.

Late that night, for almost an hour, Charlton questioned a bewildered Aubrey about the movements of the girls. Gloria must have kept quiet about their previous escapade. Aubrey smiled and laughed, unable to absorb what he was hearing. The twins – in trouble? Impossible. They could be a bit irritating at times, but criminals, burglars, arsonists – they were incapable of any such thing. Too good, he had always told Gloria, not like the other kids on the estate. Charlton produced a search warrant and asked Aubrey to show him the twins' bedroom. There, under the bunk bed, stuffed behind unwashed clothes or hidden underneath manuscripts, were the jackets, tapes, ornaments, pencil cases and office equipment missing from the cars and buildings the twins had burgled. Charlton began to read some of the manuscript, then he saw by the bed one of the red five-year diaries lying open at the previous day's entry. He read it with delight. He found the second diary and soon all the twins' writings and the loot was being collected into black dustbin liners to take back to the police station.

Aubrey and Gloria watched from the top of the stairs as the police ransacked the bedroom. As parents, they had never been allowed to interfere with the twins' possessions, let alone invade their room. Gloria tried to protest, but it was too late. She watched the scene and knew it had been bound to happen – a few weeks before she had dreamed that four policemen had entered their living room asking about the twins. Then the twins had come in and everyone had started to sing. But this time there were no twins and no singing.

The next day, the story made the headlines in the *Western Telegraph*. All his life, Aubrey had feared being singled out in any way: now he and Gloria would have to come to terms with the fact that their twin daughters were criminals. On 10th November 1981, June and Jennifer were remanded on a police statement that they should be held in custody for their own safety, and that if granted bail they were likely to commit further crimes.

CHAPTER SEVEN

War Games

She should have died at birth. Cain killed Abel. No twin should forget that.
Jennifer Gibbons

'June Alison Gibbons.' The officer looked across the room to the closed door of a wooden cubicle. There was no response. She spoke more harshly. 'June Gibbons.'

The door of the cubicle opened and June stepped out. She made no response but stood in the centre of the reception room, clutching the pillowcase into which she had rolled up all her clothes except the bra and underpants which she still wore underneath a coarse navy-blue striped dressing gown, prison regulation. She had no idea what to expect next. Would they shave her and make her go to the showers as she had read in books about the Nazi concentration camps? Did all the women and girls at Pucklechurch remand centre have to strip and wear dressing gowns, even in the middle of the day, as she was doing now? She must look so ugly standing there. She heard the sound of running water coming from another cubicle at the far side of the room and steam rising from over the partition. She felt afraid. She looked around for Jennifer. If only she were here, she would be able to reassure her. Where was she? Had she been taken to a separate block? June began to panic. She wanted to shout for help, but her lips remained closed.

There was a rattle of keys, a door opened and Jennifer walked in, still wearing her jeans and tee shirt. She gave June a pitying look. She knew just how bulky and vulnerable her twin was feeling in the prison dressing gown. 'June Gibbons,' the reception officer repeated. 'Would you please move over to the cubicle? Mrs MacCarthy will give you a bath and wash your hair.' June did not move. 'C'mon, June.' She tried to sound friendly, thinking that maybe the girl was frightened. 'It's just a bath. Everyone has one when they come here first.'

June did not respond and remained rigid, her eyes downcast. The reception sister became impatient. The girl might be shy but in remand centres such as Pucklechurch, with their steady turnover of all kinds of prisoners, there was no time for psychological niceties. She summoned an officer and together they dragged June across to the bath cubicle, undressed her and lifted her into the disinfected water. They had never come across such powerful, albeit silent resistance. After June had been safely placed in the bath, they released Jennifer from a second locked cubicle. She, too, stood rigid, clutching her pillowcase in exactly the same position as her twin sister. This time the officers did not wait to ask and cajole, but lifted Jennifer peremptorily across the room and hoisted her into the bath in the cubicle adjacent to June.

Now that they were clean and disinfected, the nursing sister gave each twin the 'Pucklechurch twirl', an intimate examination of all the bodily cavities. They then took it in turns to stand in front of the reception desk, and the officer, looking pleasant and official in her navy-blue prison officer's uniform, logged their possessions, handed them two pillowcases in which they were instructed to put their sheets, towels, a nightie and pair of slippers each. She gave them her usual welcoming speech. Her main task was to make sure of their identities and to fill in the forms naming next of kin and medical history. Since the girls made no reply, she failed to elicit any information and was forced to leave the forms blank. She would have to get in touch with the girls' solicitor or the police. The interview over, she handed them each a green booklet of prison regulations and prisoners' rights and a piece of paper and envelope for their first letter. 'We're strict but fair here,' she instructed them. 'If you have any problems or complaints you can ask to make an appointment with the chief officer.'

June did not even seek a glance at Jennifer. In some ways this was what they had hoped for: people to take care of them, to protect them from the disorder of their lives. The officer was not too bad either. She had smiled at them in quite a kindly fashion. What frightened them most was that they might be put into separate cells. Escorted by two officers who appeared to be of lower rank, the girls were propelled down a corridor. Sinister bunches of keys rattled on the officers' belts.

Although they did not look up, June and Jennifer were aware of the stares of other inmates whom they passed. Who were they? Murderers, prostitutes? Drug pushers? Was this the sort of place they would meet Myra Hindley? Along the ledge of the glass windows of the corridor connecting the reception area to the block where they were being taken, they saw rows of plants. Glancing sideways, they glimpsed, beyond their reflections in the glass, what looked like cloistered gardens. Then as one of the officers unlocked the door of block A, the assessment block, they faced the onslaught.

There was noise everywhere. Radio 2 was blasting reggae music through a Tannoy system, dozens of girls were chatting and shouting. It was bath time and some were singing, others banging on cubicle doors. 'Hurry up. Stop sticking your fingers up there and get out.' 'Ah shurrup, you bitch, or I'll put 'em up your arse till it fuckin' bleeds.'

June and Jennifer were terrified. They had envisaged sitting together in a peaceful cell, listening only to the sound of their own whispers, but all these girls or women were gossiping so coarsely, laughing and shouting. Surely, they were not to be exposed to this wild lesbian pack? And the officers? Wasn't one of them holding on to her arm just a little too tightly, thought June? Wasn't she deliberately rubbing her hips against June's own slender body?

An officer unlocked a door and the girls found themselves pushed forward into the room. 'Now, settle down. You can make your beds and get into your night clothes. Mrs MacCarthy will bring you some supper.' Jennifer stood behind June, as they did years ago when they would form a queue in front of the headmistress at school or the shopkeeper at Tordoff post office. 'If you need a pee, you'll find a pot behind the door.'

The door slammed and they heard the key in the lock. They did not move but observed their new home with care. At a first glance it was very small and squalid, but better than the police cells they had been in up till now. Along one wall were bunk beds which looked as though they were meant for children, but not much different from their old ones at Furzy Park. The room had a steel-cased window. Inside the larger window there was a smaller casement which could be opened – at least a few inches.

Beneath the window there was a thick central-heating pipe. About two feet from the bed along the opposite wall were a locker, a desk and two school chairs. In the corner they saw a row of multicoloured plastic buckets and jugs. The one with the lid they assumed was the chamber pot. They wondered how anyone could ever use it. Neither girl moved or spoke. Jennifer glanced back. The door which looked so ordinary was absolutely flush, apart from a spy hole, and without a handle: there was no escape. They both just stood there in their striped dressing gowns awaiting their fate.

'It's over an hour and they haven't budged. They don't seem alive.' Mrs Junor was looking through the spy hole in the door and discussing the new arrivals with the night officer who had just come on duty. 'I brought them some supper on a tray half an hour ago, but they haven't touched it. They didn't reply to anything I said. Perhaps they can't hear or don't understand. We know so little about them.'

The two women returned to finish their hand-over report. As she was going off duty, Mrs Junor was curious to see what had happened to the black twins. She looked through the spy hole and saw them still standing, one behind the other, their pillowcases held awkwardly in their hands. She could swear they had not flexed a muscle or shifted their balance since she had first left them in the room. It was uncanny. The girls looked as though they were guests at Sleeping Beauty's party, suddenly caught, still standing, by sleep.

Mrs Junor decided she must act and summoned a member of the night staff before entering the room. 'You can't stand up all night. Why not get into bed and have a nice rest?' Silence. The two staff removed the pillowcases from the girls' hands, took out the sheets and made the beds. Then they hoisted Jennifer, still rigid, onto the top bunk and June onto the lower one. As she was leaving the room, Mrs Junor looked back and saw them lying as still as effigies, their heads raised at exactly the same angle above their pillows. She was a kind woman who had brought up children of her own. These girls were unlike any of the other inmates she had looked after in her long career in the prison service. They looked so tiny, so fine-featured, more like deaf and dumb children than teenage criminals. She could not leave them in that painful posture. She reached up to the girl in the top bunk and pushed her head back against the pillow; but the girl's eyes stayed open, staring straight ahead. In a gesture of pity and tenderness, she pulled the lids down over her eyes. She shuddered and bent down to do the same for the other girl. It was like laying out the dead.

Early next morning Jennifer and June were woken with a loud banging on the pipes. There were other noises. Doors being unlocked, people shouting, trolleys rolling past outside the door. The girls in the room next door were curious about the newcomers.

'What's yer names? You can speak through the pipes. There's such a racket goin' on, no-one else'll hear.' But June and Jennifer lay motionless on their beds.

Their door was unlocked. An unfamiliar officer wearing the standard navy suit swung into the room and looked at the girls still in their dressing gowns. She went behind the door and opened the lid of the pot.

'What's this doing empty? I hope you haven't wet the beds. I'll have to tell Chief and she'll put you on report.' But the twins' beds were dry. When threatened, their bodily functions seemed to freeze. They had tremendous will power. 'Right, I want you up immediately. Officer Barry will show you where to go and wash. Then I want this room swept out and dusted before breakfast.'

June and Jennifer were propelled into action and followed Miss Barry to a room at the end of the corridor. There was an unpleasant smell of urine and they glimpsed a few girls in pink or floral nylon dressing gowns emptying the plastic buckets down a long trough. They were led into another room with a basin and handed some soap.

'Back in your rooms by 8.10 for room inspection,' Officer Barry called out.

Pucklechurch is one of the four female remand centres in England with a catchment area which encompasses all of the southwest of England and the south of Wales. There are seventy-three women and girls looked after by all female officers. The centre also has boys under twenty-one years old who have been convicted. The female side is divided into those awaiting trial, the 'remands' and about twenty-five convicted prisoners. It is a modern building surrounded by high fences topped with barbed wire. The low blocks are laid out between well-kept gardens and tarmac exercise courts and although the buildings are quite compact, the prisoners from each block, particularly the male and female, are kept very separate.

The days at a remand centre follow an inflexible routine. At 7.45 am cell doors are unlocked and the inmates told to empty their pots, wash, make their beds and sweep out their rooms and, as June and Jennifer had discovered, be ready for room inspection at 8.10 am.

Breakfast was the next ordeal. It was what they most feared. They were escorted to a large room, handed two trays and pushed into a queue of girls. June began to panic. Memories of their old secondary school and of Eastgate assailed her. She would have to eat in front of all these girls. She looked at the door. She would escape. But a young, sturdy officer was standing there legs astride with folded arms. June looked at the windows but they did not seem to open. Maybe if she were to throw the tray at the glass? After all, she was supposed to be experienced at breaking in, why not at getting out? The windows looked thick, probably made of special bulletproof glass. Three other officers were posted around the room, watching the twins as they stood immobile at the self-service counter.

The inmates behind them were getting impatient and began shouting obscenities. What was Jennifer doing? Why didn't she move first? It was her turn. The radio news was coming through the Tannoy. The heat in the room was overpowering. And all those eyes – that stared. There was a crash as June's tray fell to the ground, and a hush as the chattering girls looked round. The officer near the window moved swiftly towards her colleague. When June, head down, charged to the door, they were ready for her.

At 9.0 am, unless the weather is freezing, the prisoners are pushed out into the exercise yards. According to the rules, 'remands' have the right to refuse both exercise and association but the prison officers are reluctant to grant them this right. Marching around the yard for half an hour at least gives them some physical exercise. For the rest of the morning they are allowed to attend various classes in shorthand and typing, child development, arts and crafts or English.

At 11.45 lunch is served and at 12.15 inmates are locked back in their rooms to check on numbers and allow the staff to go to their lunch. Three patrol officers are left on duty. When the staff return at 1.30 pm, doors are unlocked and if anyone has visitors, they are allowed to go to the visitors' room. There are afternoon classes in workrooms and the gymnasium, a modern hall adjoining the centre's chapel. There is then a further half hour of exercise, followed by tea. Between 5.15 and 6.0 pm everyone is locked up again until evening association, an informal get-together in which the inmates can gossip or read, watch television or a film on video. The day ends at 8.45 pm with a final medicine round and locking up for the night.

The first weeks at Pucklechurch were agony for June and Jennifer. It was not at all the place of safety they had imagined, but beset with new horrors. They had hoped to be left in peace in a quiet cell reflecting on their lives. Instead they were made to join in with the other inmates: they had to 'associate' with them, walk around the exercise yard even in hostile weather and, worst of all, they were expected to eat in front of people.

The girls were hungry and even prison food, prepared by a team of convicted boys on the male wing and wheeled across to the female wing in heated trolleys, appealed to them, but they could not bring themselves to eat it. After June's outburst, the twins became meek and obedient, but they could not be persuaded to collect a meal from the serving counter, and when the staff put a plate of food in front of them, they ignored it. As happens with any inmate who refuses food for several days, they were soon transferred to the prison hospital, a two-storey building across the garden from the assessment block, where they were put under observation by the senior medical officer.

The twins' eating disorder was far more complex than just refusing food. They suffered from anorexic behaviour and bulimia nervosa – alternately starving themselves and gorging, then making themselves vomit. In the hospital wing they evolved a new game in which one would fast while the other ate steadily through the complete meals for both of them. Then at some stage the roles would be reversed. Disagreements broke out between them on when the changeover should take place. They competed to look the slimmer, with the most prominent cheek-bones and hunger-dilated eyes. If one twin looked as though she'd lost weight, the other became jealous and there would be an enormous row which, if unresolved, meant two untouched plates would be left by the cell door. They also used water both as a means of dieting and as a purgative, sometimes drinking so much that they would be doubled up on their beds with stomach pains and vomiting.

Water, food and fire. They used every available symbol to live through their inner despair, eating two of everything or disposing of the food in their morning pots or through the narrow opening window pane. Like many prisoners they used hunger strike as a symbol of resistance but soon turned it against each other. Food became their mutual weapon. Some mornings the hospital staff would find the girls covering their faces with hands smeared with blood from scratches inflicted during a nocturnal quarrel over food.

The staff, who had been given little background on the girls' problems, decided to separate them. By Christmas 1981, June had been moved back to the assessment unit and would stare furiously across the garden at the window where her twin was now enjoying the luxury of living and eating alone in their old hospital room. The rooms they were each placed in became a bitter source of friction between them. Together they fought over whose turn it was to eat for two, and apart they could never rest for fear that the other was breaking their pact, eating when she should be fasting, fasting when she should be eating, or enjoying a moment's privilege or freedom which the other could not share.

It was the beginning of another period of intense creativity. Jennifer was attending art classes in the occupational therapy room and both girls began filling exercise books with their dreams and poems. In the few moments when they could rest from their internecine struggle, they began to reflect on their lives and their future:

On the wall shadows perform
Quietly displaying dark motions
Of a group so dim
Yet with expiring visions.

Gliding smoothly figures unwind
While others continuously whisper
Rising waves of stories which bind
Together a legion, born only out of disaster.

Predictions spelled out for a lingering fate
Only they know: secrets, dangers.
Enveloped in arrival of each date.
For they are your astrologers.

Silently shadows perform
Shimmering in welcome moonlight.
Silently shadows perform
Throughout the sleeping night.

Jennifer Gibbons, 21st January 1982

The only events which broke the routine of the twins' early prison days were a series of postponements of their court appearance and a visit from June's solicitor. Michael Jones was a young clerk from the firm of Eaton-Evans and Morris in Haverfordwest, which was recommended to them by the police. June had met him once or twice before she had been taken to the remand centre. Both girls received legal aid and Jennifer, because of a possible conflict of interest between them, had a different solicitor – Ivor Rees from another Haverfordwest firm, Price and Son – but at June's insistence Jennifer was asked along to the visit and Michael Jones did most of the work for both girls.

Michael Jones's arrival in the prison was a surprise and a challenge. The girls were taken to the chief officer's room, but once there they decided they were unable to meet their solicitor face to face. Through their usual muttered and written negotiations, they persuaded the chief officer to agree to a new scenario for the encounter – over the telephone. Miss Barry and Mrs MacCarthy were on duty that afternoon and were astonished to overhear the conversation. June was talking on the phone in the chief's room while Jones was replying on the phone in the adjoining office. Yet both were so close they could be heard as though they were in one room. Neither officer had heard June or Jennifer speak fluently before; they had believed they were almost mute. The clarity and sharpness of their joint interview was a revelation. From the twins' accounts and the recollections of the officers, it went something like this:

June: 'How long do you think we'll get?'

Jones: 'It's difficult to say. It depends on how you get on.'

Jennifer: 'We believe we are entitled to have our property back from you and the police. Could you please return my diaries?'

Jones: 'I'll see if I can fix that.'

June: 'Is there any drug or treatment such as hypnotism which we could receive?'

Jones: 'Yes. I'm talking to a Dr Spry about that. But first, can you tell me, was there any particular reason for you to light those fires? Why did you do it?'

Jennifer: 'We only did it so we could remember . . . June and I would like to have our pen-pal letters back.'

Jones: 'Yes, we'll see if we can arrange that. Any more questions?'

Jennifer: 'Can you tell us what is going on behind the scenes? We have been here over two months. What does the judge think about our case?'

Jones: 'He's more concerned with your progress now than with what you have done. It is very important that you start to talk if you want me to help you to get out of the remand centre. Next time I come I hope you will agree to meet me face to face.'

June: 'I will talk to you if you will help me. Can you please arrange for me to return to my sister in the hospital wing?'

Jones: 'I'll do my best. Is there anything you would like sent to you?'

June: 'Some books by D. H. Lawrence and some more exercise books, please.'

There was a muffled giggle from the chief's office as the conniving pair put down the phone. They were delighted with their manoeuvre: no pact had been broken and the negotiations had gone pretty well. Miss Barry and Mrs MacCarthy walked on down the corridor, still stunned by what they had heard. As far as they could make out both girls had been talking. Who were these twins? Why had no-one told them they could talk like that, let alone manipulate the young man? Were they just making fools of the officers and the establishment? Like the staff at Eastgate, the remand staff began to feel they were being cheated.

Through the next months the twins caused havoc with the officers, not by any overt misbehaviour, but by their increasing resistance to the regime. They were sent to the governor, put on report for days at a time; they were separated and put together again; one or both would be sent to the hospital wing and one or both returned into the same room or different rooms on block A or B1, the remand inmates' block. No move seemed to work. If they were in their room together they would sometimes chatter to each other but whenever they were forced to eat in the dining room or join in with the other prisoners in the exercise yard or in the association room, they would clam up and defend themselves by walking very slowly, their eyes on the floor and with their heads always shielded by one arm. Each twin would hold the opposite arm across her forehead. When they got tired of one position, they would change over arms, but the movement was made in perfect synchrony with the precision of the Changing of the Guard.

Once in the association room, they would sit with their arms still raised, facing each other at the table nearest the wall. Only when something went wrong, when they could not get their 'safe' table or if they wanted something, would they break their stance and approach an officer. Even then they did not speak but pointed and muttered, so that it took some time for their needs to be understood.

Some of the officers became curious about the twins and began to spy on them when they were in different rooms or even blocks, to see if their synchronized behaviour depended on signals they passed to each other. They discovered that even when the twins were unable to watch each other or pass any messages, they would be sitting in the same posture, doing the same thing, at the same time but in different places. If Jennifer was reading over in the hospital block, June in the assessment area would be reading. If Jennifer were writing, June would be writing. Not only would they be doing the same thing, but they would be posed in mirror image, like carved African bookends. There seemed to be something spooky about the sisters, as though they were one mind split into two bodies. It was something better left alone.

The explanation was probably quite simple. The girls spent a lot of time reading and writing and had played their games so long that they would automatically take up 'standard' positions. The staff, already caught off balance by the twins' eccentric behaviour, finding them doing the same thing or in similar positions in separate places, were susceptible to a supernatural explanation.

The bewildered officers also suspected that the twins were playing identity games with them. Even the most regular of the day officers found it almost impossible to tell them apart. When they asked for June, they felt sure Jennifer answered and vice versa. The only tag they used was the silver bangle which June had worn for the last three years and believed brought her luck, but the staff suspected the twins swapped the bangle to exchange their identities. They were either extremely clever or something was very wrong. As usual they were an enigma. 'They were never aggressive to the officers like so many of the others,' recalls one senior staff member. 'They were just aloof. They reserved their emotions for each other. Most of the time they ignored each other, then suddenly they would fly at each other. They spent the day reading novels from the prison library, highbrow literature which their family sent, or huddled over exercise books.'

It was in these dusky pink HMSO exercise books that the twins kept their diaries. The entries for each day were drafted, and sometimes revised, on any paper they could find – brown paper bags, bits of cardboard, the dust jacket of a book. When the entries were satisfactory they were transferred, weeks later, to the exercise books, between 2000 and 3000 words for each day. The diaries written in these months are a fierce and unrelenting testimony to the growing rage they felt against their predicament and against each other.

Some of these diaries were thrown away by an unsympathetic officer, the others were kept with the twins' private property and went with them to Broadmoor. The first entries of the remaining diaries start in March 1982, after the twins had spent nearly three months in the remand centre. They cover the next three-month period as the twins waited for the trial they believed would bring them both fame and help.

The staff gradually gave up trying to integrate the twins with the other inmates, and left them locked up in their room for longer and longer periods. The girls were delighted to escape into their own world and to funnel their feelings into their writings. So much so, that they often provoked the officers in the hope of being 'banged up' all day.

The diaries are extremely personal: nothing is censored, every thought, every soliloquy is confessed to the diary. Events are reported with photographic accuracy. People are described with extraordinary insight and sensitivity. Only in one respect can they be faulted. The girls often say 'had a good talk with' someone. But none of the officers with whom they claim to have 'talked' remembers more than a few muttered, barely intelligible syllables, which were mostly misunderstood. Even the diaries admit their communication problems, and stress the difficulty of making other people understand what they were trying to say. In most of their negotiations with the staff June and Jennifer found it easier to use the techniques they had developed at home of mime and scribbled notes.

Juxtaposing June and Jennifer's descriptions of the same day is an extraordinary experience. They were like two cameras, each focused on the other and recording her every movement or gesture. From time to time, one or the other would swing away and look at the prison world around them, but inevitably they would return to their strategic positions. The battlefield had now been reduced to a 10 by 8 foot cell, and the two enemies would sit only a few feet apart, eyeing each other, preparing their artillery of angry words. June and Jennifer describe the same events and emotions in extraordinary detail, yet the two diaries never quite fit. All the distortions of each twin's vision of the other make the double perspective as disconcerting as a surrealist painting. Reality lies somewhere, exhausted, between their furious perceptions.

Even when separated in different rooms, they could not escape the suspected thoughts of the other. Together or apart, both girls began to experience a new loneliness. The dynamics of their relationship became even more unstable and they longed for other friends or partners with whom to share their lives.

Jennifer was alone. It was the evening of 21st March 1982. She had been locked up in a separate room following one of their dining-room fracases. Relishing her independence, she slowly stripped off her nightdress and strolled around the room.

I felt as though my lover were in my room with me. He watched me. I felt slim, feminine and beautiful. I gazed soberly through the window, watched the hospital with intent, mild eyes. My lover slowly came behind me, he gently caressed my bare shoulders and we held each other close. We kissed, his warm hands cupped my small breasts. He led me to the bed. I lay sad and exposed on the bed, my hands caressed gently, but I felt they were the hands of my lover. I felt so sad and alone. I puffed gently away on my unlit cigarette. I will remember that night and I will imagine that a lover was really with me in that dark and lonely cell . . .

The next morning she was put back in a room with June, but her loneliness was only made more intense.

I feel suddenly like a lost soul. If I were a child again I could not see the problems that enclose me. I wish I was at peace with the things I do, like writing this diary. I'm not totally satisfied with the way I express things on paper. I have to draw. Sometimes I feel a failure. Something weighs heavily on my consciousness, my brain is trapped and I cannot set it free. I need to be one, to be an individual, I need to know that only I exist in the world. My sister has somehow turned cold towards me, she seems so occupied in life, I feel cut off, all alone. I think it would have been better if I had stayed in my isolation.

That night June was in the winning position. She was calm and at peace. Sitting with her feet in the bucket of warm water which the inmates were allowed during the evening lock-up time, she looked out of their window on the little cloistered garden with the spring flowers and the almond tree in the central bed, just moving into blossom – a beauty denied them all those years in Haverfordwest.

A cool, mystical evening. I feel nostalgia rising and the sensation of pure happiness which I felt last summer. I remember Carl and hours of smoking, drifting about in a drunken stupor. Outside the sky is deep blue, my mind is peacefully clear. What would I be doing if I were free? Perhaps I would be lying in the arms of my love. Now I hear the chirping of birds, a thrush, a sparrow. Each moment it grows a little darker. Pure summer air breathes all around me, like a misty vapour, like a glass of cold water (which I now drink).

June's mood of peace continued but was always shadowed by the presence of Jennifer. The two girls danced together to imaginary music, enacting their strange ballet of inner thoughts.

I want someone other than my twin. I want someone to understand me, my moods, my beliefs, my reliability. I want someone to appreciate my loyalty. I just want someone to recognize what I was born for. What in hell was I born for? What course was laid out for me to follow and when I do reach the end of that road, will I look back and regret it? Will I want to change the whole thing round? Maybe I'll say to myself when I'm an old granny, I should have taken the other road, the other direction, but it would be too late.

June looked at her mystic silver bangle and then at Jennifer. Maybe if she could find pliers and cut it off, the curse, Jennifer's curse on her life, would drift away.

It could indeed be the cause of this misery. Haven't J. and I always been at loggerheads? Even more it could be the cause of this endless barrier in my life, watching life go by, wanting desperately to participate and not being able to, this everlasting feeling of being cut off. Could it be why J. and I were unable to speak to our parents? Why we shunned them? Perhaps I would not have done all these things, smashed up buildings. It could all have been imagination. Supposing I had never worn this bangle, would my life be the simple mess it is now?

But for Jennifer, the stress of seeing June dominant was too much. She had been making herself follow a strict dietary regime, almost a fast, which would give her the advantage of being slimmer and more desirable than June. But on Wednesday 24th March, to her shame, her will broke. It always seemed to happen on a Wednesday. And it was no minor deviation. She had two whole breakfasts: two porridges, six slices of bread, two sausages and tea. 'I have fasted for two days,' she revealed, 'and it should have been three. I blame Satan. He made me do it.' And he was still tempting that lunchtime when Jennifer enjoyed a great deal of spaghetti Bolognese, carrots, potatoes (June contributed hers in a rather two-faced sisterly gesture), sponge, custard and tea. Immediately Jennifer was assailed with conscience. 'I will gain control, control over my mind, my body. I must be at peace with myself. I will want death if I have no peace. And who will cry at my funeral? Teenager dies from DIET, BINGE, LIFE. To die, without achieving my ambition.' So next day the fasting started again, and within hours hungry Jennifer was depressed and suicidal again. By now June's mood, exasperated by the lack of news of a firm date for the trial, was equally black.

Then, unexpectedly, there was a diversion. Next morning there was a whirr of activity in the garden. Faces appeared at every window. A man with a bald head, 'strong, slim and virile', was cutting the grass. There was also a short young man and a man of about fifty and an officer in charge of them. The girls were ecstatic: this was life. Alison, the woman in the room next door, already had her window open and was hurling obscenities at them. 'Hey, what yer inside for? C'mon, give us a kiss.'

The older man looked up. June was convinced he was a child molester or rapist. He looked strong as he pushed the electric mower – really strong with bulging veins. A murderer? A sex maniac? He could be famous, but neither June nor Jennifer recognized him. The officer, trying to drown out the obscenities coming from the women's windows, turned the mower on again. June was appalled: 'I mean they're actually handling giant garden shears, rakes and tools. They could have easily attacked the warden and run riot. Especially in a woman's prison too. Chief doesn't know what she's playing at.'

As June was looking out of the window, the oldest of the three prisoners passed by and handed them two daffodils. She hung them up over the door of their room. But the sound of the mower and the smell of the freshly mown grass triggered a new despair.

I blame the daffodils. I blame the daffodils for the misery and depression that has suddenly been forced upon me. Who wants to hear summery sounds while they're in prison? Who wants to hear summery sounds even when they're free. Not me. I hate summer. The same old outings, happy people (but are they really happy?) Going on long-planned holidays (turn out to be disaster and tragic). Children sucking icecream, pregnant women wearing large, blousey dresses, feeling sticky and hot. Men in shorts and vests, bare-chested, sun shades. Why can't it be winter or at least autumn the whole year round. Do we really need summer? It may seem strange to you. I mean here am I a West Indian girl admitting that she detests summer. Yes, I do hate the crowds rushing to the beach. The sick, almost repulsive sound of the disc jockey on the radio playing records, damn records which we'll have to remember sometime in our lives or look back and listen and say 'What were you doing that summer? Who were you with that summer of '82?' So depressing isn't it? I mean you have got to admit half the population would be going through a crisis in their lives, divorce, death, accidents, murder, not only happy events. A child could lose its mother, a family may split up. A man may lose his sight. You've got to think, haven't you, what summer really means. It's a damn desperate race for September. Who actually comes out unscathed to reach that cool, quiet month? Who will survive the holocaust this summer to feel cool, sweet rain on his hot forehead? What lucky family will pack up their last summer picnic and actually drive home to face September? Sometimes I'm filled with a morbid gloom when on a terrifying hot day everyone seems to have deserted the whole face of earth. The place is as if the sun had fallen and everyone run from it. There I'll be, alone and parched, meeting myself who I suppose is just as lonely as I am. Walking barefoot, longing for the shade, longing to sleep but hating to go to bed because when I do it's like the inside of a tumble dryer. My sheets hot and sticky entangled in my sweat-soaked body, my feet searching feverishly for a cool place at the deep end corners of the bed. Even at night, the sun will not leave me. The sounds will go on tormenting me. Happy smiling pathetic faces of humans will go on bringing out all the pity I can muster; pity for the humans who now give up or give in. Submit to those stupid vocations, mowing the lawn, weeding the garden, looking at girls in bikinis or summer frocks. They are swallowed by summer's guile, bewitched, poisoned by her tantalizing ways. Her rays of hope and warmth are blinding headaches to me, a roasting of ball-like flesh in constant use of sun lotion . . .

The diatribe against summer was a little premature in March, but for all that it improved June's spirits. Perhaps it was June's ascendancy that brought about disaster the following night. Reluctantly, the twins had agreed to attend association that evening. Just after 6.0 pm the doors on B block were unlocked and the girls went in excited little groups to the association room. 'June, Jennifer,' called out an officer. 'Time for association. You know you promised the chief to go.' When they could not avoid going to association, the girls made a point of sitting at a table just inside the door and alongside the wall. They took it in turns which of them should sit facing the wall and therefore out of the gaze and attention of the others. Tonight, it was June's turn to face the crowd.

Jennifer noticed how slowly June was walking. Unless she hurried, someone would have taken the secluded table. When they arrived it had gone and they were forced to make their way across the crowded room to another table on the far side. It was then that June fired the first shots in the new battle. Looking straight towards Jennifer, she carefully, deliberately dragged a chair behind her and placed it so that both of them could face the wall. The pact was broken. Jennifer felt anger possess her, June had betrayed their game. She shook with fury, her head felt dizzy, her heart thumped as she longed to seize her sister by the neck and throw her off the chair. Instead she bent down and pretended to read her Edna O'Brien book. June sat back on her seat and stared at her sister, waiting for the reaction she knew her action would provoke. But Jennifer's anger had turned her cold. She was determined to keep calm, remain superior. She felt June's eyes watching, hovering over her, and she knew that June was scared.

All the rays of her fear attracted me like a net. She knew, I knew. All I had to do was snap. All the girls would see me fighting, screaming, hissing and attacking like a cat who is sure of its revenge on a very weak rival. She would be dead and I would be free in my own mind. Free to do what I liked, to become me. I would control myself because I would know that I had killed my enemy. People will just have to understand. It is all a matter of the heart, the spirit, the mind. She's scared. She knows that one night I will get up. I will stand over her bed. I will tighten the noose in my hand . . . It would be the best thing I would have done in my life. I will laugh at the past, stamp on her grave.

The next day they were friends again.

As the days passed the girls became more introspective. They looked back on their past, mourned for the family they had never talked to, worried about their mother and most of all about their own futures. 'The best part of my youth is gone,' wrote June, slowly running away from me. Only older people like my mother will say that I am intensely young with a life ahead of me. Am I really young? When I was 17 I dreaded being 18. I looked upon it as terrifying old age; a woman and still a virgin. But now I am approaching 19, this bitterly crucial age, nearly two decades on earth, I feel wasted. I should have done something great by now. Not crime. Marriage, a child, travelling the wide world. I should be a real woman – who has walked up the altar, had a baby, even a divorce. If I had babies, a home and a husband I should feel wanted and secure. I would worry about my children's future rather than my own. I wouldn't worry about my age. Too many people would be needing my existence. Then again, if my kids died and my husband left me, I'd read the Bible again. I'd take an overdose or help in a mental home . . .

Until at last I reach the age of 40, sit back in my own house, look out of my window, watching my teenage children. Then I know I might be satisfied, I would have done my duty. Then when I have written two best-selling novels, I would be blessed, got my reward for this endless anger and suffering. I can see myself in my late thirties, I might be childless, I might be in a mental home. My parents will be old, almost helpless. My nieces and nephews will be reaching puberty. My sister Rose will be in her twenties. My days of crime will be over and forgotten. Where will J. be? Will we, unbelievably, still be together, sharing a flat, recluses, writing books, inferior to the world? Would all the treatment fail us? What about the News in the papers? Who will be Prime Minister? Lady Di's child will be going to school. Perhaps she will be Queen. I will remember with conviction, that the best part of my life is the part I'm living now . . .

June got some gratification from the news, in her weekly letter from Gloria, that 'Pepsi-Cola Addict' had at last been published. She was now famous both as a criminal and an author: perhaps this might encourage the judge to give her a less severe sentence. The news was no encouragement to Jennifer. In any case, the trial still seemed remote. Both girls were desperately lonely and had been unable to make any kind of friendship with any of the inmates with the exception of poor half-witted Alison, who had been transferred elsewhere. They each blamed the other for their lack of social success, but it was hardly surprising because they now did not communicate at all with the other girls. The only person who really took notice of them was Maureen, a coarse woman in her thirties, and even she was tiring of trying to get a rise out of people who did not respond in any way.

The twins decided to revive their previously unsuccessful attempts at witchcraft. But while the necessary ingredients were hard to find in Haverfordwest, they were almost impossible in Pucklechurch. There was one girl they liked the look of, and they cut out from magazines pictures of rings and bangles in the hope that they would work as well as the real thing in bringing her to them. That was not successful. They then tried deep meditation and chanting, to make a particular girl come and talk to them. The magic did seem to work on one or two occasions and one or two of their 'targets' spoke to them. The tragedy was, the twins were far too embarrassed and frightened to say anything in reply.

In some cases, the meditation on a girl seemed to have the opposite effect. 'I reckon we actually made her go,' wrote Jennifer about a coloured girl to whom they were both attracted. 'Instead of getting the dear soul to speak to us, the magic flew back in our faces. She's been sent to Styal prison.'

Both girls felt the other inmates found them very unapproachable and they longed to step out of themselves. 'I'd strive to be the person I was born to be,' wrote Jennifer. 'I'd drop my name and pick up a new one by deed poll. Everyone's doing it, shedding themselves in all kinds of ways, putting on new ways, new noses, new faces, new hairstyles, dropping their lives and escaping to some far-off country, and being new.'

But such daydreaming did not help the present situation, for once more the twins had been inveigled into attending evening association and though they were hunched over their books on their favourite secluded table, they still attracted the unwelcome attention of Maureen. 'C'mon, you two. When did you ever get a bit of it?' she leered over the table. The overheated room was filled with cigarette smoke and chatter. Three officers sat at one table near the door and gossiped. The twins buried themselves more deeply in their books. All around there was laughing, joking, argument and badinage.

Maureen seemed set to shock the twins when there was a flutter of excitement on another table which sent her scurrying to join it. Indira, a half-caste girl in her mid-twenties, was boasting about the baby she had had. 'Prove it,' shouted Maureen. 'How did y' get it? By kissing?'

Indira, whom the twins judged to be subnormal, nodded and smiled. Maureen leaped forward and pulled up the girl's dress. 'C'mon. Show us your stretch marks then?' Indira looked frightened. Laughter was spreading in ugly bursts around the room. 'How often d'you do it?' Others joined in. 'You'll dry up inside if you don't . . .' The 'screws', noting the change of tone, quickly moved in and removed Indira.

June and Jennifer carried on reading as though nothing had happened. But the seedy little incident triggered memories of their own sexual experiences. June recalled how she had had to put brandy on Carl's penis to help him penetrate her. Even then it had been a struggle. But worth it. She was no longer a virgin. There could be no worse fate than to be locked up in this room full of frustrated women – many of them, she suspected, lesbians – and to have still been intact. No, the others were not superior, more mature or more worldly. She had experienced all of that – and more. She longed to tell these bragging girls a thing or two, but as usual she could not speak. Her tongue lay heavily in her mouth, she knew if she uttered any sound it would be a squeak. Everyone would turn round and stare.

'Look, girls, it's a full moon. Hey, that's the kind of night makes you randy.'

The girls rushed to look out of the window. June was about to take the opportunity to look up when she felt Jennifer's disapproval. She was reading the D. H. Lawrence book June had handed over to her. But was she really? Jennifer was motionless. Not even a glance, not a raised head. June was so possessed she could not turn the pages of her own book.

I see my hand coming up to turn the page. Waiting, choosing the right time to make this move, to turn a page. A hush in the room, I wait until everyone is talking once more. They can't be watching me. I'm invisible. Not there, a statuette turning the page. Someone pours tea into my mug, I drag it towards me. I'm a normal girl drinking tea, holding on to her mug, still reading, eyes down, absorbed in the book. I pick up my cake, take a bite, a square Cromley cake, a few currants. I eat without really chewing, even the motion of my mouth is too embarrassing. People to see me happily munching, never. I eat as though bored, as if it was water. I swallow, hardly chewing, gulp it down with atigue. J. is looking miserable, a frown. I find myself nearly always glancing at

J., trying to read her mind. Angry, mad, ready to explode. Terribly, painfully self-conscious, self-aware.

'How big's 'is cock then? C'mon, black beauties, tell us who 'e is.'

Maureen, bored with discussing Indira's stretch marks and looking at the moon, had turned her attention back to the twins. A snapshot attached to a letter in neat, sloping handwriting had slipped out of the book Jennifer was reading. Maureen grabbed at it and started to show it round. The photograph was of a Ghanaian boy in his late teens. Mark had been one of the first to reply to Jennifer's advertisement in the pen-pal magazine. He had come to England in 1979 and taken up work in a restaurant in Old Woking in Surrey. He dreamed of becoming a chef. He and Jennifer had exchanged letters so formal and circumspect they would have met with approval by the most rigid Victorian parents. They had even arranged their own marriage, a subject of much soul-searching to Jennifer who was not sure whether committing herself to a boy she had never met was quite the right thing to do in a permissive age. Yet she believed in him and dreamed of him. He seemed like the hero in the D. H. Lawrence story she was reading, 'The Captain's Doll', mysterious, from an alien background, but magnetic.

The story got me thinking about Mark. Do I really love him? I still want to meet him, and I will. I can imagine us two as perfect lovers. He'll admire me because he's a Leo. Leos always admire we Arians. Give me a kiss, sweet Mark, I long to say those words to him. I imagine us holding hands, talking, laughing, romancing and making love.

'C'mon, tell us then. Don't say 'e's your brother. 'E looks a bit puny.' Maureen was gleeful. She had been longing to provoke those poker-faced girls ever since they had arrived, just to see if they could talk. But the humiliation only made Jennifer more withdrawn. June was inwardly pleased. She had been both encouraging and envious of Jennifer's 'fiancé'. She took an elder sister's interest in their affair and offered Jennifer advice. She told her they must meet and warned her that he may lose interest if she were to be locked up for many years in prison or a hospital.

'Never seen 'im 'ere? Sure 'e's not one of your imaginings? Why don't you invite 'im to visit? 'E'd love it 'ere, wouldn't 'e, girls?' All the obscene comments, the giggles and laughter could not take away from the purity of her relationship with Mark. But a visit? Meeting him in person? She would have to reflect upon the wisdom of such a move.

One lunchtime a week later, Jennifer was lying on her bed waiting for dinner. An officer handed her a letter.

My heart skipped a beat. I recognized Mark's handwriting. His letter was heartful. He wants our friendship to continue, so do I. He expressed how worried he was about me. I had not written for months and he thought our friendship had ended. He was puzzled over my letter. He recognized my handwriting but the stamp was not my own, it was government property, the rubber one. When he read it, he told me how worried he became. I'm in a remand centre charged with criminal damage. With his heart he tells me that I should ask the Lord, my God for my freedom. Seek and ye shall find. Knock and it shall open to you. He told me where to find this passage. Matthew verse 77. I thank him. He'll be 22 this summer. I no longer care about age. It's love that matters. I feel I love Mark now, and will love him more when I meet him. How long must I wait? I need security, Mark will give it. Yes, my dear Mark, we shall be married some day. We shall be married in style. We could be married in prison. It will not matter, at least I will be a wife. I will belong to somebody.

While Jennifer lived with her memories of Carl and her hopes for Mark, June was planning to eliminate Jennifer from her life: Jennifer was the wicked one, who had got them into this place, who had decided on the pact that had, all these years, kept June from her family and from making outside friends. As the weeks in Pucklechurch grew into months, June felt Jennifer was intent on possessing her mind and soul, and began to fear her with a new intensity.

Trapped in the tiny airless room, the power struggle between the two girls escalated. They were enemy submarines, their periscopes trained on one another, both moving on a similar course, but under opposing commands. The Pucklechurch staff explained their odd behaviour by the belief that the twins were like one mind split in two. But their unison was only an artefact of the years they had spent playing games against the world. They had practised the skill of appearing to be identical. Even the twins themselves believed they could read each other's thoughts, but as they probed more deeply into their inner selves, it became clear their minds did not match.

Despite the identical front they presented, there was almost as great a divide between the twins as between them and the rest of the world. They were always watching, but usually misinterpreting the movements of the other. They each developed exaggerated scenarios of what the other was thinking and planning. War was bound to break out.

Aubrey and Gloria at their daughters' trial. *'These parents shouldn't carry the blame for everything.'* (June)

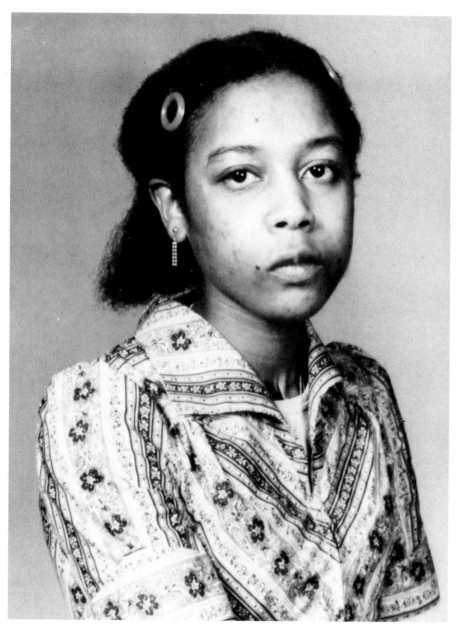

Jennifer in Broadmoor, 1982.

Opposite: June in Broadmoor, 1982, and one of a series of letters to Marjorie Wallace.

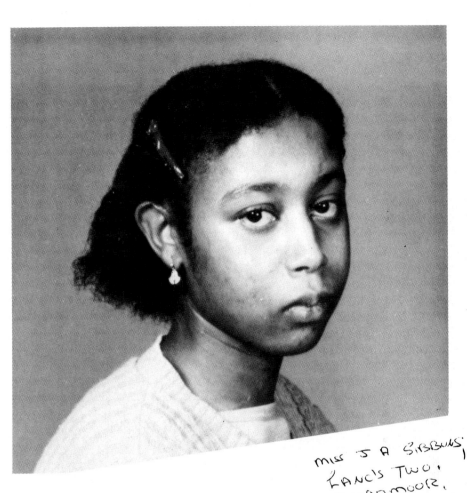

P1

Miss J A SIBBONS,
LANC'S TWO,
BROADMOOR,
HOSPITAL,
CROWTHORNE,
BERKSHIRE,
RG 11 7EG.

Weds. November 24th 1982

Dear Marjorie,
hello, how are you? It was nice of
you to visit on Sunday. Hope you had a pleasant
journey home. I am alright at present.
I'm going around in a kind of "limbo", trying
to think what kind of stories to write. It
doesn't really matter what the story is about, just
so long. It is written in a sensible style.
To set my sleepy brain's writing again, I believe,
I need these two little more booklets, then I might
fin myself, writing from midnight, until dawn.
.... I'm doing quite a bit of reading, when
...... as when I was in Parkle-church,
.... Finnister "The

July 28th 1982 (Wednesday.)

Dear Diary, I feel mentally depressed. Why can't my life ever be perfect. That's just it, life never is. I am disillusioned. Feel lonely, defeated, & I want to commit suicide. I feel it's the only way. Death can only help me.

Extract (reproduced to size) from one of Jennifer's prison diaries.

CHAPTER EIGHT

Shadow Play

Nobody suffers the way I do. Not with a sister. With a husband – yes. With a wife – yes. With a child – yes. But this sister of mine, a dark shadow, robbing me of sunlight is my one and only torment. *June Gibbons*

It was a lazy Sunday afternoon in early April 1982. The Pucklechurch staff were taking a long lunch and the inmates from A wing were locked in their rooms, except those who had been called to see visitors. It was unusually quiet. Outside the sky was stuffy and grey, inside the twins' room the air was stale. Lack of staff that day had meant long hours left to their own devices. For the last two hours June and Jennifer had sat immobile, eyeing each other over the top of their books. Neither spoke. The radio was playing some of the songs of the summer of 1981. Time was weighing heavily on them. They had been on remand in Pucklechurch for almost six months, and the previous day had learned that their trial had been postponed once more, for at least a month.

The twins were on red alert. Tensions had been rising all day as in turn they made their move to escalate the confrontation. At lunchtime Jennifer broke her agreement to eat both June's and her own meal. She had gone too far: the shoot-out seemed inevitable. Then, at the last moment, they reached a compromise. Jennifer ate June's potatoes. June ate Jennifer's rice pudding. But there was no basis for an enduring peace.

Now, sitting barely two feet apart, the adversaries recognized the endgame had started. June was writing her diary as she waited for the next move. In just over a week's time it would be their nineteenth birthday. She could feel their youth draining from them.

'Now I am here perhaps for another month, two months, six months, maybe for another year in this cell. Familiar voices yet change: new people, different atmospheres; summers, winters, autumn I will still be here,' June wrote.

Each day the twins analysed their feelings towards each other and their imprisonment in their diaries, more perspicacious than any psychiatric reports. The memoirs they kept during April and May of 1982 are masterpieces.

June looked through the barred window at the garden and the small almond tree in the central flower bed.

I get visions of that tree suddenly losing those blossoms; and me looking up one day to find those blossoms turned brown, lying at the foot of that lonely tree. I won't still be here, will I? Goddamit. I won't wake up and find winter approaching and cold rays of sunlight shining on the wall of this cell; those pink blossoms one day turned brown. A cold breezy day. Me still here in this cell, waiting. My punishment – this age, this craze, this phase, this anger. I try with all my heart to accept my life as it is. My weariness, my heartaches, my moments of tension, loneliness and anger, I try to live with them. Now I ask myself and probably my soul and you, will they ever find a solution to my problems, to J.'s problems?

The tune on the radio bored into June's mind, jangling recollections of that warm summer in Welsh Hook. She glanced at Jennifer, reading, motionless. Had she recognized the song? When she did, her mood must change, she would feel envy for June, envy for her past. She longed to reach out to change the channel, but did not dare.

Jennifer had noticed the tune, and was silently observing the telltale tremors of June's discomfiture. 'She wants to turn it off,' thought Jennifer. 'She is afraid of memories because she knows she has less to remember.' Jennifer returned to her book, a religious tract, 'Precious Thoughts for Every Day', which Gloria had given her. But spiritual thoughts were not uppermost in her mind. Like Mr Pugh in *Under Milk Wood*, she was quietly dreaming up recipes for removing her irksome lifetime partner.

June's thoughts were no more charitable. As she looked across at her sister she felt creeping through her limbs the paralysis that Jennifer could induce in her. Her lips and tongue were anaesthetized, her whole body was numbed. Only her perception, her intuition remained clear.

Jennifer was the cause of her troubles. Jennifer prevented her from communicating with her parents, with the world. What would happen when they went to court? Would Jennifer win again and make them self-conscious, uncommunicative, act like zombies?

June wanted to star. Why shouldn't she walk, talk, face the judge alone? She imagined her voice ringing out through the courtroom. She would put her hair up, her eyes would sparkle, she would look jaunty and elegant in her floral skirt and everyone would comment on her exuberant personality. She would win them over with her arguments and she would tell them about her problems – and how she had been imprisoned all her life by an evil double of herself. That double would be nowhere near her to let her down and damage her moment of glory, the trial of her life. The hunchback creature with the craning neck and sullen eyes which was her twin would not be there to injure their parents, upset the judge, the solicitor and the officers. But she would not blame the judge, she would tell him how it was all her sister's doing. She would tell the world about their troubles, about the game. She would be released. June saw herself rushing to embrace the world which she had been forced to reject and which had rejected her all these nineteen years. For a moment she felt intoxicated with freedom.

Then she caught sight of her face in the unbreakable mirror which stood on the locker. She looked again and she was sure that the reflection had altered. The outline was the same – but there was something happening to the eyes. They were glinting and growing hard. She looked at her mouth. It was moving too, the corner of her lips began to curl into a mocking grin. Yet her mouth was not moving, and she was not smiling. She realized with horror that the face in the mirror was not hers. The grin was enlarging into a chasm, she could hear her sister's laugh. But Jennifer had not even raised her head, she was still bent over reading or pretending to read.

She saw the veins on the back of Jennifer's neck pulsing. She could feel the hairs on her own arms stiffen. Slowly, June let her arm slide along the top of the locker towards the radio, perched on the top of a pile of library books. She waited, then reached for the tuning knob. In a final act of provocation, she spun the knob off the station that was irritating her.

This was Jennifer's cue. While June was examining her face in the mirror, Jennifer had staked her position. She edged her own chair a few inches nearer, let her book slip onto her lap and tensed her fingers around the bars of June's chair. She jerked it backwards, throwing June against the desk. Then, as an enraged June turned round, she grabbed the chair and thrust it in her face.

'You bitch!' she cried.

'You're evil, you're a witch,' June shouted back. 'I hate you. I've always hated you.'

Jennifer was triumphant: she began to chant in a way she knew would drive June wild. 'The witch will kill the bitch. I am the wicked witch.'

The evil forces June had perceived in the mirror were filling the room. Jennifer seemed possessed and determined to resolve things. She would strike her sister unconscious with the chair, then suffocate her with a pillow and set fire to the cell. Jennifer alone would rise from the ashes.

June reached for the bucket and hurled it at Jennifer. 'Shut up! They'll hear us. They'll hear us talking,' she yelled. Jennifer felt the lump which usually blocked her throat disappear. The hatred inside her had released her voice. 'Let them, let them all hear,' she shouted. By now she had dropped the chair and her hands were around June's neck.

The cell door opened and Mrs Murdoch and a patrol officer burst in. They looked at the wrestling girls, the upturned chairs, the spilled water, the green bedspreads curled like snakes on the floor. The senior officer grabbed Jennifer's wrists to drag her out of the room. The patrol officer took June by the shoulders and pinned her against the bunk bed.

'Put this one next door,' grunted Mrs Murdoch. June was not going to leave it like that. She was not going to let Jennifer go into a new room smiling. She broke free from the officer and lunged at Jennifer, her right hand clawed, her nails closing in on her sister's face. By the time the officer had wrenched back her arm, blood was already running down Jennifer's cheek.

June was left alone in their cell. Slowly the hatred evaporated, leaving her depleted. She lay on her bed, glancing from time to time at the empty bunk above her. The night ahead alone frightened her, yet she still could not forgive her sister. Their relationship was destroying them both and no-one could understand or help. She felt like crying. The radio which a few hours ago had been the object of such intense irritation, was now her comfort. She listened to the Leo Sayer song, 'Have You Ever Been In Love?' The words reminded her of Jennifer, she confided to her diary.

J. and I are like lovers. A love-hate relationship. She thinks I am weak. She knows not how I fear her. This makes me feel more weak. I want to be strong enough to split from her. Oh Lord help me, I am in despair. Can J. and I get back together? I really aim to be alone. Yet, even as I say this, I am deceiving myself. Can I stand being alone? I need someone to talk to, a friend. J.'s bed is empty . . . I wonder if she will ring her bell to come back to me? My heart does not beat so fast now. It only beats fast when J. is around, always with J.

As though she could hear her twin's lament, Jennifer sat smiling with satisfaction in room six, opposite. The previous inmate had left her transistor radio on the window ledge. Relishing her freedom, Jennifer tuned through the channels and chose some operatic music. She had been given a bath and her face had been bathed in disinfectant. It still felt raw where June's fingers had dug into her cheek but she welcomed the discomfort. She did not even mind the thought of having a scar. It would be outward proof to the world of the inner suffering June had inflicted on her. She was pleased that they had fought and that she was now alone. She wondered if June was regretting her behaviour. Would she plead to have her sister back? But Jennifer was not going to forgive her so soon.

I forgive too fast. It was always like this in the past. One minute fighting, next we are friends. At home, my bedroom was a room of blood. Will J. and I ever grow up? Is it a matter of growing up or are we two very wicked women? Pray for me, my friend. Wish me well. Love, Jenny.

P.S. This is the last Sunday that I shall ever be eighteen. Such a cruel, cruel world.

The next day June was put on report for attacking Jennifer. She was given a two-pound fine. By midday, they were together again. 'J. and I are now reunited. No more fighting. I had two dinners. It was shepherd's pie and cabbage, rice pudding. J. only had rice pudding.'

It was the start of a birthday armistice. For a few days there was harmony and all seemed to be going well for the twins. Jennifer had a letter from her pen pal, Mark, in which he referred to her as 'young and beautiful as the colours of a rose'. They had never met and it was months since he had last written, but Jennifer was flattered and worked hard on a suitable reply. But the day the letter came, she had dreamed about a rat, which she interpreted as meaning someone was deceiving her. Could it be Mark? 'My instinct now is to tread warily. Not that I don't trust Mark. He is to be, hopefully, my husband. I yet have to ask him a rather personal question. Is he a virgin? It wouldn't sound right if I ask him so openly in a letter. We have some very nosey officers around here.'

In the end, she decided to invite him to visit and her decision was rewarded: Mark could not accept, but he sent her a birthday card, large and red with a gold rose on it.

The same day June was summoned to see the chief officer. On her desk lay a copy of the long-awaited 'Pepsi-Cola Addict'. She looked at the shiny blue cover with its drawing of her cola-drinking antihero, Preston Wildey-King. She was delighted but critical. She could have drawn it better herself. She examined the thumbnail reproduction of her photograph on the inside cover and regretted she had never been able to get a more glamorous likeness. But it was there. For real. With a caption about her. She read the book again, carefully, and began to wonder whether she was right to set it in California with 'yankee-doodle dandy' dialogue. Surely the Americans would find it phoney, and would prefer to read a book written by a British author with English dialogue?

Pucklechurch was not used to housing novelists and 'Pepsi-Cola Addict' caused quite a stir in the remand centre. So much so, it could easily have destroyed the delicate equilibrium between the twins which had made the Easter armistice possible. But Jennifer had her relationship with Mark and both girls were looking forward to their parents visiting them on Easter Saturday, the day before their birthday.

It was a long and tiring journey for the Gibbons family, so their visits were infrequent. Aubrey and Gloria, Greta with her baby Helen-Marie, and Rosie had got up early to catch the train which meanders round the coastline of West Wales to Swansea, Cardiff and, ultimately, Bristol. There they took a taxi to Pucklechurch, ten miles away in the Avon countryside. As they came close to the prison Gloria felt the oppression of the high walls and barbed-wire-capped fences. At the gate, a warder explained that only two visitors were allowed at a time, that visits were limited to fifteen minutes, and children were not permitted. Obedient as always, Aubrey accepted the restriction without complaint and told Greta and Rosie they would have to stay outside with the baby. Gloria and he went inside and waited for their names to be called. In due course, an officer escorted them to a small room with a dozen or so tables around which prisoners and their visitors were sitting.

After some time the twins arrived, holding on to each other's arms. They sat at the table, heads lowered, and mumbled occasionally. Gloria tried bravely to carry on a one-sided conversation with them. She noticed the scratches on Jennifer's face which had not yet healed. It was very familiar. Gloria had seen the twins' faces torn by fighting many times before. But surely in a prison the officers could stop the girls from damaging each other? She ignored the wounds and babbled on inconsequentially, telling the girls news of Haverfordwest, discussing clothes, anything to fill up the canyon of silence.

Aubrey was more impatient. His few bluff comments and half-jokes had elicited no response from the twins. The visit was not a social success. He fiddled with the brown case with clothes the girls had asked for in their letters: the blue floral skirts, some tee shirts and sneakers.

To bring the flagging visit to life, he brought out the clothes, the two silver crucifixes Gloria had bought for their birthday presents, some boxes of chocolate and two Easter eggs. The girls' eyes shone with delight. But the feast had been spotted by a prison officer who rushed across.

'They can't have those,' she explained to Aubrey. 'You'll have to pack them up and take them home with you. You're not allowed to bring anything in unless it appears on our sheet.' With a resigned shrug Aubrey began to repack the case.

'You've got to book it in advance. If you fill in a request form, your parents can bring clothes for you next time,' the officer told June and Jennifer.

'But it's their birthday tomorrow,' said Gloria. 'Couldn't they just have something?'

'I'll let them keep the chocolates and Easter eggs,' said the officer. 'But that's a special privilege that won't be repeated. Now I'm afraid your time's up.'

There were subdued farewells, then Gloria and Aubrey slipped silently away, back to Wales. The visit might have appeared disastrous, yet that evening Jennifer recorded in her diary: 'A most amazing and glorious thing has occurred. My parents actually came to visit me. It means more to me than anything. I always wanted something big to happen before I was nineteen.'

The twins' birthday was on Easter Sunday. The day started with an officer delivering a pile of cards from the family. The beds were stacked with the sweets their parents had brought, ready for a birthday feast. For once, June and Jennifer tasted the popularity they craved as the other girls, glancing through the door, saw the glitter of confectionery and the birthday cards. One young girl, Cathy, came in weeping, saying she was pregnant and the last time her parents visited they had forgotten to bring her sweets. June, moved by the story, offered her a chocolate. Then Indira came in, eyeing the gold-papered goodies. She was readily persuaded to eat one. Like many of the inmates, Indira found the twins eerie, and was normally frightened to visit them in their room. But the candy lure overcame such prejudices.

'Why can't we make friends, break down the barriers? Why can't we join the group?' reflected June.

Why can't I be the free, happy, 19-year-old I want to be? All I have to do is hang on to Cathy next door, follower her around. Talk. Laugh. Association would hold no more terrors. I'd sit on a table, be in a group. J. and I would go our own ways. It is up to my mind, my subconscious to change. People won't be hostile because I will not be hostile. If I were alone now without J., I would have a friend. Probably in here, next door. Everyone would get used to me and this friend going around with each other. I would eat in the dining hall, walk happily on exercise, go to association with the feeling I would love to go. Life wouldn't be so threatening.

Soon there was a little group of visitors munching away and attempting to gossip with the mute twins. But conversation did not flow. 'We all ran out of words to say. It was embarrassing,' recalled Jennifer. The guests felt uneasy and drifted away, leaving June and Jennifer on their own, eating chocolates, trying on their new sneakers, sent as presents, and dancing together in the confined space of their room. The truce was holding. For that day the two could meet in the no-man's-land between them without fear. But the armistice soon came to an end.

'C'mon, you two!' Mrs Murdoch shouted. 'If you don't move you'll get constipation, piles and bad breath. Now get marching.'

The girls had been forced out on the exercise yard. Even though it was their right, as prisoners on remand, to refuse exercise and association, the officers always insisted the Gibbons twins joined the other inmates for two half-hour exercise periods a day. It was cold and foggy. June walked on but Jennifer refused to keep pace with her. Instead she shuffled a few steps behind. June was furious:

She's not even footing with me. Tension. Agony. We don't speak at all. Two robots really. I must get away from her. I can't stand to see her deteriorating in front of me. Her moods affect her bodily positions. But I'm not like that. I'm more responsible. I fear Court in her state. She would let me down, standing in the box with such a terrible shaped body, her knees slightly bent, neck jutting out, a self-conscious paranoid look on her face, her hands holding onto the front of her jumper. I grew out of that habit years ago. I could push her. I could just give her a shove. I pity Mark. In his mind he sees a lovely straight-backed girl, smile on her face, young, brave and well-developed. But what is Jennifer in here? Cowering, afraid of eyes, people watching . . .

Whenever one twin examined the other, she could see only lies and distortions. At one moment she saw reflected in her twin all the faults she feared were in her own appearance. The next, she would see only the ideal and envy it – a young girl, with a gentle expression and profile which could rival that of Greta Garbo or Audrey Hepburn. June, riding high in her new confidence, portrayed Jennifer in her mind in the harshest tones. She decided to turn her technique of silence against her sister. The staff were puzzled at the extent to which one girl could ignore the other.

After exercise the twins returned to their cell, silent, uncommunicative, independently storing an armoury of invective in their diaries. June was examining another solution: suppose there were only one of them? There could be no question then of inferiority or bondage. June looked across at Jennifer, a few feet away, as she wrote:

It is a cool evening. J. is a miserable bitch, how I could kill her. At the moment we are arguing about nothing. My book? Is she jealous? I want to escape her. One of us is plotting to kill one of us. A thud on the head on a cool evening, dragging the lifeless body, digging a secret grave. I'm in a dangerous situation, a scheming, insiduous plot. How will it end? At 19 I want to be an individual, independent from that bitch. I'm in enslavement to her. This creature who lounges in this cell, who is with me every hour of my living soul.

We have become fatal enemies in each other's eyes. We feel the irritating deadly rays come out of our bodies, stinging each other's skin. We scheme, we plot and who will win? A war which has gone on much too long, when will it reach its climax? Tonight, tomorrow, Sunday? A deadly day is getting closer each minute, coming to a point of imminent death like hands creeping out against the night sky, intentions of evil, blood, a knife, a mincer . . . I say to myself, how can I get rid of my own shadow? Impossible or not impossible? Without my shadow would I die? Without my shadow would I gain life? Increase my situation or decrease it? Be free or left to die, feel weak or sometimes powerful, without my shadow which I identify with the face of misery, deception, murder.

June spent days fostering her hatred, but still lacked courage to make her challenge. Jennifer seemed unconcerned by her threat and that was already sapping June's confidence. But June misread her twin. Jennifer's calmness in the face of the challenge was because she was unaware of it; oblivious of the hatred and internal pressures June had built up. Like lovers lying side by side in bed, their physical proximity served only to increase the gulf of misunderstanding through failure to communicate. June's fury was now tempered with doubt.

She doesn't deserve bail or another prison. She needs to be locked away – from me, from other girls, even from Mark. Who could tolerate that passionate bitch – full of intense hate, full of senseless obsessions about her looks? That endless starving or bingeing. God help her! Or better, God help me. She's ten times more the bitch than I am. She learned that from sweet Carl. Always calling her obscene names because he loved her, and wanted to change her. But do I love her? Oh, Christ! what a painful question to ask myself. What about 'Do I hate her?' It isn't strong enough. How about, would I kill her if I had the chance? How? Morphine in a glass of milk? A cosh over the head? Or a stab through the heart? I am a would-be murderess. I wouldn't kill a flea. But J.?

June, attempting to break the impasse, tried to goad Jennifer into attacking her, which would bring the officers to separate them. She succeeded in needling Jennifer into aggression. 'Once again the old rebellious tiger came out,' wrote Jennifer. 'I seized June by her pretty head and shook it. She grabbed my hand but ended up clutching my neck. I yelled at her.'

Jennifer was dragged out, taken to a different room, and next day fined the usual two pounds. Both girls were put on report. June was well pleased. It was almost a victory. But it was short-lived. Alone once again in her room, June reflected on her fate.

21st April 1982. The troubles of my dear heart are enlarged, beating within me like a flame of fire; like a rocket about to take off. To be free. But I am not free. The pain, the weariness of life; the anxiety always for peace. For I long for escape, but from whom? From what? My own irresponsible life of mundane thoughts, of seeking for a restored life, free from burden, free from pain. But I believe hope always boomerangs back to me. I hate the life I am leading now. But why do I say leading? For I do not lead my life at all. It is pulled along by an invisible string. By whom? By what? A circumstance of the past. A force. I am just an onlooker. Yet I suffer as an onlooker would not. For if I came up to two people quarrelling bitterly, I would be suddenly glad of my own being; yet as an onlooker, I would still pick out one of the quarrellers and have deep pity in my heart. For one would lose. Looking at oneself as a character from a story. Born to lose. A character who deserves all sympathy; yet what sympathy there is in the readers is all doled out to the other characters. Who will ever guess she suffered? Perhaps her eyes, dark and brooding. Perhaps a discontented look upon her brow. Perhaps a twist of sadness lingering upon her face. Only a sensitive person would know. This person would be intrigued. Compare the sadness of himself to hers; be puzzled. Finally he would delve into her past. She will hesitate to pronounce her past; feel afraid, yet terribly anxious to reveal all her pain. She will be somewhat like a martyr, special. She will feel chosen. Ah! she will sigh. Sympathy at last. There is understanding in this world after all. So I and she will weep uncontrollably: only for herself. Like as though she were watching a sad film in the movies. And she will weep for the character, only because she recognizes this character to be herself. She will cry partly out of relief to know somebody in the world understands her; like the man she met at the party; like the time she laughed and out-laughed her friends. Why was she laughing? Partly out of anxiety, out of grief. No, she was not really laughing. She was laughing like a disturbed child who goes to a Punch and Judy and laughs; only for that split second does the child laugh, forgetting all his troubles. All his intense hate. A laugh as false and unrealistic as the hot yellow sun at night . . .

June's fantasy was no more than an image of herself and her own struggle. She had become convinced that, as in primitive African belief, creating two identical human beings was Nature's unpleasant joke. She and her sister were the result of some ancestral curse. Their silence and lack of communication were said to be an expression of resentment against the world and in particular against their parents. But June's anger was not directed towards her parents. They had committed only one mistake: allowing both twins to live. 'Poor parents,' she commiserated. 'They take the blame for everything. And they shouldn't. It was fate: Kismet.'

Jennifer, in contrast to June, sought refuge in being a twin. She felt herself to be the inferior. She could not tolerate June's superiority and independence.

Somewhere I have a real twin in this world. J. can't be my real twin. My real twin was born the exact time as me, has my rising sign, my looks, my ways, my dreams, my ambitions. He or she will have my weaknesses, failures, opinions. All this makes a twin – no differences. I can't stand differences. J. hasn't got my mind, my looks, not even my build. My mother when once she measured us told me I was slightly taller than J. I was not exactly pleased.

Their disagreement on the nature of twinship only served to tighten the bonds by which each had ensnared the other. However much they wrote about breaking free, the two girls were trapped in their cell. One twin could not stir, breathe or swallow without irritating the other. In that brittle atmosphere their childhood rituals became, as June described, a form of mutual torture.

This morning in bed I lay there. I didn't move. I didn't breathe. For I knew it was the beginning of a game. I heard the breakfast trolley go over. My heart beat; I began to sweat. I wondered to myself, should I call her? She was up there snoring, breathing heavily. But was she really? She lay there like a person awaiting execution. Paralysed. Afraid to move, lest the guillotine slice her throat, lest she did something which would anger her all day. She did not think of moving. One move would be the biggest mistake she made. Fatal. So she lay unmoveable, I lay likewise, as though paralysed by her stillness, her refusal to move. For I knew it was a refusal; it was not an inability. She had not lost her power to move. And all her perception was sharper than steel. So sharply cut, it sliced through to my own perception. They clashed, cutting into each other. Sinking in. Finding out. And so it was this. I read her mind, I knew all about her mood, in that split second I awoke from my unconsciousness to the sound of her perception; her perception which made mine ten times as sharp. My mood. Her mood. Clash. Like spilled blood. My perception. Her perception. Twisting and clashing, knowing, cunning, sly . . .
And where will it all end? In death? In separation? I cannot help it. She cannot help it. It comes over us like a vague mist. It sends murder into my heart, rage into my head, this early morning anger. Time to unlock. The officers are here, opening each door. I wait. Tense. Like a cat ready to spring, but not springing. Without a sound, using the hustle and bustle to drown out the slipping of my body from the sheets, I touch ground. Then she is moving. Angry, raging. For who has won the war? Not I really. I still feel rage in my soul. But if she is angry, I see no reason to be angry too. For only one should lose. Not both. This is the game.

A quarrel, punishment and separation were inevitable. The following day, alone in a cell, June wept for the first time in weeks. Just as life with her twin was intolerable, so life without filled her with a terrible sense of loss. Either way she suffered. Alone in the room, waiting to hear Jennifer's tap on the door or to see the two familiar eyes peep in through the observation slit, she had to endure physical loneliness: when she was with Jennifer it was different – the deeper loneliness of two people locked together yet failing to make contact.

That morning June had her period. In her present mood, Jennifer was to blame for that. 'It is J. who put this curse on me, the curse of the red, running river,' she complained. 'It was as though through the rivers, was my own child, like inky dye.' Both June and Jennifer believed that each would steal the other's children. Babies had become an obsession which symbolized their need to be recognized. 'For I do not want to reach forty without children. I do not want to pass away from this world without someone to remember me as important in their lives.'

She knocked at Jennifer's door. Jennifer knocked back but that only filled June with more ambivalence.

She too will miss my company. No. We don't really hate each other as much as that; for if I died, she would probably succumb and die too. Should I tear her face to bits when we meet again? Or should I stay calm, accept my position, being pushed out into this cold, bitter cell. Last night I dreamed of a mirror and in that mirror was J. I looked in it as a spy would, and I could see J. A mirror means illness or loss, yes, J. is gone from me.

Jennifer next door was also feeling desperate.

I wonder what June is doing now? Who is really mad – J. or me? Is J. possessed by a demon? Am I? There must be a spirit that won't leave me alone. All my life it has been with me. I call it the beast. I am now thinking I should like be rid of J. forever. She is just a bag of misery. Because she fails to co-operate with my beliefs, I cannot help myself. She thinks me so aloof, she doesn't realize that beneath my image, I too have a heart. I feel so forsaken. I always seem to lose. June has won all the battles. I always suffer with the knowledge I have lost. Even though she was dragged out, I felt she'd won. It is not the material things I speak of, it is the mind. Her thoughts, her words, her wicked, beautiful words make her a winner. I don't forget the words. They haunt me. Her criticism haunts me. Her past haunts me. She is the ghost and I am the mortal soul, the soul that some day must die. I feel as though I have just put J. in her grave. I have thrown her in, never to come up again but her words will always pick a way to come back and haunt me. June is too much of a powerful force . . .

As the month of April moved slowly by, the twins' pattern of fights, separations and reunions dragged on, though with diminishing fervour. June made no further attempt to impose her will, and the girls' attention turned more to the continual delays in bringing them to court. At first they had been because the prosecution was not ready to proceed. But now the defence was deferring the trial.

Wynn Rees and Michael Jones, the solicitors, were aware the prosecution had such strong evidence, including a diary of June's eulogizing on the delights of arson, that there was no chance they would be found not guilty. But the diary sounded so bizarre, the lawyers thought there was a chance of getting the twins treatment in a mental hospital rather than a prison sentence. Hospital must surely be preferable to prison? Michael Jones discovered a psychiatrist, Dr William Spry, who specialized in treating young offenders, and arranged for him to visit the twins while they were on remand and later in Pucklechurch.

'Miss Gibbons, you know that I have been called in by your solicitor to talk to you about your case. Mr Jones felt that I might be able to help understand some of your problems.'

June was sitting on her own, her head lowered. Dr Spry was a man in his early fifties, soft-spoken, with a grey goatee beard and curly brown fringe. He had a habit when speaking of blinking slowly like a nocturnal animal. From his opening remarks he somehow triggered June's resistance.

'Now, June, the police found some material in your bedroom. There were some diaries which you kept at the time of your alleged crimes. Tell me, have you and your sister always kept diaries? The chief officer tells me you spend most of your days here writing?' There was no reply. 'You got yourself in a bit of a mess and we feel that a spell in a special hospital would help you and your sister sort yourselves out. Dr Hamilton and I are trying to find one suitable for your needs.'

There was still no response. Dr Spry flicked through a file containing copies of the diaries the police had found. 'Hmmm. You write here you used to carry a knife with you? Now what would that be for?'

'Does he think I'm daft?' thought June. 'Of course I know it's a male sex symbol. He's excited by my diaries, I can see that.' She muttered the word 'protection'.

'If a man or boy were to waylay you, would you use it to protect yourself?'

'What else?' thought the unresponsive June. 'Surely he didn't think I would use it to threaten him into having sex with me?'

'Isn't it a bit unusual for a girl like you to be carrying something like that?' Dr Spry persisted.

Still no reply. June was beginning to find it amusing. 'It was only a small penknife,' she recalled, 'not even sharp. Anyway, it was stuffed down my wellie. I wouldn't have known how to use it if I had tried.'

As the interview progressed the unspoken conflict grew – at least in June's mind. Then Dr Spry said, 'You write here about rape. Tell me, June, do you enjoy –?'

June exploded: 'I'm sure he said the word "fuck". Why not say "make love" or "coition" or even "intercourse" itself. But not "fuck". It sounds like "suck", like stinking mud; like bubbling porridge, the way holes get sucked in. Of course I say "Fuck off". But "Do you enjoy fucking?" It's so damn well obscene. "Fuck" takes a lusty second and it's over. The boy satisfied, the girl all sore.'

Dr Spry maintains that he did not nor ever would use such a word, but whatever he said, or she thought she heard, offended her. He went on to question her about the fires.

June was inwardly triumphant. 'Ah, he's got there at last! Arson and sex. Surely he knows that all we arsonists are only looking for sexual fulfilment? Everyone knows about that.'

After June was escorted away, it was Jennifer's turn. Apart from three or four interviews with the uncommunicative twins, Dr Spry also visited the scenes of the twins' crimes, and met their parents once. But his main source was the diary June had kept during the five weeks of their summer orgy of sex and crime. This diary is aggressive and crude, quite unlike the thousands of pages which preceded and follow it. Spry did not meet the twins' teachers, nor the psychiatrist, educational psychologist and other staff who worked with them at Eastgate, although he asked for a report from them. He had learned very little about their history and thought their literary ambitions and their intensive programme of self-education irrelevant. He was only vaguely aware of the Kennedy boys and did not know the extent to which they had introduced the twins to glue, alcohol, drugs and sex, and probably also put the idea of arson into their heads. But he did see for himself the intense hatred that existed between them. In a later interview one of the twins began to speak. The other immediately set upon her and they fought like tigers, drawing blood from each other's faces.

Spry felt the twins were mentally sick and needed treatment: a prison sentence would be 'totally inappropriate'. But what was wrong with them? He decided they could be classed as psychopaths. The Mental Health Act defines 'psychopathic disorder' as a 'persistent disorder or disability of mind which results in abnormally aggressive or seriously irresponsible conduct'. Spry may have been unaware that the twins' criminal behaviour dated only from the time they had been left by the American boys and could hardly be described as persistent, and that they had no record of aggression except to one another in the heat of their rivalry. He felt the 'gang bangs' June referred to in her diary were very aggressive acts towards boys of their own age, although the boys were hardly innocent victims. The twins' silence Spry described as 'aggressive mutism'. But the arguments were tenuous and do little but demonstrate the inadequacy of the definition of a psychopath.

The solicitors accepted Dr Spry's report, and decided to base their defence on it. If the twins were to avoid prison on the grounds that they were psychopaths, a hospital with a secure unit had to be found which would admit them for treatment. Spry was unable to find such a one. There were two problems: first, under the DHSS rules, the twins were only eligible to go to one of the mental hospitals in the catchment area in which they lived, and none was suitable; secondly, no hospital was keen to admit two mute psychopathic arsonists.

In the end Dr Spry approached Dr John Hamilton, consultant psychiatrist at Broadmoor hospital. Broadmoor and other special hospitals can accept patients from any part of the country. Hamilton was keen to bring to Broadmoor a reputation for effective treatment of its dangerous patients, rather than keep it simply a secure place in which to confine and forget them. In his eight years as a consultant there he had set up a unit for young men with personality disorders. Hamilton was interested in Spry's description of the twins, and arranged to visit Pucklechurch to see them. He had no unit for adolescent girls, but Broadmoor had engaged a communication-skills therapist who he felt might succeed in getting the silent twins to talk. Broadmoor was not ideal, but it appeared to be the only chance of getting the twins treatment instead of prison. The decision was made and the lawyers agreed that either Dr Spry or Dr Hamilton would appear as psychiatric expert at the twins' trial.

While these arrangements were being made, the twins were growing impatient. They wrote letters demanding new solicitors, immediate trial and a release from their limbo. Three or four times the hearing was postponed. They continued to prepare themselves for the court appearance, to slim, to make themselves more attractive, but the delays were demoralizing.

Always pining for a different face, for I am never happy with it. My eyes seem like small holes; when I smile or grin my face just enlarges. It is only when I draw my cheeks in that I am temporarily satisfied. But I cannot go on living all my life drawing in my cheeks. I do so want this Greta Garbo look, the hollow-cheeked urchin appeal.

The pressures of the wait and successive postponements began to tell on the girls and both suffered nightmares, often the same nightmare, a particularly terrifying experience which they called the Beast. It was a sensation which would overcome them when they were dozing or just waking up or falling asleep. On 29th April they both record such an experience. It was just after dinner. Jennifer had eaten and enjoyed kidneys and cabbage and two sponges in custard. June had eaten her main course but donated her sponge to Jennifer. For once, there seemed to be harmony. Both girls lay on their beds and fell asleep.

June woke an hour later. She felt a great heavy breathing weight enveloping her as though a fat man had lain on top of her, smothering her in the folds of his flesh. She lay scared and rigid, unable to struggle against the hands which she felt were moving towards her throat. The Beast had in the past tickled her stomach as though in play. She felt like a tiny baby who was being suffocated, too weak to struggle against the presence. Both girls likened the sensation to what a baby must feel before a cot death. June heard Jennifer moaning in the bunk above her. She, too, was lying paralysed under the unknown weight, but June did not know. 'If I don't struggle to move, I know I will die,' wrote June. 'Will he ever leave me? Perhaps when I die I will die in my sleep, though you and I shall only know the truth; the monster has won.'

The twins could offer no explanation of their nightmare, which they had experienced for the first time only two years before. It may simply have been an extension of their waking quarrels, or perhaps it was some subconscious recollection of an infant trauma. Did someone, a jealous brother or sister, hold a pillow over the faces of the toddler twins? Or did June and Jennifer's rivalry start in Gloria's womb because there was not enough room for two of them to grow and flourish there? The position in which they were born – June head first, Jennifer breech – may have meant that June literally was sat upon by her sister. They had, even before birth, crowded each other out. The Beast was the other twin.

The long wait was relieved by another visit from Dr Spry, together with Dr Hamilton, who told the twins that Broadmoor was willing to accept them. He described the village atmosphere of the place, the comparative freedom (provided they behaved well), the therapist and nurses who would help sort out their problems, the hairdressers, the gardens, the sports facilities. Over the next weeks, both girls began to build fantasies around this wonderful hospital, this utopia in which they could luxuriate and resolve their difficulties.

From then on they expected each day to hear their names called to go to the governor to be told the date of their trial. The trial and the hospital they would be sent to afterwards became their only hope. 'When I get to the hospital,' wrote June, 'I won't be suffering. I'll be sitting with other people, enjoying the sun. I'll be moveable and approachable and TALKATIVE. If I'm quiet one day it will be because of my mood; not that I'm slowly deteriorating.'

The call came early in May when, full of hope, they were summoned to see the chief officer. 'June, Jennifer, I am afraid that we have just had a message from your solicitor to say that Dr Spry has to leave the country tomorrow for several weeks. I'm afraid your trial has had to be postponed.'

'I can't imagine myself in Pucklechurch all the summer,' reflected a despairing June. 'Just sending my life away, eating, ageing with J.; no visitors, no contact from the outside world; no trial. Just getting fatter and older and more withdrawn.' And Jennifer told her diary:

I thought I'd just say this to you. I am just 19 and already I feel the disillusionment of a woman who is growing old and is miserable and full of grief and pain. Dear friend, my heart is weary. I brood and remember and regret. My cell window is watching me. My cell door, oh it just stares and it never opens without keys. Four white walls and then there is me. Pray for me . . . My name is Jenny and I am slowly getting to know myself. Remember me, Jenny.

Then, as the twins were reaching their darkest moment, an officer arrived with a letter from their solicitor. The date for the trial would be in a week's time, 14th May 1982, provided accommodation had been confirmed for them at the hospital. June's excitement for the approaching day transformed her and soothed the tensions with Jennifer.

It is all God's doing. He has cut my problems in half; so I only remain with one half of my burden. My worries, my impatience, my anxiety have all ceased for a while. I shall count the days, the hours, the minutes: I shall await Thursday. Then, on Friday the morning shall arrive. All I need do is to hold on until next week.

Together the sisters planned how they would look: they set about putting in requisition forms for their floral skirts and black jackets. June embarked on a desperate last diet to appear the more beautiful. They started a new programme of exercises for their bodies, touching toes and jogging on the spot in their cell.

On 13th May, the eve of the big day, both girls were summoned to see the chief officer. She informed them that due to a lack of a second psychiatric report, their case had been postponed again. Back in their cell, June tore down the few late wallflowers which were hanging above the door and threw them out of the window. She wrote to her solicitor, accusing the judge of racial prejudice, and of putting aside their case, just because they were 'black and daft'. The twins were set on revenge.

It was six o'clock on Monday evening. The day had been full of tension. The girls hardly spoke to each other. They went to fetch their tea and saved some butter which they concealed in their socks. Back in their room, June took the cover from one of their drawing books and put it over the observation panel in the door, while Jennifer knelt down to spread butter over the screws fixing their bunk beds to the wall, in the hope of loosening them. In silence, they stripped their beds and pushed their nightclothes and exercise books into their pillowcases. June hung one of the new green bedspreads across the lower part of the window. They waited for the evening patrol to come on duty, the cell doors to be unlocked and the inmates summoned for association.

It was not long before they heard the familiar sound of officers' footsteps and the rattling of keys. 'These two are coming,' they heard Miss Neal calling. That was their signal. They resented being called 'these two' by all the officers and neither girl had any intention of going to association. They were going to show the officers, the judge, the doctors who they felt had neglected them, and their solicitors, what they were feeling. For once their rebellion was going to be one of action.

As the keys turned in the lock, the girls hauled down the mattress from the top bunk and used it as a barricade. June pushed forwards while Jennifer leaned with her back against the door, propping her leg on the desk.

'One, two, three,' said Miss Neal and she and two other officers heaved. The door moved but the twins had wedged the mattress firmly and they were able to hold it back. The door was locked again as more help was summoned. June and Jennifer could hear voices in the garden outside. Jennifer rushed to drag her mattress from the lower bunk to put across the window, while June held the fort at the door.

'C'mon, girls,' a male voice shouted outside the door. 'It's silly to go on. We can get that door down in a few minutes and you'll get hurt.'

'It's only a mattress,' they heard another voice outside their window. It was followed by a laugh. 'They're just little mites and they think they're strong!'

But the twins felt exhilarated by their performance. They knew they had little chance of holding out, but they were not impressed by their opposition. The door was unlocked again and this time a piece of wood like a broom handle was pushed through to wedge it open. 'We're used to this sort of thing,' warned the man's voice. 'One of the boys tried it and he ended up with his head jammed between the bed and the mattress. If you won't take it away, we'll have to fetch a jack.'

There was a short lull before the male warder returned with a jack. June and Jennifer watched with alarm as the door shook loose from its hinges. They put on their jackets and grabbed their pillowcases. Just in time. A triumphant Miss Neal walked in. She was relishing her handling of the situation.

'Right! Let's be having you.' She took hold of June and jerked her out of the room. The night orderly seized her pillowcase. June struggled.

For the first time in their six months' stay the girls describe how they were subjected to some physical bullying. Until now, the officers on the assessment wing and the nurses in the hospital wing, according to the twins, had treated them well. Indeed, some had shown positive kindness and sympathy which the girls registered, but never outwardly acknowledged. While June and Jennifer confined their protests to each other, they had received little or no punishment – a fine of fifty pence, a pound or possibly two – just enough to deprive them of a few bars of chocolate or packets of nuts from the canteen. At worst they would be put on report and given room confinement, which meant they were deprived of the 'privilege' of eating with others in the dining room or mixing with them at exercise or association. If they had injured each other in their skirmishes, they would be separated for a time, an outcome which the twins had usually planned. If they had any complaints, they were allowed to book an appointment with the chief officer, who would listen – or try to listen – to their needs. Like most of the staff she could seldom make out what the Gibbons twins were saying and usually misunderstood their requests.

But putting up a barricade was different. It was an act of hostility against the officers and the regime, a serious offence, punishable under rule 20 of prison regulations. June was pushed roughly down the corridor to the 'dungeon' in an annexe off A wing. 'It was like being raped,' she fantasized. 'Raped by a pack of wild lesbians.' In an anteroom she was undressed, even her bra and underpants removed, and a piece of material which looked like brown sacking was pulled over her head. She felt angry and embarrassed. Her slide and rubber band were wrenched out of her hair. 'There was a sexual element in it. I almost enjoyed the whole hassle. There was I helpless, yet defensive.' One of the officers grabbed her wrists and tried to remove her silver bangle. Her grip was painful and she did not let go until June was safely inside the strip cell.

June looked around her. The floor was concrete, as were the walls. There was no window, only an opaque skylight in the ceiling. There was no furniture, except a wooden bench attached to the floor and, screwed to the wall beside it, a small tabletop. There was an oblong concrete platform in the shape of a mattress, covered by wooden slats. Two navy-blue quilts were folded on top of the 'bed', which looked disturbingly like one of the Welsh family tombs in St Mary's church-yard in Haverfordwest, which she and Jennifer had used as a table for their secret binges.

The door was unlocked and she looked up to see three officers staring at her from the entrance. She was being treated like a dangerous animal and it amused her. She wondered which of them would have the courage to step inside. Much to June's admiration, Miss Neal walked in and placed a polythene cup of tea and a polythene plate with a rock cake on the shelf. 'Your supper, June,' she said without looking at the girl. June felt sure she was embarrassed.

The door was locked and there was silence. Every quarter of an hour, according to regulations, an officer checked on her through one of the spy holes in the door or the wall. June lay on her stone slab without moving, gazing up at the skylight, a smile on her face. The night staff could not understand. It was usual for girls to rant and rave when put in the strip cell. They would scream, bang on the door, or keep pressing the internal bell. This black twin uttered no sound and made no movement. It was difficult to ignore the irony of locking a girl whose main offence against society was being mute and withdrawn into a silent cell.

June lay and reflected on her life so far. The slab was hard and she was frightened by the thought of earwigs creeping about in the wooden slats. She looked across the room and saw a small hole in the wall where she thought rats could come in. But it was warm in the cell and she felt at peace. She was determined to refuse all food and water. As her mind dozed, she was sure she could hear Jennifer's breathing. She looked around the empty cell. Perhaps they had no other room and had taken Jennifer to this one while June was sleeping. Where was Jennifer now? June spoke seriously to her subconscious and meditated. She came to the conclusion that Jennifer was in the hospital wing. The thought of Jennifer lying in their own room and not suffering was too disturbing. But was she also in strip dress in a punishment cell? Did she have a mattress? Had she also refused her food?

Jennifer in her silent cell over on hospital wing was in turn torment-ing herself with the thought that her sister was having the better deal. She was quite pleased to be in strip dress, it was a dress after all, if not particularly flattering. At least she had a mattress and there was a window overlooking the garden. She sat on the grey mattress in the centre of the room, opposite the spy hole. There was a noise as the flap at the bottom of the door opened and a cup of tea and a cake were pushed through. Eventually she wrapped herself in the one blanket and fell asleep. The day had been a success.

'Good morning, June. Wakey, wakey.' One of the day officers entered the strip cell. June had been dreaming of her mother. The morning sunlight streaked in through the skylight. Her eyes were dazzled by the white starched blouse Miss Neal was wearing. Miss Neal looked at the uneaten rock cake and the unused pot. She handed June a pink quilted dressing gown and a pair of purple slippers. 'Button it up,' she admonished. 'We don't want you flashing everything to the governor.'

The governor came from the male wing of the remand centre. 'I felt downright offended to be seen in this state by a phony, weasel man,' June wrote later. The officer who had been on duty the night before read out the statement describing the barricade. It read quite dramatically. June felt proud. Then came the questions:

'Why did you do it? Your sister said it was because you did not want to go to association again.'

June knew that it was much more than that. It was the delays in court, the frustration and the impossibility of being confined with Jennifer in a cell. But it was not worth explaining all this.

'You must understand, June, that it is no use running away from society.' The governor launched into his speech. 'You can be obstinate outside but you will always find society is stronger than you are. It will win in the end. If you want to live in this world then you must accept its conventions. You will be taken back to A wing and have three days' confinement.'

June was disappointed. Is that all? she thought to herself. Surely it should have been a week or three weeks. Three days of safety and then back to life with Jennifer? She would lie wrapped up in her own world, refusing food and drink to make sure that she would come out of confinement so weak that they would have to demand a court appearance and her transfer to the special hospital.

June searched for the answers in the horoscope she had found in a newspaper in the room in which she was now confined. It told her she would lose a friend. 'I hope that doesn't mean you,' she told her diary. 'It also says that I won't get my way with my man this month. I either put "my man" as my solicitor or J., for it is as though I am married.'

Time and again the twins returned to this theme. They saw themselves as the ultimate unhappy couple, Jennifer as the quirky, irascible husband, June the victim wife, and although they switched roles in most of their other games, in this they remained consistent.

When a husband knows too much of his wife, her faults, her thoughts can drive him crazy. He will feel like killing her. The wife when she knows too much of her husband, his faults, his thoughts, his ways, will want to kill him. Some people only live together because they hate each other. It adds excitement to life.

By the end of her three days June was desperate and lonely. 'Lord rescue me from my mute-like state,' she prayed. She listened to a symphony on the radio and thought about freedom and home.

My father used to play this music on the radio. I'm sitting somewhere looking out the window; one of those lovely, windy, romantic days, green grass blowing, poppy heads swaying, silent cars passing, silent children playing. Waiting for my mother to come back from town. Ah! to be dying, slipping away from this world. I want my heart crushed out from me, release from this chasm, release from this loneliness. I shall write to you soon, if I make it through the night. Your ever faithful but suicidal friend, June Alison G.

It was a relief for both girls to be back in their room together again.

The days drew on. The men from the open prison nearby pulled out the daffodils and wallflowers and prepared the beds for geraniums. Michael Jones, the solicitor, and Anthony Evans, their counsel, paid a visit and told the girls a definite date had been set for their appearance in court. They explained that if they pleaded guilty, there would be no trial as such, and that the judge would probably send them to the special hospital. But the discussion was not very fruitful. 'J. and I had lost the power to talk. We were answering their questions with nodding and shaking of our silly heads. They were bored with us.'

They dreamed of the hospital they had been told about. 'I hope there is a gym there and a swimming pool. I'm sure they have discos. I'll be going every night. It'll be like living in a hotel. We'll eat in small groups, just like a family,' thought Jennifer.

They dreamed of 27th May, the big day. They would, after all, wear their flowered skirts in May.

CHAPTER NINE

Blind Judgement

It will be a life filled with people; a secret underground society, which I shall neither fear nor hide from. For these people will be acquainted with me.

June Gibbons

'One for sorrow, two for joy.' Jennifer, alone in a room, looked out of her window at a single magpie pecking on the grass. 'Damn it, it's nearly summer and I can't find another one.' Her dreams the night before had also seemed portents of disaster for the big day: graveyards and coffins and being chased by a black hand. 'It all adds up to one thing,' she thought. 'Court will be delayed.' She stripped her bed, kept on her nightclothes as she had been told and sat down to read her latest Bible booklet, 'Our Daily Bread'. The morning bells went.

It was 7.30 am. They were due to leave Pucklechurch at 8.0 am. She heard the breakfast trolley stop outside her door. An officer delivered her porridge and bread and butter. 'I have to bite into something today,' she thought. 'The victim is bread.' Over two hours later she was still waiting. She was now sure this would not be the big day.

Then keys rattled in the lock. 'Hurry up,' said Miss Humble. 'You're needed in reception at once.' Jennifer's excitement and relief soon turned to anger. In the reception room, she saw the clothes she was to wear for court laid out on the table. There was her striped polo-neck top, her turquoise jumper and a pair of fawn corduroy trousers. She stared at them in dismay. Where was the flowered skirt her mother had sent which she had asked to wear?

'It's too late now,' said Miss Humble, interpreting from her gestures. 'We're in a hurry. I don't know what happened, but there's no time to get it out.' She opened Jennifer's pillowcase, stuffed with exercise books and newspaper cuttings. She checked hurriedly down a list in her hand. 'What a mess!' she exclaimed, taking out the cuttings and some exercise books which Jennifer had been using for her memoirs and poems. 'They're not on your list.' She threw them into the disposal bin and, before Jennifer could protest, took her over to the cubicle and handed the enraged girl her jumper and trousers.

As Jennifer emerged, she saw June approaching. They had been separated for the past few days but this had not made her thoughts towards her sister more charitable. She noticed June's breasts showing through the opening of her dressing gown. To her sisterly eyes, they looked awkward and droopy. 'Busting out all over just like the month,' she commented. June in turn stared at Jennifer's trousers with disdain, followed by dismay as she saw that on the table laid alongside her pink jumper was an identical pair of fawn corduroys. 'We aren't actually going to walk out of Pucklechurch in style,' June bemoaned to herself. 'No skirt, no socks for the big day.'

Both girls gazed in misery at their reflections in the glass of the cubicle doors. Jennifer's disappointment over the skirt was temporarily lifted by a trick of light which seemed to make her face look thinner than her sister's. She had probably been the one with the strength to diet in these last days (except of course the bread that morning). June, being weak, had no doubt given up. June saw the reflection, and whispered her acknowledgement of Jennifer's superior looks.

Both girls watched as Miss Humble emptied out June's pillowcase and threw all her papers and exercise books into the bin, too. Nothing was going according to plan. They had hoped to sit side by side in the minibus which was to drive them to the crown court at Swansea. June was put in the back with Mrs Roberts while Jennifer sat in front with the new officer whom they had nicknamed Badger-Eyes. Mrs Simmonds placed herself beside the driver.

The six sat in silence as the bus drove across the Severn Bridge and dipped into Wales along the motorway to Swansea. It drove up beside an expanse of lawn across which men with briefcases were hurrying towards the courts. Opposite the court buildings, there was a swing park where some mothers were sitting watching their children at play. It was turning into a sunny May morning. June felt even angrier that on this historic summer day, *their* day, they could not walk past the waiting policemen looking elegant. She imagined the judge, their parents, the witnesses, the people whose goods they had stolen and whose buildings they had vandalized or set alight – all staring at her.

The bus pulled up into a yard behind the main building. They were being taken in by the back entrance, not as they had dreamed, in front of waiting rows of press and photographers. The driver got out to ring a bell and the officers ushered the twins into a dark corridor in the basement of the court. They were locked into adjacent cells, each guarded by their escorting officer. They were taken to a room for lunch, and for once they allowed themselves the luxury of eating one meal each. Then they were locked in separate cells again. The cells were very much like the police cells they had been in when they were first caught: no furniture, and a tiny barred window high up in the wall.

Each twin waited, tapping occasionally on the wall to the other. Mrs Roberts offered June a cigarette. The tension was broken by the arrival of Dr John Hamilton, the consultant at Broadmoor who had visited the twins after Dr Spry during their period on remand. In his late thirties, short and bearded, John Hamilton was not a threatening figure to June. She felt sympathetic to his slight stature and hesitant, Scottish accent.

'How are you then?' he asked quietly. June nodded.

'Now you know you are pleading guilty to all the charges.' When she did not reply, he repeated his statement. 'It was as though he wanted desperately for me to plead guilty,' she later wrote.

'You know that you must speak up, otherwise the judge won't hear.' June tried to tell him about her idea that she should use a microphone.

'There are no microphones but if he can't hear you, the judge might get irritated – and that won't help you.'

June giggled. But his cool response reminded her of her serious role. She had to impress him. He was the one who could get her into the special hospital she dreamed about. What was it like? Would she and Jennifer find it the haven they sought?

As though anticipating her thoughts, Dr Hamilton tried to tell her about Broadmoor. It was difficult to explain as he had no idea what she knew about special hospitals. He had no idea either of the vision his words now evoked in her. He found it difficult to make out her questions and much of the time had to guess. 'It's more like a town,' he reassured her. 'There are shops and classes, there's a hairstylist and gymnasium. There's a woman who will help you with your speech and a team of people with special skills to care for you. You'll have a chance to tell us about your problems.'

For June, this sounded like paradise; an end to her lonely soul-searching and those years of enslavement to her sister. All she had to do was talk: to say 'Guilty' in a loud, clear voice. She wondered whether there was a church in the hospital. 'I shall pray, sing and shout "Alleluya!",' she thought. 'Thank God for where I am. I shall treat the girls and staff there as my family. I will no longer be afraid.'

In the cell next door, Jennifer was waiting for the lawyers, Michael Jones and their counsel Anthony Evans. A slightly pompous, distant man, Evans did not seem to find the girls particularly interesting. 'Hello, old girl!' he said, with a friendly pat on the back, as he came into Jennifer's cell. She was offended; this best-of-pals, how-do-you-do method seemed inappropriate. Her attention was focused instead on the young solicitor, Michael Jones. While Anthony Evans was reading out the sixteen charges, Jones was busying himself with the written papers, passing them over for Jennifer to examine. Jennifer indulged in her fantasies.

Was he making a romantic gesture? His elbow advertently touched my arm. I could tell it was being done on purpose. What he was doing was pretending to play with his chin. Meanwhile he looked at the papers. Meanwhile his elbow was resting on me. I wonder if he got an electric wave when he touched me? This has happened before. This secret touching. Carl once did it too. Our romance . . . I saw Mr Jones looking at my legs, the lower half in jeans, my socks, my shoes. Probably wondering what I looked like beneath, perhaps? I shall never know the truth.

Nothing could have been further from Michael Jones's mind than Jennifer's legs. It was important to him that nothing should go wrong with the case now. He was still only a legal assistant in the firm of

Eaton-Evans and Morris. After leaving a minor public school in England, he had graduated in law at the University of Wales but after serving his articles he did not pass his final exam. He had yet to prove himself in the firm. The senior partner, Mr Wynn Rees, a patient and kindly older man, had entrusted him to handle the case, thinking the twins might respond better to someone younger.

'Come on. You must speak louder than that. Say "Guilty" so that the court will hear,' Anthony Evans exhorted her. Jennifer tried. She would have liked to co-operate, but the clear confident response she wanted to make just would not come. 'Please, Jennifer. You must talk louder than that. Now, say "Guilty". '

Just after 2.0 pm June and Jennifer were led towards the court room, escorted by Mrs Roberts, Mrs Simmonds and Badger-Eyes. The girls looked frail and insignificant, standing heads bowed, shoulders hunched, flanked by their bulky escorts. Their image of themselves was sadly incongruous with their appearance. 'I stood proudly,' Jennifer recalled. 'I knew people were watching.' It was far more impressive than the theatre the twins had been to in Haverfordwest. There were chandeliers hanging from the ceiling; a man in red robes and white wig was sitting on what looked like a throne; there was a woman in black robe and hat at the door and a younger man, also dressed in robes, holding a large blue book. He looked across to the girls standing side by side and asked: 'Are you Jennifer Lorraine Gibbons of 35 Furzy Park, Haverfordwest, Dyfed, Wales?'

Jennifer was taken aback to be addressed so directly. Anyway, she was expecting June, the elder twin, to be dealt with first. She felt herself flushing, looked down, then nodded her head and grunted an affirmation.

'And are you June Alison Gibbons of the same address?' June nodded. The clerk of the court proceeded to read out the charges: '. . . That you did, jointly, between the 2nd and 5th day of October 1981, at Haverfordwest in the county of Dyfed, enter a certain building, namely Portfield adult training centre, as a trespasser and steal a transistor radio, an electric clock, a pair of scissors and a carton of Play-Doh of a value together of £40.50, the property of the Portfield adult training centre. What say you, Jennifer Lorraine Gibbons? Guilty or not guilty?'

Jennifer saw this was her chance to star. In a voice which she imagined rang out through the court, she muttered her plea. The clerk turned to June. 'What say you, June Alison Gibbons? Guilty or not guilty?' June's response was barely audible.

Jennifer eyed her sister with disapproval. 'She was making the mistake most people make, saying "Guilty" before the clerk had completed his sentence. Even then she had to repeat it. No-one could hear. My voice changed all the time, one moment low, another full of expressed proudness. June's was flat and monotonous.'

The clerk continued to read out the sixteen joint charges for burglary, theft and arson. That you did jointly, between the 15th and 18th of October 1981, at Haverfordwest in the county of Dyfed having entered a certain building namely Tasker-Millward school, as a trespasser, steal therein drink and foodstuffs, value £5.24, the property of Dyfed County Council education department. What say you, Jennifer Lorraine Gibbons, guilty or not guilty?'

Again Jennifer whispered her plea, followed by June.

The clerk's voice droned on, punctuated by silence as the court waited for their responses. '. . . Between the 17th and 20th days of October 1981, without lawful excuse, damaged by fire a dormitory at the Portfield special school, Haverfordwest, belonging to Dyfed County Council, intending to damage such property or being reckless as to whether such property would be damaged . . . Having entered as trespassers a building known as Haverfordwest VC school, Barn Street, Haverfordwest, stole therein five phonic tapes, three picture frames, a pair of scissors, a paper knife, a toy motorcycle and a quantity of keys.'

The memory of the paper knife, which June had then carried around in her Wellington boots, reminded June of Dr Spry. Where was he? Why hadn't he turned up? Could he still be abroad? He hadn't even been to visit them recently. He must be late.

At last the clerk reached the sixteenth and final charge. 'On the 9th day of November 1981, . . . enter a certain building, namely the

Pembrokeshire technical college, Jury Lane, Haverfordwest, and steal therein a pair of scissors, four cassette tapes, a packet of adhesive, three dictating-machine cleaning heads, a quantity of envelopes and sweets and a carrier bag.'

Every detail of their five-week spree of crime was framed in language which made the often trivial nature of the crimes take on heroic dimensions. 'I felt quite proud,' said Jennifer. 'To tell you the truth, I was rather enjoying it. It was a day to remember for when I'm old. Me, in my sweet youth.'

Everyone sat down and John Diehl, the barrister for the prosecution, brought his evidence. To June's delight and dismay, he began to read extracts from her diary which had been found when the police raided their room.

'It deals with personal matters, my lord,' he was saying, 'whether real events or imagined ones, and is a somewhat bizarre document.' Diehl handed the judge, Mr Justice Leonard, the jotter in which June had recorded their days of crime. 'June in particular revelled in the offences and she expressed particular delight in the damage caused by fire,' the prosecution continued. 'She showed pleasure in the publicity which resulted from such incidents.' He quoted from the transcript: 'Yesterday we broke into Tasker Millward canteen. We nicked food, swiss rolls and pies.' Later in that entry she had recorded, sinisterly, 'I'm going to be the biggest arsonist around.'

Diehl continued, using extracts from her diary to construct his scenario of their crimes, but making some effort to establish the twins' previous good behaviour and pointing out that the stolen items were of little value and nearly all recovered from the girls' bedroom or their hiding place in the wasteland. Indeed, the list of their thefts when read out in his rich voice was more pathetic than criminal – an ashtray, a dictaphone, a soft toy, the odd pen or ruler, the stubs of a used chequebook. Even their more prized thefts, the radio stolen from the American limousine and a set of tools, were valued at only £25 and £20 respectively.

When counsel described their break-in and arson at Meyler House, the headquarters of the Welsh Water Board, June was tempted to giggle. 'Amongst the most annoying consequences was that certain records had been destroyed which it was estimated amounted to 470 man weeks to replace,' Diehl accused. The twins knew the water authority was unpopular. Like the schools and colleges, their other favourite targets, it is a bland red-brick building, one of many soulless institutions which have grown up in Haverfordwest during the last decade. Setting fire to those mausoleums of a bureaucratic age was so impersonal, to the twins it didn't seem such a crime.

When counsel came to describe how they were caught in Pembroke technical college with gloves on and how June had a lighter in her sock, she thought she could see Mrs Roberts looking at her with a shocked expression. June was sure she was thinking, 'Fancy stuffing things like that down your socks.'

There was a hush when Diehl said he could not continue his excerpts from the diary as parts were too disturbing to be read in open court. 'I was numb with emotions,' June recalled. 'Triumph. Shame. Embarrassment. Ah, who knows what I suffered sitting there?'

The girls were too far forward to see the nearly empty courtroom behind them. It was just as well. Few people had turned out for their big day; only Aubrey, Gloria and Tim Thomas sat in the second to back row. June heard her mother's cough and became worried. Could she be ill? She felt a wave of remorse that her mother, whom she loved dearly, should have to listen to such a painful recital of their misdeeds.

Gloria and Aubrey were upset. They found it all hard to believe and were apprehensive about the outcome of the trial. Would the twins be sent to prison? For how long? They had always been such good girls. No trouble. Was there a hope they might be put on probation? Neither the lawyers nor Dr Spry had told them of the plan to have the twins committed.

At last Diehl had finished with June's diary. She watched as their counsel, now almost unrecognizable in his wig and gown, stood up. 'If it please my lord, I call Dr Hamilton.'

June's attention was drawn back to the court. 'He looked strangely small in the box; so humble with his glasses and suit, my heart went out to him,' she wrote. She listened as Dr Hamilton answered the judge's questions. 'There he stood, fighting for my happiness, fighting for my success. Someone who cared. He stammered quite a lot. It seems that he needs a speech therapist too.'

It came to the serious moment. The courtroom grew tense. 'Dealing first with June Alison Gibbons,' she heard her barrister question Dr Hamilton, 'is she suffering from a mental illness, psychopathic disorder, subnormality or severe subnormality ... of such a nature or degree as to warrant her detention in a hospital for medical treatment?'

Dr Hamilton replied, 'I believe so.'

Evans: 'What sort of period of time would such treatment be necessary?'

Dr Hamilton: 'It is very difficult to forecast this until we have the opportunity for a prolonged assessment. One would certainly envisage it would be for a number of years. Certainly not shorter than that. Dr Spry and I came to the same conclusion – that detention under a special order was the most appropriate method for the court to consider. Arrangements have been made for her admission to Broadmoor hospital within twenty-eight days.'

A shudder went through the court. Aubrey drew his breath as he recognized the name Broadmoor. He heard the judge's voice: 'Do facilities at Broadmoor include facilities which people at that age require?'

Dr Hamilton reassured him: 'It is not usual for someone so young to come to Broadmoor, but we do have a number of adolescents. We have a medical staff who we believe could be helpful. In her case speech is the fundamental problem. She has an unusual speech difficulty. We have a skilled communication-skills therapist.'

June was delighted that the judge should refer to her as young. 'I felt so proud, so helpless. J. and me the youngest in that very courtroom. While they talked about us in such a sympathetic way, I felt so distressed; so sorry for us; for our parents. Ah! what sympathy does to a hardened, violent criminal; I could have wept.'

Dr Hamilton described the violence between the girls and added that June showed suicidal tendencies. 'I suggest an order for surveillance for a substantial period of time in a secure hospital.'

Evans: 'Does the matter equally apply to her sister Jennifer Lorraine Gibbons?'

Hamilton: 'Indeed, that is so.'

Judge: 'I have also read an earlier report when the matter was not quite so crystallized, and which was exploring the situation.'

The judge expected the defence to call the author of the report and principal medical witness. Evans hurriedly intervened: 'Dr Spry is unfortunately abroad and has not been able to supply the information to satisfy the form, and is not able to be here.'

'I didn't know he was abroad,' the judge said testily. He was obviously taken aback. The trial had been postponed once before because Dr Spry was in America and Mr Justice Leonard, who has a reputation for fairness and humanity with young people, did not wish to hear the case in Dr Spry's absence. In the circumstances, the choice now was to adjourn or to accept the word of one doctor, even though that doctor had had little opportunity to study the twins and represented the receiving institution.

The judge decided to accept Dr Hamilton's assurance that he and Dr Spry were in complete agreement. Evans, visibly relieved, said, 'If your lordship were disposed to make the order suggested by Dr Hamilton, then there is nothing further to say.'

Everyone stood for the sentencing, except for the twins, whom the judge told to remain seated. 'I am satisfied from the evidence that has been placed before me that both defendants are suffering from a psychopathic disorder. I am further satisfied that their disorder is of such a nature as to warrant their detention immediately for medical treatment. I have regard to all the circumstances of the case, including the nature and the number of the offences, and comparable methods of dealing with them, and have come to the conclusion that the only suitable course is an order under section 60 of the Mental Health Act (1959). Therefore I shall make an order for their detention in Broadmoor hospital where vacancies are available within the next twenty-eight days. In the meantime I order that they shall be detained in prison until vacancies become available. It further appears to me, having regard to the nature of the offences and the number of them, that there is a danger of their committing further offences if released. Also regarding the information I have as to their tendencies to be dangerous to themselves and to each other mutually, it is in my view necessary for the protection of the public that the two defendants should be subject to special restrictions which are set out in section 65 of the Mental Health Act, and in view of the difficulty of prognosis, I think the order I make must be without limit of time.'

The twins had received a life sentence, a punishment given to murderers like the Yorkshire Ripper. June and Jennifer showed no emotion as they heard their sentence. The judge addressed them by their first names and wished them well.

Inwardly they were elated by the glamour of their sentence. Their years of suffering had been vindicated and they felt the relief that sick people sometimes feel when a long unrecognized illness is given a name and therefore a status. Wrote June,

The words kept on going round my mind. Spinning in circles. Sick. Mental. Psychopathic. Imagine how I felt. Me? A mental psychopath? I only heard about things like that in Alfred Hitchcock or read about them in the papers. A dangerous, evil, ruthless criminal! Me! At last my torment, my self-consciousness, my violence is known. I am labelled! Ah! Now I know my fate! June Alison Gibbons, just aged 19, going down in history as a psychopath.

June thought back over her childhood and adolescence and all the people who had known her. What would they think? What effect would it have on them – and her family?

Ah! it is good to know that my dear beloved grandmother is in no way to know that she has psychopathic granddaughters. Yet, somewhere, somehow, she does know. She is here in our presence with our grandfather. This! To go down in our family history, the family tree. And what about my nieces and nephew? Are they actually going to have two insane twin aunties? Ah! what cruel fate!

Michael Jones, pleased with the smooth outcome of his case, met the twins at the bottom of the steps which lead into the defendants' dock. 'Well, I'll leave it to you girls now. Goodbye, June. Goodbye, Jennifer.'

'He was smiling rather sheepishly,' June recorded. But she was so overwhelmed, she could give him only a gauche nod and, much to her annoyance, ruined her first moment of heroism by bumping into the bell used to summon prisoners. She could sense Jennifer's disapproval.

'That wasn't too bad, was it, girls?' said Mrs Roberts jovially as she and the other two officers escorted them back down the stairs following a male guard towards the court cells. 'Now, we've got a lot to do, sorting out all your clothes and books. There are enough of those exercise books to keep one reading for years. What on earth do you find to write in them?' Since at least technically the twins had the chance of being set free by the court, all their possessions from Pucklechurch had been taken with them. Now that they were to return, convicted, lists had to be made out again, clothes signed for and books returned to become prison property.

Mrs Simmonds brought the girls cups of tea. She and the other officers were surprised by the severity of the sentence they had received. The twins were infuriating sometimes but, like most of the staff at Pucklechurch, she had never thought of them as dangerous or insane. Pathetic, yes, and a touch weird, especially the way they lived for each other, but apart from refusing to mix at mealtimes and association, they had done nothing very wrong. The girls stood staring silently at their exercise books. It was impossible to tell what was going on in their minds – or, as she suspected, their one mind.

'I expect your lawyer and your parents will be down any minute to see you,' she said kindly.

Aubrey and Gloria were anxious to see their daughters. They were waiting on the other side of a glass partition in the visiting room at the end of the basement corridor.

For June and Jennifer this was going to be the most dramatic, most poignant moment of the day. What would they say? How would they express the love and sorrow they felt for the parents who had reared them and were now faced by this family disgrace? They longed to kiss and hug their beloved mother, tell her how sorry they were, make up for all those years of being silent and aloof. What a shame they were not wearing their skirts and socks. Jennifer also regretted the piece of bread she had eaten so greedily that morning. If she had only stuck to her one-meal-a-day diet, or not agreed to eat June's meals at all, her face would by now have the fine bone structure which would make her beautiful.

The girls pressed their faces against the glass partition and lowered their eyes. It was as though they were waiting for their parents' benediction, to be absolved from their crimes.

'Hello, June! Hello, Jennifer!' they heard their father say in the loud voice he used when he was embarrassed and wanted to reassure the world that everything in his family was all right. It was overlapped by the shuffling echoes of Gloria's greeting.

'How are you both then?' Aubrey continued. 'You're looking well. My! Jennifer, your face is plumping out a bit. You're getting even fatter in the face than your sister.' He was relieved to have broken the ice. 'Your mum and I were saying in court how much weight you'd both put on. They must be feeding you well at your place. Or is it the beer?' He laughed.

Jennifer reflected furiously on the fawn corduroys. They had made her look fatter, they were to blame. What distressed her even more was that both her father and mother seemed more interested in June.

'You do look well.' Gloria joined in. 'How are they treating you? OK?'

'You're getting into being quite pretty young women, you know,' said Aubrey. Unaware of his gaffes, he was beginning to feel more at ease. 'Isn't it time you wore some make-up? Your mum could send you some when you get to the new hospital.'

'No, Aubrey, I think they look best natural, they've got such nice skins.'

Mrs Roberts, standing beside the twins at the other side of the glass divide, was delighted that the tensions between the family were easing. It was not often that, as an officer, she had had to be present when young people, let alone two young girls, were meeting their parents after such a sentence. She felt sorry for the Gibbonses, who seemed to be charming and caring people.

'I'm sure you'll be able to send it to them,' she reassured. 'Broad-moor is a hospital, not a prison. It's a very nice place. I've heard the food there is lovely.' She turned and patted June on the head. 'You'll be surprised, my dears, after a year there, things will be quite different.'

Gloria and Aubrey, quickly blocking the past hour from their minds, exchanged whispers and Aubrey reached down and pulled two black donkey jackets out of a small case and handed them to Gloria.

'We brought your black jackets as you asked,' Gloria told the twins, 'and some grey tights. Oh! You know those jeans you wrote about –'

'Skirts,' June muttered. Aubrey didn't catch her odd monosyllables but Gloria guessed.

'They've got some nice flowery ones in Tesco's. I'll send you some.'

The male guard who was standing alongside Mrs Roberts looked at his watch and signalled that the visit must come to an end. Something had to be said about the sentence, the crimes. 'It won't seem so long,' said Gloria. 'You've got your whole life ahead. You just get better and you'll be home in no time.'

Mrs Roberts beckoned June and Jennifer. They took one last look at the reassuring faces of their parents and followed the officers back to the cells. 'How does it feel to lose two twin daughters for so many years?' June thought about how desolate her parents must be. 'Just imagine them telling all their friends, Greta's husband, David's wife, the whole neighbourhood! At least all this waiting is over. They must be relieved. I hope they are at peace with themselves.'

June felt less peaceful now as she realized her day was over. What had happened? No-one but her parents, Tim Thomas and three or four reporters had witnessed her drama. The trial had been no trial at all. Just one mingy hour. There had been no witnesses, no eloquent arguments explaining her plight. She would have written the thing much better in one of her books.

As they were leaving the yard at the back of the court in the minibus, they had a minuscule taste of the drama they had missed. Suddenly, rushing out from behind a parked car was a photographer, followed by a woman with a notebook. 'Quick! Down!' Mrs Roberts shouted. For one wonderful moment, the twins thought there were guns and that shots were being fired into the windows of the bus. 'TWINS

ASSASSINATED.' They would make the headlines, after all. Mrs Simmonds pushed Jennifer's head down, while Mrs Roberts flung one of her substantial arms across June's face. 'Don't look! Turn!' she commanded. The photographer ran alongside the bus but gave up as it gathered speed and drove off.

It was late afternoon and clouds were closing in on the May sun. The countryside had lost its colour and even the water stretching out under the Severn Bridge towards the Bristol Channel had turned a melancholy grey.

The sense of anticlimax deepened as they returned to the remand centre and their possessions were checked off against a list for the third time that day. The senior officer on duty wrote out new log cards to be put on the doors of their cells; white cards for convicted prisoners. This time, the officers were taking no chances. June and Jennifer were taken to separate rooms on the assessment wing. They were too late for tea. Each girl, locked alone in her cell, put her few clothes and books into the locker and reflected on the day.

'All I need do now is wait,' thought June, as she sat staring at the graffiti-covered walls of her squalid cell. 'Wait for the word "success" to take shape.' She imagined the taxi driving her and her sister away from the prison towards Broadmoor, the beginning of her new life, the life she craved, needed, the ultimate haven. She signed off her diary: 'Life shall be grand for J. and me in less than twenty-eight days from now. Your lonely friend, convicted burglar and arsonist. J.A.G.'

The governor and officers at Pucklechurch were surprised the girls had been sentenced to Broadmoor. Usually, it was very difficult to get places there for offenders, even the most violent. The courts were generally reluctant to send young women there, partly because of the expense (about £20,000 a year per person) and partly because there were no special facilities for teenage girls. Pucklechurch prison doctor, Peter Trafford, who had had them in his care for six months, was not called. 'In the majority of cases I would be asked to give evidence, but in this case I was not consulted. I think it would have been better if I had been involved. It did seem a bit strange that the defence organized Broadmoor without my being consulted.' Dr Trafford clearly did not think the twins were dangerous or fulfilled any of the normal criteria for psychopaths.

The day after the hearing, the chief officer sent for June and Jennifer. It was usual to make certain a prisoner understood her sentence, but in the twins' case, she was more concerned. Deprived, like the rest of the world, from access to their thoughts, she was worried by how badly it might have hit them. 'You know you are convicted now and that you have been sentenced to Broadmoor for an unlimited time,' she explained to June, while Jennifer waited outside. 'Is there anything you would like to ask?' June shook her head. 'How do you think you'll cope? How do you feel about it?'

'All right,' June muttered. 'What else could I say?' she thought. 'I could hardly be impolite and say I can't wait to get there out of this smelly dump?'

Later that afternoon, during wing association, while the doors were unlocked, June slipped into Jennifer's room. Jennifer was reading a gaudy religious pamphlet, 'Precious Promises', which had a picture of mountains and a lake on the cover. She was excited. 'Mark's written,' she whispered. 'He's very concerned about me.'

'Show me the letter,' hissed June, snatching at the pamphlet in Jennifer's hand. A letter filled with Mark's thin, sloping writing fell out. Both girls made a grab for it, but June was there first. 'Why doesn't he visit us then?' she added, putting on her sinister voice. 'Maybe he'd think you're me.'

Jennifer made a mental note that she would *not* meet Mark with her twin. Mark was her beloved friend, her fiancé, and she was not going to share him with this jealous bitch. But she was worried about the relationship. She needed to talk to someone about it. Should she tell him about the sentence and going to Broadmoor? Should she wait until she looked thinner and had her hair straightened by the stylist in Broadmoor? Should she remind him about the marriage agreement which he failed to mention in his letter?

'Do you think he'll wait for me to be released?' Jennifer asked anxiously.

'It depends,' came June's unreassuring reply.

During the wait for their transfer to Broadmoor, Jennifer became obsessed by Mark's letters and impending visit. Eventually, on 4th June 1982 she plucked up courage to write to him, reminding him about the wedding: 'Are you still on with the agreement we made last July?' She also told him it would be more suitable if he postponed his visit until she was in Broadmoor. He was living in Wokingham, which was not very far from the hospital. The truth was that she was worried a visit might be embarrassing. 'Supposing it doesn't work?' she thought. 'Wings of the devil, rush it and it goes wrong.' She recalled the catastrophic first meeting last year with her pen pal Peter, when no-one said anything. She was worried that the officers would laugh at her. Her subconscious had warned her in a dream in which she was ringing a bell on a doctor's door. When she looked up, the notice which read 'Appointment' changed to 'Disappointment'. No, she would risk hurting Mark by putting off the visit.

June also spent much time thinking about her sister's romance. She had read Mark's letter but didn't quite trust his sentiments. He seemed to have forgotten about Jennifer's proposal last year, although he had accepted at the time. Probably, he was just being polite. She thought about Jennifer and Carl Kennedy. This week, the first week in June, was the anniversary of their first love. Yet even then, it was Jennifer who had been the object of Carl's passion. He fought Jennifer only because his love for her was so urgent and angry, he was like Tom Brogan in D. H. Lawrence's *The Rainbow*. June feared she had meant nothing to Carl. He had deflowered her, but that was a week after her sister on that famous night in the church. June recalled how Carl once sent her out while he made love to Jennifer on the bed in his room. The Kennedys were away that night and June went downstairs to help herself to their brandy. Drunk and miserable she had returned to watch the violent couple.

June shivered. The cell felt lonely and bleak. Her memories could not console her. In all things Jennifer had won. She looked out of the window. The little garden, which had been so pretty a month ago with its wallflowers and cherry blossom, was desolate today. The daisies were strewn untidily over the grass, the flowerbeds raked over waiting for the summer geraniums to be planted. The skinny branches of the almond tree were rattling in the wind.

Tree; wind; sun. The shallow air and wind. Silence. Cut off from hearing the wind; cut off from sound. As though the tree, the sun, the wind are a different barrier from me. Ah! the solitude of a prisoner. The aftermath of the trial. Outside the beautiful sun is shining, but something is missing; I am missing from the outside world.

Increasingly, she was saddened by the disgrace and disappointment she had inflicted on her parents.

My father, my mother, were they ever over the moon and proud to make two adorable twin daughters? Did they lie awake at night, thanking God for their beautiful gift? Did they wonder what young girls we would grow into? What kind of life was awaiting ahead for us? Did they even know our fate, the fate that entangled them? Did they know we were to be different from the rest of the family – that we were to be written into public papers for offences; that we would be law-breakers; that we would be condemned, sick – not fit to face society. Did they look into our cherubic baby faces and see the troubled, evil wickedness, the desire for destruction, which lay before us? How could they. We could not possibly have been born like that. It grew on us, as the years developed; self-consciousness, frustration, thwarted ambitions. Finally, it snapped.

As the days went by, Broadmoor became more and more like the New Jerusalem, not only a place where they would be safe from the outside world, but accepted into a loving, caring family.

I see visions of Broadmoor on a warm sunny May day. What will I be doing next year? Probably sitting outside on a lawn, sipping lemonade. Nurses in white, walking around, lounging around. And I'd be free to sit there, perhaps sewing or knitting. Still young but more mature, more communicative, more flexible.

June's reverie was interrupted by the grating cries of two crows swooping down on the grass. Other birds joined the quarrelling pair. She was sure that Jennifer, who was in a room at the end of the corridor also looking onto the garden, must have thrown her bread through the window. June's tranquillity turned to fury. 'The cunning bitch!' she muttered to herself. 'We agreed we would both eat bread this month.'

The girls had been told that they were to have their photographs taken before going to Broadmoor. There was the inevitable competition as to who would look the best. They both decided they would try to look fierce and stern, not actually dangerous. But the Audrey Hepburn urchin look was still fought over.

Now that the twins' future had been decided, the staff at Pucklechurch left them in peace. There was no more trouble over joining with the others at exercise or association. During these final weeks of waiting, they started again on their relentless seesaw of starving and stuffing. Their food was usually brought to them to eat in their rooms. Lonely and hungry for consolation, they found it difficult to refuse: the effort of starving became unendurable. With the long hours of waiting, and with the memory of Aubrey's misplaced jocularity, food became an obsession, particularly for June. 'Am I in love with food?' she confided to her diary, in a passage which must rank among the great descriptions of the fifth deadly sin.

It is an affair which is full of bitterness and regret. I loathe the food which destroys my soul, my face, my body. Yet I go on eating out of duty, out of weariness. I bite into the body of my very enemy and as I chew my food will win. It can take dominion over my flesh, making me corrupt and depraved, exposing me to a plumpness of flesh, a fattening of the heart, over-healthy, rarely satisfied. And today, the first day of June of this year, 1982, I eat. I am making love all over again. I ate my breakfast. Ah! this cold porridge. I stuffed it down my throat and it revelled into my stomach, puffing it out like a swollen face of someone who has drowned. No, I must destroy this energy of mine called porridge. Why did I ever come back to it? Why was I compelled to touch the grey, vomit-looking stuff? Now it has me. But I shall not surrender. Tomorrow I shall simply eliminate it from my soul. Tomorrow I shall give my love only to bread and toast. But not for long, since this wicked, guilty thing called bread shall soon go beyond the barrier. I was a fool to fall in love with it again, for it is against me. It is bringing my face out in spots. And what about potatoes? Ah! I am so reckless. I am becoming what J. used to be, not so disciplined with myself. And carbohydrates, so many carbohydrates! I am treating myself as an invalid until this period is over.

June saw herself increasingly in the image of the young nineteenth-century heroine, dying from broken dreams and refusing food, too fragile to talk to anyone or leave her room. She paced the eight feet of her cell in a twilight trance, watching the shadow of birds on the barred casement windows, and fancied herself like the Lady of Shalott, weaving the memories of a world she was determined to abandon.

She imagined how she would look in a few months' time – 'as light as a baby, as helpless as a rag doll. My hair dropped out, my eyes big and vacant. The little of what skin I have stretched across my nose.' She worried about what would happen to Jennifer after her death. Would she too starve or die of a broken heart? A tragic story!

June began to dress in black. She requisitioned her black jumper and corduroys, even her black shoes. 'I am in mourning. I have no colour on me. Shall I sit with my feet in a bucket of hot water every evening and dream my life away? Be one, celibate to all? I want to sound like one of those Edwardian girls, who write so passionately and lustfully, long letters which will be appreciated and applauded.'

In her room, Jennifer was brooding over Mark, waiting for him to reply. Days went by and still no letter came. She began to fear the worst. Maybe she should not have asked those questions so frankly, recalling her marriage proposal and asking him about his virginity. On the other hand, she saw herself as stormy and forthright, with something fiery beneath a strong, solid character.

Every evening, alone in her cell, she took out the flowered skirt she had been prevented from wearing to court, solemnly tried it on, twirled it round and prepared for her bridal day. For a few moments each day, she became a young woman with a lover and about-to-be husband. 'What d'you think I look like?' she asked her diary. 'A lady? Is that what you said?' She saw herself married to Mark with six children. There was Mark putting on reggae records while she changed the baby's nappy.

But was she asking too much of him? Could she expect him to marry a woman with a criminal past, to take on a wife who was a psychopath? Would he wait four or more years until she was free, like a tree listening to the wind, as the music of his life slowly slipped away?

'He may be African, but he's not daft,' June whispered to her as they both emptied their pots down the sluice. Jennifer noticed a strange odour which she decided must have been the stew they had for dinner. June must be on a diet after all.

'I told you you shouldn't have said about going to Broadmoor. He's scared of you, scared of all that prison stuff!' Jennifer felt chastized. She had to agree.

'It'll ruin his reputation, getting involved with a maniac criminal like you,' June persisted.

Jennifer walked back to her solitary room, thinking about what June had said. She was overcome with guilt. Poor Mark! He came all the way over to Britain from Ghana only to get tied to a girl in trouble. He had not even seen her face or heard her voice. She wondered whether she should have made a video tape to send to him. Instead she took the 'Daily Thanksgiving' booklet which Mark had sent her from her small library on the window ledge and turned the pages. 'How often are we restless and worried.' She underlined the word 'worried' in her red Biro. 'But the worst troubles are those that never happen.' Maybe things were turning out for the best. If she were to marry him it would not be out of love but just for the sake of marriage. June had warned her about using people in that way. But she needed to know one way or the other. She tried to recall some of her occult recipes. Focusing on Mark's unknown image in her mind, she repeated again and again: 'Mark, please write back. Jenny loves you.'

Both June and Jennifer had much sympathy with the man's position in a world dominated by scheming females. 'Ah! the suffering of men,' June had written, stimulated by reading *The Rainbow* and remembering Wayne Kennedy. 'The suffering of males in a world full of women. Men are dazzled by them and think they are their superiors. They are caught up in a painful web of hurt, filled with wrath, desperation, with loneliness. They hate women but cannot be without them . . .'

June thought of her 'marriage' to Jennifer. She recalled the many days and nights as they were growing up together, quarrelling like lovers, arguing into the night, aware only of each other. June's pencil tore the page of her prison-issue art book. During this last lap in Pucklechurch, both girls had taken to drawing – usually sad faces of white girls with the sharp, bitter cheekbones they both craved. Each was jealous of the other's talent, although June rightly acknowledged Jennifer as the one with more artistic ability. Each put her twin's drawings up on the wall above the table, alongside posters of Princess Diana. In the prison cells as in their bedroom on the estate and throughout their lives, their aspirations formed a poignant counterpoint to the squalor in which they lived.

The month of June was slipping by and there was still no definite date set for Broadmoor. But the court had ordered that they receive treatment within twenty-eight days so the ordeal at Pucklechurch must be over by 24th June 1982, not much more than a week away. It was a period in which both girls became aware of the seriousness of their situation, and they bitterly regretted the pain they had caused to their family.

June in particular spent many hours thinking back over her girlhood. She recalled her 'crimes' – the day they had both played truant from the secondary modern school, the afternoon when they had stolen a bottle of Coke from the crate their father kept under his bed. She recalled how depraved she had felt when they were sixteen years old, on the dole, and had asked their mother to buy two bottles of tonic wine which they hoped would provide a miracle cure, loosening their tongues and making them extrovert. Poor Gloria! She knew so little about her cold, aloof daughters. In some ways June felt that the crimes and their imprisonment were a good thing, in that it gave their parents a chance to look into their minds. Both June and Jennifer took great care with their letters home, writing and rewriting them to make them ring true and help their parents understand.

Why am I so mother obsessed? I haven't had the chance to be acquainted with mine properly. I mean I don't lack a mother, but I long to be that devoted teenage daughter who has a loving sisterly relationship with her mother. We ought to be at home, sitting talking to her, going shopping together, cooking dinner, doing the household chores and at the same time having a tender conversation with the woman who has reared us to what we are now.

June decided to write a poem for her mother to enclose in her last letter from Pucklechurch.

Here in Bristol, I think of Wales.
Here where the traffic roars, I think of the country.
Give me the little things.
Give me mountains for the city,
The hereafter for brambles,
An old farmhouse for these grey puddings.
Give me seagulls for the crows . . .

The punishment was not being locked away from the world, they had both wanted that. It was being so far from their family. 'Without them, I am nobody,' June reflected. 'I need to know that someone is behind me watching my progress. I want people to remember me as someone important in their lives; wife, mother, friend, companion, daughter. That's all I need to go happily to my grave.'

At last, on Friday 18th June, the waiting was over; the twins were called to the chief officer's room and told they would be transferred to Broadmoor on the Monday.

For Jennifer, there was more good news that day. One of the officers on duty came into her cell, delivering two envelopes. On one she recognized her mother's handwriting; the other was from Mark. The Lord had answered her prayers. She read her mother's letter first. It praised June's poem and expressed her delight in the talent both girls were showing. Jennifer felt the usual pangs of jealousy but they soon passed.

There was a crash of thunder and the cell walls were streaked with lightning as she slowly opened her second letter. A new photograph dropped out. She picked it up and painstakingly examined her husband-to-be. He was dressed formally in a white shirt, what looked like a school tie and black trousers. He was sitting in an armchair facing the camera and looked more like a fifteen-year-old than a mature twenty-one. He was a far cry from the husband and father she had daydreamed about looking after her and their several children. She regarded his bulging eyes and thick lips and her eyes burned with disappointment. She kept looking at the photograph, holding it at different angles, hoping it might change. She already felt June's scorn. She read the letter, written in a stilted, formal English. It puzzled her.

She did not quite understand what he meant. In her last letter she had asked him to express himself better but he was still unclear. He said he missed her and that he was sorry she was to be locked away for so long. About the agreement, he said he was not sure what question she was referring to or what she meant.

'I told you, you talk in riddles,' June told her the next day when Jennifer visited her room. As Jennifer handed over the photograph, her sister took one glance, shocked at first and then breaking into mirth. 'It's not a man at all,' she giggled. Jennifer was wounded but had to agree. She realized how naive she had been but it was difficult to admit her mistake and discard the hope which had sustained her during these six confined months. She decided that she would ask him for another photograph and in her next letter make her question about marriage clear. Then, once they had settled into Broadmoor, she would invite him to visit her there.

The last weekend in Pucklechurch proved quite exciting for the twins. For seven months June and Jennifer had isolated themselves from almost all their fellow inmates. The staff at Pucklechurch never heard them in conversation with the other girls and although the twins write about the occasional attempt at communication, it seems their muffled efforts were usually either not heard or misinterpreted. When this happened, both June and Jennifer found it more comfortable to nod and point and let things be.

One woman, Alison, had made an impact on them. They looked on her as their source of inspiration and laughter. She was thirty-four and had lived in and out of institutions most of her life. In their early days on A wing, she had 'adopted' the twins, encouraged them in their romances and told them how special they were. They realized her behaviour was bizarre, but they were flattered by her attentions and missed her when she was transferred elsewhere. She had recently been returned to Pucklechurch. In the last few days before their departure, the twins wanted to feel they had made friends who would remember them. Jennifer even practised her old witchcraft recipes and holding Alison's image in her mind, she repeated 'You like Jennifer' again and again. She did the same with Janet, a twenty-nine-year-old inmate who, since their sentence, had shown some interest in the twins. The magic worked. During the last weekend before Broadmoor, both Alison and Janet paid them several visits.

It was Sunday morning and A wing was almost deserted. The officers and most of the girls had gone to the little chapel beside the gym. Only one officer and a handful of inmates were left behind. The women clustered together in Jennifer's tiny room and exchanged sweets and gossip. They giggled, blushed, discussed intimate subjects and crunched crisps and chocolates like any group of schoolgirls enjoying a dormitory feast. It was June and Jennifer's first taste of communal life, and they relished it.

'Don't let them stick injections into your bums or stuff you with pills in that place,' advised the worldly Janet. 'You'd better watch the TV and join in, or you'll be drugged up to the eyeballs and walk round like fuckin' zombies.'

Alison, who hated Janet, had ideas of her own. 'You'll be locked up like loonies anyway. I've been there.' She stared ahead of her, her mind wandering. 'I'll miss you. Why don't you marry Richard Burton? 'E'd look after you.' June was touched. 'I didn't know she valued our friendship so intensely,' she thought to herself. She tried to ask Alison about having psychoanalysis.

'Oh, yeah! You'll be spending 'alf the bleedin' day lying on a couch talking to a silly quack. You'll come out cracked, mental. At least you'll 'ave a man in the room!' She winked. June and Jennifer were overcome with embarrassment. 'Expect you're still virgins, though,' Alison added.

Jennifer shook her head proudly. 'How many times, then?' said Janet. Jennifer put up five fingers. 'D'you suck cocks?' Janet carried on. 'I did with my boyfriend but I think it's more fun to masturbate. Everyone does it here.'

'The screws?' whispered a shocked June.

'Oh, don't bother about them. They're used to it. I even do it with the light on. Are you two lezzies, then?'

Jennifer felt her face grow hot. Both she and June had developed crushes on some of the girls. Once they had used some lipstick to smear a love message on Alison's pillow. Did she guess it was them? Did everyone think they were bisexual?

'No need to worry,' Janet reassured. 'We get a lot of lezzies here.'

'Remember you're my babes.' Alison, who had been miles away, returned to the conversation. 'I'll miss you.'

Jennifer unwrapped two pieces of chewing gum and handed them to her new friends, carefully smoothing the wrapping paper to keep as souvenirs. Everything in these last moments was important.

Locked up again in their separate rooms, June and Jennifer ate their last dinner in Pucklechurch. They bade goodbye to the little almond tree in the garden, to the windows of the hospital opposite where they had spent most of their first three months, to the walls, the door which had contained them. 'Farewell! Pucklechurch.' June raised her spoon between mouthfuls of rice pudding. She had visions of the glorious new world which awaited her. She thought about who would follow her into the room. Would they sense all her suffering? Would they overhear all those conversations with Jennifer about wanting husbands and babies – and their bitter fights? She found a pen and scratched her name on the wall. 'Gone to Broadmoor. 21st June 1982.' She filled in her last diary entry in Pucklechurch.

Tomorrow I shall be leaving, going like the sun behind a cloud . . . But I am not the sun, I am a passing breeze ruffling people. And Pucklechurch will be glad to be rid of me; freedom from those 'terrible twins'. Only memories which shall leave a dent in the forehead, a pucker on the brow, a strange and radiant silence to fall over and within this cell.

Jennifer in her cell was also having her last rice pudding.

Please God! Don't let me suffer as much in my new life as I have here. Let me be bold enough to speak openly. Let me trust the doctors and nurses and no longer be afraid of people. For the past seven months I have been a soul with no hope. Don't let this disease paralyse me again, destroying my abilities, tying up my tongue like firewood.

As the night patrol came on duty, her cell door was unlocked and she was sent to fetch her water for the night. She walked slowly down the corridor, intending to say goodbye to all her new friends. She knocked on Alison's door but there was no reply. When she opened it, Alison was sitting on the floor, looking towards her. Jennifer waved but Alison did not appear to recognize her. Jennifer shut the door and tapped on the next room. Again there was no reply. Its inmate, a girl to whom Jennifer had never spoken, was sitting on a mattress on the floor, her head bent over some knitting. She did not even look up.

At the end of the corridor, Jennifer found Janet's room. Her spirits rose, but as she opened the door she saw her friend lying on the bed, the blankets tucked under her chin, her eyes staring at the ceiling. She was no longer the wise, comical girl who had been giving her so much advice a few hours past; she looked sad and vulnerable. Jennifer slipped hurriedly away, pushing a note she had written under the door. 'Write to us. Don't forget us. J. and J.'

The dawn was grey, with a dark summer's drizzle. The birds were sheltering under the roof above June's cell window. She lay and listened to the familiar sounds of the breakfast trolley, the doors unlocking, the shouts from inmates and the greetings of the officer. She read part of St Paul's Epistle to the Thessalonians and Psalms 54, 55 and 57. She packed her pillowcase, took out her diary and pen and wrote:

In a few hours I shall be driving out of Pucklechurch gates for the last time. I shall be taken further to the Land of Hope and Glory. There I shall stand in my flowered skirt and black jacket; aged nineteen years. And one day I will look back on that day, Monday 21st June; and what will I think? All I will see is my sister and me, as vulnerable as flowers in hell, unimportant, yet important; flying towards another phase of life.

CHAPTER TEN

Flowers in Hell

What a senseless degrading havoc I have made of my poor sweet human life.
Jennifer Gibbons

Broadmoor did not turn out to be the New Jerusalem the twins had dreamed about, although at first the spacious Victorian villas with their wide corridors, overheated rooms and large windows overlooking the countryside were a welcome contrast to Pucklechurch. They were delighted that instead of plastic utensils, they were given 'silver' cutlery, the rice pudding was better and there were separate television lounges for BBC and ITV. There were no noisy bells. Instead a voice would summon patients over a loudspeaker. 'Dining hall, ladies,' or 'Letter for Miss Jones.' They were also delighted with the large bathrooms with mirrors, and the greater privacy they were allowed.

For the first night, June and Jennifer were placed in York House 2, locked in separate but adjoining rooms, so they could just see each other at the windows. The following day they were taken to the hospital store room and invited to choose three new outfits, either dresses or separates, a tweed coat each, new underwear, nightclothes and three pairs of shoes – one flat pair for work, one for the ward and smart shoes for social events. With her new social life in mind, June chose a blue dress with an elegant tie belt. Jennifer picked a red one. Later that day they were summoned to take part in a video session which Broadmoor was using for their assessment, where they relished their opportunity to 'act'. That evening the girls played a game of Scrabble with the nurses. They were offered cigarettes followed by an evening snack tray of sandwiches and biscuits. 'Your reward for being good today,' said the nurse.

'Progress upon progress,' Jennifer reported. 'Read *Over 21*. The star signs look encouraging. Had chatty talk to J. through the window. Hope each day gets better.'

Jennifer's optimism was not rewarded. By the third day, she and June were in conflict again. While Jennifer was throwing her energies into making the most of her new luxurious lifestyle, June began to withdraw. Faced with eating in the dining hall in front of so many strangers, she found the old paralysis creeping up on her. She began to walk slowly, refusing to move until the nurses were forced to drag her down the corridor from her room to the bathroom or lounge. Her head was bent, her eyes downcast and any attempt the staff made at conversation was met by dismal silence.

The nurses observe us, I observe June. She is trying to ruin my reputation, my life. The day will have to come when we are both of us behaving in a normal manner, talking, moving fast, laughing and living. I must get my life, my mind, myself in control. June is being deliberately cold to the nurses. She has too many faults and now they are showing particularly.

'Look up when you reply,' Sister Bevan, the vivacious Spanish sister in charge of York House 2, admonished June. Jennifer gritted her teeth. If June went on like this, they would never be treated as normal nineteen-year-olds and they would never get out of Broadmoor.

By the end of the first week, June had resumed her puppet pose. Jennifer felt forced to imitate but felt that if they did not escape now, history would be repeated and they would end up, years later, as resident zombies. She had noticed in the bathroom there was a small window which did not appear to have the usual bars. She could slip her slim body through the window. June would follow her into the bathroom with a 'ladder' of knotted towels and clothes which they would tie to the washbasin taps. They would then lower themselves to the tarmac court and run to the wall. They had overheard other women on the ward talking about how some years ago a woman had managed to climb on the shoulders of another patient and leap over the wall. Since in the time Broadmoor was built, women were considered feebler than men, the walls on the female wing are not as high as on the male side. The woman had twisted her ankle and did not get more than half a mile towards Crowthorne station before she was picked up by the police, but she had tasted freedom.

Jennifer was facing June in the corridor outside the bathroom. She had tried to signal to June that she must hurry as tonight they would make the break. But June did not respond. She stood there with one arm over her face and the other shielding her body, staring obstinately ahead. Jennifer knew there was no time to lose. It was nearly 8.0 pm and there would be no chance to go back to the bathroom.

'Jennifer and June, what do you think you're doing? It's time for bed.' Samantha Bevan came between the silent pair. Sister Bevan had started work with the women and girls of Broadmoor hospital at the age of nineteen. Over twenty years later, she had come to regard her patients as almost closer to her than her own family – she spent so many hours each day locked up with them, sometimes over ten years or more. June and Jennifer worried her. She had never come across girls who were so mute and rigid. She summoned help and dragged first June, then Jennifer, down the corridor into their side rooms. Like the officers at Pucklechurch, they had to lift the girls into bed.

Samantha Bevan looked at Jennifer's impassive face, then knelt down to tuck the covers around her. Jennifer watched as the nurse stood above her. The nurse, whom she had first seen as friendly, seemed to take on June's knowing, aloof expression. Jennifer looked at the barred window and the walls of the room closed in on her. She felt her fingers come alive and her body vibrate with a rare energy. It was the first time in her life that she had felt such a powerful rush of anger which was not directed solely against her twin. But like her twin, this woman was preventing her from breathing, from being free.

Within seconds, her nails were tearing at Samantha Bevan's face. 'You bastards!' Jennifer screamed. Shocked by the words shouted so clearly by the silent girl, as much as by the pain in her face, Sister Bevan cried out. Jennifer let go and, looking up, met the frightened stare of a young nurse who had rushed to the door.

Lancaster Ward 1 is used as an 'intensive care' unit for the female patients at Broadmoor. The lower rooms resemble the silent cells in

Pucklechurch with bare walls, barred windows high up on the wall, and only a mattress on the floor. When a patient arrives on the ward, she is put into the bottom room in the hospital, reserved for the most violent and dangerous women. Then, as in a game of snakes and ladders, she has to make her way up through the twenty-three rooms in Lancaster Ward 1 to the next ward, Lancaster Ward 2, and from there back to the more open rooms and dormitories of York House, the block to which the twins were brought when they first arrived. With each incident, depending on the severity, the patient is put back several rooms or wards, until, after an average of six years without too many 'snakes', she reaches one of the top rooms on the rehabilitation ward, York House 3.

There are constant rewards on the way up. The more you fit into the system, the better 'office' you have, not unlike a BBC executive or government civil servant. Good behaviour on Lancaster Ward 1 is rewarded with promotion to a room with a bed and some items of pressboard furniture. Once in Lancaster Ward 2, you can progress through the twenty-two rooms, gaining at best a room with a chair, wardrobe and desk (made of real wood), a mirror and a rug on the floor. In the privilege rooms, you are allowed to keep your cosmetics on your dressing table, whereas in the ordinary rooms, all your possessions are kept in a locker outside. There are also upgraded hours of freedom, ranging from Lancaster 1, where rooms containing aggressive or self-mutilating patients are kept locked during the day as well as at night, to York House 3, where the patient is issued with an internal passport or 'parole' card, allowing her to move freely within the hospital. Some patients who have been in Broadmoor for many years and are unlikely to be discharged are more permanently settled on one or other ward, but for others the privilege room system operates until they leave.

Lying alone on her mattress in the seclusion room in Lancaster Ward 1, Jennifer suffered the darkest moments in her nineteen years. All the expectations she had nurtured during those final months in Pucklechurch had vanished behind the walls and doors of her new prison. 'I would welcome Death as a child would welcome candy each day,' she wrote. 'Death is always ready, smiling his sweet smile, anxious to be friends.' She could not speak. Her tongue felt tied up like a bundle of dried firewood. On Sunday, when the day-room at Lancaster 1 was converted into a church, she found herself unable to join in her beloved prayers and when the priest offered her the sliver of communion bread, her lips would not open. They remained unhappily pressed together as he held out the wine. He blessed her and moved on. She remembered all the wine and vodka she had drunk last summer and looked across the room at her fellow inmates on Ward 1. They sat in rows, listless and staring, like soldiers about to be shot. Carl, Lance and Wayne seemed far away.

June, too, separated from her twin, became deeply depressed. At dawn on 11th July, thirteen days after Jennifer's attack, she was found trying to garrotte herself in her room. She had tied the belt from her new blue dress around her neck and tied the other end to the silver bangle on her arm, in which she had invested so many magic powers, and pulled.

The twins were swapped over. June took Jennifer's place in the intensive-care unit, while Jennifer jumped the intermediate stages and went back to a dormitory in York House 2. Both girls deteriorated and June retreated into a comatose state as she had four years ago on the ward at the Carmarthen hospital when she had been first separated from her sister. She refused to eat in the hall and her weight went down to under seven stone.

It was during these weeks in early July that I made my first visit to Broadmoor and watched June being lifted by two nurses into the visitors' room. Jennifer, who was led in immediately after her sister, was also silent and unresponsive at first. Then in a breathless rush she spoke to me. 'Please tell the doctor that June must come back. It's not right. We want to be together. Please help us.'

Jennifer's grief was less dramatic than June's but she pined for her sister's return, like a young wife awaiting her husband from the battle front. Every new footstep in the corridor outside made her think June was coming back. She gazed at the empty bed beside her and longed for it to be filled by June. She spent hours looking out of the window to see if she could catch sight of June in the garden. 'I am doomed unless J. gets back,' she wrote, 'I'm desperate to see her. Something evil is going on. Do they mean to separate us for good?'

As the days went by, even the most ordinary movements became an ordeal. She would hover in the corridor, too scared to enter the day room. Once sitting there, always on the chair nearest the door, she would be afraid to leave. If she got up to leave on her own, she felt that everyone in the room would stare at her. If, on the other hand, she waited until someone else left before she got up, she felt sure others would think she could only move because that person had moved first.

It was hot in the garden. End-of-July temperatures had encouraged swarms of flies. Jennifer listened to the sound of the jumbos making their way from Heathrow to America or beyond. But there was a girl sitting smoking on the seat which Jennifer normally took in their recreation periods. What should she do? It was too embarrassing to join her. What if the girl talked? Or offered her a cigarette? But to walk straight past and sit on the next empty seat would make her look snobbish and antisocial. 'I really am getting fed up with my lack of self-confidence. Why can't I just say "Hello!" and break the barrier?'

Jennifer's self-consciousness became so acute, she even gave up drinking tea in front of the nurses or patients. She found that picking up the milk jug or teapot became an impossible task, especially if they were in awkward positions and the handles were turned round the wrong way. 'Don't keep asking her, she'll have a cup of tea when she wants one.' Vi, a girl from her dormitory, talked across her to Sara. Jennifer felt as though she were invisible. Sara needed the teaspoon beside Jennifer's place, but she either thought Jennifer was deaf or she, too, was embarrassed. Jennifer knew that she should just pick it up and hand it over, but could not bring herself to take action. Why didn't Sara just ask her to pass it? Jennifer could not tolerate silence from other people. 'It gets on my nerves,' she thought. 'They're playing a game with me, these long, irritating silences. Why won't they talk and put me at my ease?' She was worried about getting a reputation for not drinking tea in case it gave people too big a shock when she finally plucked up the courage.

It was Monday 26th July 1982, almost a month since Jennifer attacked the nurse and the twins were put in separate blocks. Jennifer, as miserable as ever, was climbing the steps to the occupational therapy room. As she reached the top, she heard Vi calling to her: 'Your sister's here!' Jennifer felt numb. She looked ahead and saw June sitting at one of the long tables. She was wearing one of Jennifer's jumpers and the green skirt their parents had brought when they visited the week before. Gloria had told Jennifer the colour, saying how she thought Jennifer would prefer a gold-yellow one. Oblivious of the curious looks around them, the sisters met and talked.

At tea break the two girls sat together and chatted rapidly. Both girls admitted their unhappiness. 'When I'm alone,' confessed June, 'I make myself think I'm you. Your face, your body. I am you.' Jennifer was astonished. 'But that's what I have to do, imagine I'm you.'

'No! You're Miss Independent,' replied June. 'Do you remember when you went alone to see your pen pal? When I think of that, I feel strong.'

They decided that from then on they would help and support each other.

'I got a letter from this guy who read about us in the paper. He's got a speech defect too and wants one of us to become his girl friend. Has Mark been to see you yet?'

Jennifer did not have time to reply as a nurse led June away with the rest of the patients from Lancaster House.

It was just as well. Jennifer did not know whether she should tell her sister that Mark was due to visit in five days' time. She was so anxious and excited that the week passed in a blur of anticipation. His visit presented some problems. Patients in York House are expected to make their own tea for guests and carry it on a tray to the visiting room. Tea, cups, sugar and biscuits have to be bought at the canteen shop and milk has to be requested on the day. Jennifer also spent many hours wondering what she should wear. (As part of the special hospital reforms in recent years, patients at Broadmoor are encouraged to choose the design and colour of their clothes. A London store is contracted to the hospital and once a year they arrive at dawn with vans laden with clothes. By 9.0 am the women from each ward are filing past, choosing one outfit donated by the hospital and one they will buy with their own money. As each patient receives between three and six pounds for good behaviour, together with social security allowances, and has no outgoings, the money they keep in their hospital account can quickly mount up.)

If Jennifer wore her new red dress, it might appear too obvious to the staff that this was a special occasion. But she knew Mark's first impression of his wife-to-be had to be favourable. 'He'll know if I'm shy or self-conscious. He'll notice everything about me, all my mannerisms. This is what I dread most,' she told herself, longing for June to advise. She worried about the colour of her petticoat. White would be nice, but inappropriate, as she was no longer a virgin. She would wear a black one with black tights. In preparation for the visit, she even braved the hairdresser and allowed her usual plaits to be undone and her hair washed and styled into a ponytail.

The day for Mark's visit arrived. Visits at Broadmoor start at 2.15 pm and finish at 4.0 pm. Jennifer dressed in a green skirt and cardigan, prepared her tea tray and waited for her name to be called. By three o'clock, she was still waiting. Where was Mark? She began to blame her choice of dress. Green is an unlucky colour. Perhaps Mark had been involved in a pile-up. Maybe his boss hadn't allowed him time off? Maybe she had been too outspoken and hasty in her letters and he had never intended to come at all? She heard the sounds of thunder and a dark burst of rain washed against the window. A storm in July? What terrible message was it trying to bring her? She heard the sounds of banging outside, maybe some crates being overturned by the wind. She began to doze. By the time she awoke, visits were over.

Mark had set out to visit, she learned later, but had got lost between the trains and buses from Aldershot. He then had to walk the mile and a half up the hill from Crowthorne station, just as the sky darkened and the rain fell. He was carrying a parcel of books for his dear pen pal and a postal order for ten pounds in case she needed to buy anything. He had little idea what kind of place Broadmoor was and he was nervous of having his first rendezvous in such curious circumstances. Jennifer had told him she would be in a hospital for some years, but in a fit of pique when she had not replied to his letters, he had burned all her letters and could not remember exactly why she was being kept behind those high walls. It was 3.30 pm as he rang the bell at the main gate. He waited in the cramped room beside the desk while two other groups of visitors signed the book. He eventually plucked up courage and asked for Miss Jennifer Gibbons. 'Oh, she must be on the female side,' said the reception nurse. 'This is the male side. You have to go out of here and it's down on the right.'

By the time Mark reached the female side, it was a quarter to four. A large, bossy nurse on reception duty glanced at the soaked black boy. 'You're too late,' she said, unsympathetically. 'Visiting ends at four and there's no time to arrange an escort down from the ward.' Mark asked if he could leave the books and money he had brought. 'You've got to take those to the visitors' box and sign. Nothing's to be left at the desk.' He was frightened by her attitude and did not dare ask where the visitors' box was. Still holding the gifts, he started back on the long walk to the station.

During the next weeks, June progressed to Lancaster Ward 2, but remained sad and mute. Jennifer settled down better to the daily hospital routine and began to make efforts to communicate. She was so out of practice, however, that she could seldom make herself understood.

'Don't you ever get tired of writing?' Sister Bevan asked. Jennifer was sitting in her usual seat in the dayroom, hunched over her exercise book, working out the plot for her next short story. 'Why don't you come to the office and we'll see if we can find you something to sew?' Jennifer could not believe her luck. She had watched the other girls sewing and had dreamed about making a beautiful rag doll, like those she and June had made in Eastgate, but she had never felt confident enough to ask. 'Perhaps you'd like to make a soft toy, something which you could put in for the exhibition?' said Sister Bevan.

Broadmoor specializes in the soft-toy industry. Animals and dolls of all shapes and sizes are lined around the visiting room and in the dining room for sale either to the public or to the patients themselves, who have the cost of materials charged to their hospital accounts. Jennifer tried to explain about the doll, but failed. She followed Sister Bevan into the office. 'What colour would you like?' Jennifer made a sound which seemed to come through her nose. 'Dark brown,' she muttered. It would remind her of the teddy bear she had left at home. But Sister Bevan misheard. 'You don't mind? Then, what about this one?' She handed her a kit of beige material, a colour Jennifer disliked, and started to thread a needle.

The teddy bear which Jennifer had set her hopes on turned into a small beige dog. By mistake, she sewed his tail onto his leg, giving him a lopsided look. But Jennifer thought him quite cute, christened him Russell and signed a requisition slip to buy him. At least he would be a memento, something to remember from the summer of 1982.

The twins had physical examinations, and tests revealed that they shared the same blood and that they were, indeed, identical. Gloria had always maintained that they were not identical and no doctor before had thought to check her story. The staff psychologist visited both girls, using a stopwatch to time how long it took them to respond and giving them the usual battery of questionnaires, personality and intelligence tests. It was like Eastgate all over again.

The teacher from the school also paid a visit but, like the others, failed to understand anything June said. 'If you want to come to school, you'll have to do better than this!' he admonished. 'You won't be with your sister. I don't want you two muttering and giggling together, like the staff say you do.' He told her about the classes she could join and she signed on for English, mathematics, typing and art. The girls recall that he made an unfortunate remark which, unknown to him, may have put the girls off any attempts at learning: 'It's not too difficult telling you apart from your sister. You're the chubbier one, aren't you?'

Both girls were visited by Jenny France, the speech therapist. 'Why is the cat pleased?' Jenny France was showing the standard set of cards which are used in speech therapy; a goldfish bowl with a fish, then a cat looking up and finally a cat and a smashed bowl. 'What's missing?' she asked. Jennifer knew this one well. She felt as though she were five years old. She giggled. She wondered whether June was laughing too.

The twins found their separation intolerable. They both turned their thoughts to suicide. 'Could I drown myself in the bath?' thought Jennifer. 'Or should I get a pin from occupational therapy and stick it in my heart? What would J. do? Collapse? She shouldn't really be in here behind bars. She's too pretty to miss out on life.' They prayed each day and consulted their horoscopes for any hope of change. 'God, you've got to help me,' Jennifer shouted when alone one day in the toilet, banging her fist against the wall. 'Give me a date when my sister comes back to me. I need her. Won't you please, please help me?' The girls met occasionally when both wards used the same occupational therapy room, and sometimes as a reward at weekends. The nurses had struck a bargain with them. If they both behaved well and made an attempt to speak during the week, they were allowed to meet on Saturday afternoon in Sister Bevan's office. These meetings made the separation policy even more difficult to carry out: the girls so obviously came alive when together and pined when apart. But the psychiatrist was adamant.

Dr Boyce Le Coutcur is the responsible medical officer in charge of Broadmoor's female wing. He took the decision that the twins would have to be separated after the first incident and from then on nothing would persuade him to change. A lanky, lugubrious man in his late fifties, he started his medical career in Australia, where he was born, and came over in 1960 to practise forensic psychiatry in Britain. After twenty-five years working in Broadmoor he still retained the dehydrated look of a thorn tree in the outback. A psychiatrist of the old school, he has a reputation for extreme caution in recommending restricted patients for release.

His attitude towards the Gibbons twins when discussing them with me appeared outwardly to be one of indifference. Yet he took the courageous decision to telephone me, a journalist, following the publication of an article I wrote about the twins in the *Sunday Times*, and invited me to Broadmoor to talk to them. He was anxious that I set up some writing courses, allowed me access to their diaries and, often against the wishes of some members of the Prison Officers' Associ-

ation, the union to which the Broadmoor nurses and other members of
the staff belong, he encouraged my visits over the next three years. But
he was and still is adamant that the twins are in need of very long-term
treatment in maximum security. Maybe because he had not read the
microscopic diaries that reveal the more vulnerable side of their
personalities, he did not feel much sympathy towards what he saw as a
malevolent partnership.

June and Jennifer wrote letters begging him to let them go back
together, but he was forewarned by reports from Eastgate and Pucklechurch. They needed a long period of separation and treatment
before he would allow them to be together again. Treatment in
hospitals like Broadmoor is based on behaviour modification. It is the
only treatment considered appropriate to a person suffering from a
personality disorder. Reward and punishment operate in every moment of the day's routine, giving the patients no let-up, no moment
when what they do or say is not being monitored and used to place them
a rung or two higher or lower on the privilege ladder. For her efforts at
making a soft toy and co-operating with the staff, Jennifer was rewarded by being allowed a bath in the evening. 'People who have
afternoon or evening baths are better than those who have one in the
mornings,' she recorded. Any change in routine was welcome and it
would give her more time to write her morning poetry, but the
promotion had its drawbacks. Mark was due to visit again at the
weekend and she would not now be able to have a bath before his
visit.

Saturday 14th August 1982. I woke today and some birds were whistling near
my window. 'Somebody help me! Somebody help me!' they seemed to be
saying. Will Mark let me down again? Everything was ready – two cups, tea,
biscuits. I counted out eight biscuits. I waited each minute, my faith sinking. I
got up for the loo and in there I prayed, dear merciful God, please don't let me
down. Not another disappointment.

A voice came over the Tannoy. 'Jennifer Gibbons. Visit.' Jennifer
walked as fast as she thought seemly to the office where her tray was
waiting, but in her excitement she took the tray belonging to another girl.
'Who's nicked my tray?' said the girl. 'They're my cups, you stupid

bitch. Give 'em back!' She grabbed at Jennifer's tray and Jennifer was forced to unload the tray, find another and start all over again. The nurse waiting to escort them grew impatient. Just as they were leaving, Jennifer discovered the sugar was missing. She would have to go back to her locker and find some sugar and then ask to borrow a bowl. The others went, leaving her to wait for the next escort.

Eventually, she arrived in the visitors' room, carrying a tray. At first she could not recognize Mark, then she saw a nervous young man sitting alone at a table. He was dressed as in his photograph, in a smart striped shirt and grey trousers. She felt again a shiver of disappointment. He looked like an ordinary schoolboy, so different from the casual glamour of the Kennedy boys.

'Hello!' he said and just saved the tray from slipping out of her hands. Jennifer sat down and offered him a cup of tea.

'No, thanks. I don't drink tea.' After an uneasy pause, he elaborated: 'Hot drinks open your stomach and make you hungry.'

'Biscuits?' she whispered.

'No, thanks. I don't eat at tea.' He smiled. When Jennifer made no move, he offered to pour her a cup of tea. 'Please, let me help. Sugar?' he asked politely. Jennifer shook her head. All that trouble over the sugar bowl was for nothing.

A nurse came over to see how they were getting on. She looked at Mark. 'Your brother, Jennifer?' she asked. Jennifer glowered. 'You'll soon get used to it here,' she told Mark in the patronizing tone the twins had grown to despise. Jennifer felt humiliated by such a crass intrusion into their first meeting. She examined Mark's face and admired his protruding white teeth. She was determined to find him attractive.

He told her a little about his life in Wokingham, how he had few friends and lived with his boss in a small house. Most weekends, he told her, he watched television or listened to records, mainly reggae. On Sundays, he went to church. They searched desperately for some common ground. 'I now know why he talks so slow,' thought Jennifer. 'It's the charm. Even when he didn't seem to understand what I meant, he smiled.' She asked him some questions about his birth sign and his family. Their meeting, like their letters, had the formality of a Jane Austen tea party. But the main business of the afternoon had yet to be discussed. Finally, in an indistinct rush, she blurted out: 'Our agreement? Last July?'

Mark shook his head. 'Well, I don't know. I don't know.'

Jennifer felt embarrassed. 'Marriage?' She gained confidence. He seemed deep in thought. Perhaps he hadn't heard her. In any case, was he ready to be her beloved husband? He didn't seem as yet solid or stable enough. She wondered whether he knew it would cost money to get married and decided she was being a bit too forward.

They fell into silence. Jennifer was aware she was showing signs of nervousness, giggling a bit and twisting a strand of hair round and round her fingers. Did Mark notice? Were the people at the next table looking? She sipped a little of the tea he had poured in the one cup, and wondered what else she could ask him. 'Do you like football?' 'Oh, that's a game for women,' he replied. Jennifer was baffled but decided he had not heard properly. They relaxed in the mutual territory of pop songs and their dislike of cricket and golf. Mark made no moves to go until the nurse announced the end of visiting.

Afterwards Jennifer collected his presents from the visitors' box. They included a book of *Reader's Digest* stories and 'Inspiring Messages for Daily Living' by Dr Norman Vincent Peale. There was also a large box of Terry's All Gold chocolates. The box presented Jennifer with a problem. People would expect her to share the contents. She decided to hide the box away in her locker and take one or two to comfort her during the night. But her locker was already so full of diaries and magazines, she could barely squash it in. As she slunk away down the corridor, she heard a crash as the locker door burst open and the box of chocolates fell to the floor. Two girls who had watched her trying to push it in laughed. Jennifer felt humiliated as well as disappointed. Part of her had to admit the visit had not been a success. Mark had been friendly enough, but distant, not a bit like a fiancé setting eyes on his bride for the first time. 'He is after all a Leo,' she consoled herself in her diary. 'You know, the majestic lion. They have their regal ways.'

The twins' faith in star signs was severely threatened a week later when June received a letter from home. Dr Le Couteur had asked her to discover any information about her birth and Gloria had replied. She told her that, contrary to what the twins had always believed, June was born at 8.10 am and Jennifer at 8.20 am. For years the twins had worked out their horoscopes, often at considerable expense, on the basis that June was born at eight o'clock and Jennifer at ten minutes past eight. Now, all that they had believed made up the difference in their personalities and their fortunes was upturned. Jennifer had inherited June's rising sign and all those hours spent studying Jennifer's were irrelevant. 'It's all a mistake, a tragedy,' wrote Jennifer, after June had told her the news.

My horoscope has nothing to do with me. My position has been taken by June. My poor beloved sign has been snatched from me. The worst thing about it is that I am not a good, strong Aquarius. She is the one who has an Aquarius in her. Oh, dear! What a mess. Now, I have to pick up the pieces. Who am I? I will be very much on the alert when reading star signs now.

As the summer of 1982 wore on, the twins' attention focused more and more on the city inside the walls. 'We just seem to forget about people outside,' wrote June. The family visited less often. The train journey from Haverfordwest to Broadmoor is long and complicated, involving an early start, a change of trains at Reading and finding some transport from the station to the hospital. The twins' brother David and his wife Vivienne felt Broadmoor was an unsuitable place to bring their two children. Vivienne never came. The twins were forgiving. They remembered David and Vivienne's birthdays and anniversary, sent cards and even contemplated sending sums of money from their hospital account. They did send money to Greta, who visited a couple of times, and of course to their parents, whose infrequent visits brought them such joy.

I came with writing courses, books and encouragement to continue their creative writing. At first the twins tried, and wrote some short stories. Jennifer even began a new novel. When I suggested they be allowed their typewriters from home, Dr Le Couteur was enthusiastic. Aubrey and Gloria brought one typewriter from home, which was installed in the quiet room on York House 2, for Jennifer to use when she wished. She never made the effort. The hospital also paid for a correspondence course I suggested in journalism and poetry. June and Jennifer promised to try, but their interest in writing anything other than their diaries and the occasional poem had given way to more immediate pursuits. Jennifer's feelings for Mark fizzled out, too.

Now that they were behaving in a more acceptable way, albeit still refusing to talk to the doctors and most of the staff, they were rewarded by more time together and with other patients. The girls could put their names down on the ward noticeboard to go to socials, discos and bingo with the male side; they joined some boys at English and typing class and at the activity centre, a workshop and recreation area. It was not long before they were in love – and competition.

June sat drinking orangeade and awkwardly inhaling from a cigarette. Beside her was Eddy, a young, heavy-featured man. Jennifer, opposite, was chewing at an old piece of gum she had found in her coat pocket. It was one of the weekly socials with the men.

'They're waiting for each other to tell each other what to do. What a laugh!' said Eddy to his friend Ron, a more sensitive looking seventeen-year-old boy. Jennifer was mortified but could not take the initiative. June was being cold and aloof again. 'Ron, meet June.' He looked at Jennifer. 'I don't know her name.' Furious that he had remembered June's name and not hers, she muttered, 'Jenny.'

'Debbie? That's nice.' As usual she had been misheard. The girls continued to smoke and chew gum. By stares and signals, they agreed that June could keep Eddy and that Jennifer would try to capture Ron. But neither could trust the other and no-one spoke. Eddy and Ron found the pair entertaining but eventually got fed up. 'Can't decide which looks the most bored, her or her?' Eddy's finger pointed to the sisters and rested on Jennifer. 'See you,' he said, sauntering off. Ron got up to leave too but as he left he turned to Jennifer. 'Coming to the disco, Monday?'

'It's your fault,' hissed June. 'You sat there all humped up so Eddy would go off me. Bitch!' That night Jennifer lay awake in the dormitory, angrily chewing the rest of her gum and plotting to eliminate her jealous rival – or herself. She kept the gum in her mouth, hoping it would choke her in her sleep.

Monday's disco was a success. June and Jennifer had agreed that they would actually dance, if asked. 'The nurses won't be surprised,' June had murmured to Jennifer. 'We're all supposed to be mental anyway.' Both girls had chosen new shoes at a recent shoe issue and wore new dresses. Eddy and Ron joined their table. This time the music was so loud that conversation was impossible. Ron kept nudging Jennifer under the table. They laughed and danced. Eddy put a cigarette behind June's ear. 'See you around,' they both said as the music stopped and the nurses summoned the girls.

The foursome became complicated with June and Jennifer deciding to share Ron and use Eddy as an extra. Ron began writing letters to Jennifer and she replied. By the written word, the twins could entice any man. But reality soon set in. The girls found out that Eddy was in Broadmoor for arson and assault; Ron had been sentenced for manslaughter. They were shocked. 'Such heart-rending news,' wrote Jennifer.

What a mess I've landed myself in. I've been linked with a murderer and I have accepted his gifts. I feel so low, cheated. He said he didn't mean it. It could have been an accident. J. and I both had dreams in the past about being strangled. I just hope Ron didn't use his bare hands. He could have done it with a knife . . . I don't trust him now. In his letter he said I was 'very pretty'. That is overexaggerated. I'm not pretty really, and he knows it. Is he lying when he says he's in here for manslaughter? He was talking about a ghost, too. Again, he could be exaggerating. It's bad luck. He's the only seventeen-year-old around.

The twins did seem to have bad luck. All through their lives, just as they reached out and made a relationship, it was snatched away. At their primary school in Yorkshire the headmaster had taken an interest in them, allowing them to sit by him in his study. Then Aubrey had been moved to Devon. They had moved again to Haverfordwest and there, after years of silence, they began to open up to their teacher, Cathy

Arthur. Just as they felt they could trust her, she left to write a thesis about them at the university and when she returned she was too involved with her first baby. They were abandoned by all the professionals to live alone together on the dole. Then there were the Kennedys, to whom the girls willingly gave their hearts and bodies. They vanished with little warning and were never in touch again. It was the same with the local boys. On the estate the usual time of service was three years, and families came and went. Boys they became attracted to never seemed to stay for long. The hurtful pattern was established.

There was further heartbreak for Jennifer. In all my previous visits, she had begged me to find the manuscripts of her three novels. I found 'Discomania' and 'The Pugilist' but there was no copy or even notes on her first book 'Taxi-Driver's Son', which she had sent to New Horizon to be printed. I made enquiries with New Horizon, only to be told that they had written to Miss Gibbons in Haverfordwest on 8th September 1982. They had given a fortnight to reply and when they received none, they had destroyed the manuscript. 'Disposed of. 23.9.82,' was written at the top of the letter. 'I hope that as advised you kept a copy of this manuscript.'

Jennifer showed no emotion on receiving the news, but as a writer myself, I knew how devastated she would feel. From then on, in every letter or at each visit, she asked whether at least her rough notes had been found.

As autumn wasted into winter, patients 19091 and 19092 became hardened to their surroundings and began to accept that the young men they met at the socials were likely to be child molesters, rapists, or murderers. In fact, they grew quite proud to be in the same place as such famous criminals as Ronald Kray, and relished the racy social life. June and Jennifer threw themselves into the Christmas celebrations. Their letters to me were full of ward-party rounds. 'Dear Marjorie,' wrote Jennifer,

June came to visit me on Christmas day. There was a disco on the ward all day. It wasn't too bad. The dinner was all right. Everybody got presents from Broadmoor. Mine was a book. (So somebody knows I like reading.) It was about a man haunted by guilt who thinks he's being followed. A peculiar choice, mostly in the form of a diary. There were a lot of parties which J. and I attended together. June told me that she's in danger of being sent to Lancs. 1. We think it's to do with the planet Uranus which is known to be rather destructive . . . I am looking forward to your visit. Take care. Your dear friend. Jennifer.

By March 1983, a new man had come into their lives. Jennifer had handed over Ron, whose horrible crime had dampened her enthusiasm, to June and directed her affections to another young offender, Billy. Their relationship was to prove equally unhappy but was not without its excitement.

Billy is going to give me his baby. Sweet Lord Jesus! The boy has agreed with my word. I told him tonight at table tennis. He got a shock, but the real reason for his shock is that he had a dream about me, like a premonition. He was having sex with me, sucking my breasts and that sort of thing. Would you believe it? I mean, the thing is on. He's going to bring his sperm in a bottle on Monday. If it doesn't work, he'll do it again on Thursday. Oh, my God! I'm actually going to be a mother soon. The emotion inside me is one of happiness and doubt. Supposing it doesn't work? But I pray to the Lord it does. I gave Billy an Easter egg, bright yellow. What an egg!

Jennifer took out the photograph of Billy which she had hidden in her bra and kissed it. 'The young boy in the photo is gonna be a daddy soon.' She added cryptically, 'Again.'

At the weekend, she found a used cosmetic bottle and attempted to sterilize it in her bath water, but when she met Billy the following day, he did not produce the precious sperm. He said he had not been able to find a container and had put it in a bag which made it turn watery. He suggested they should try again if he found a syringe over the next weekend. But the next meetings could not take place. Jennifer's slovenly habits, her failure to wash her clothes and tidy her drawers meant that she was banned from all socials for a week. She became agitated. Would June be going and meeting Billy? Would he give *her* the specimen instead?

That fear was put at rest when June sent her a note, saying that Billy was not at the social. He, too, had been banned and confined to his room. The specimen would have to be handed over at the Easter dance.

But the real reason for Billy's confinement soon emerged. The people on his ward knew he was looking for a syringe and the plot had been uncovered, amid much hilarity.

'Goodbye baby!' wrote a distraught Jennifer. 'I've had a miscarriage and I'm crying my heart out for a child that never was. I had to spoil things by asking for too much. I'll attack a nurse, hang myself, slash my wrists and be put in seclusion. Poor Billy! Poor J.! We've come to a standstill.'

In April Billy was transferred, along with many of the men, to the newly opened Park Lane hospital in Liverpool.

June was finding life on Lancaster 2 tedious and depressing. She still missed her twin and made no contact with the nursing staff, the psychologists and the doctors, whom she now regarded as her enemies. She pleaded to be put back with Jennifer, but sympathy for the twins was running out. The nurses watched them laugh, chat and dance when together or with men at the socials, but return to bent and silent shadows when back on the ward. Such wilful hostility and antisocial behaviour were not to be tolerated. June, in particular, seemed to be going downhill. She sat alone in the dayroom listening to the other girls gossiping about boyfriends, periods, masturbation and babies. She felt excluded and unhappy.

> What can be happening to me tonight?
> I feel as though I'm swimming in a pool;
> by the sea washing up to touch my feet,
> I taste the bitter sweet smell of salt;
> salt water running in between my toes,
> salt water running from my eyes,
> to touch my cold and papery hands . . .
> What can be happening to me; I can reach out
> and touch the stars; I can see Jupiter
> and Venus; I can see the galaxy
> And then I spot the earth and see a
> missing space; my missing space; for I am
> not here or there; for maybe I'm
> everywhere, tonight.

The more pressure that was being put on June to talk, the more resistant and unhappy she became. 'It's happening, what I dreaded. Everyone is slowly turning against me. I'm talking about these so-called nurses in blue . . . I feel full of complexities and my inside soul is not quiet. I'm talking to God and I'm asking for help. I'm on my way to a nervous breakdown.'

But the staff were relentless in their efforts to make June conform. 'You know what you're doing, you're doing it on purpose,' said Jenny France, the speech therapist. She gave June two weeks to see if she would co-operate and make the visits worthwhile. The teacher threatened to ban her from the typing class for lack of effort. The staff used her love of socials as the only punishment they thought sufficient to make her talk. 'Speak louder! Say please!' said the sister. 'Nice to hear your voice,' said another nurse, sarcastically, when June asked for a new exercise book. If she didn't talk, she was not allowed to attend class in the day or social events in the early evening.

June regarded all their attempts as nothing more than blackmail and refused to respond. In the past, it had always been her nature to respond differently to individual officers and nurses, often feeling considerable sympathy with their position. Her time in Broadmoor had hardened her heart. She began to regard them all as evil and in order to let them know she was not playing their game, she adopted a new weapon – an inscrutable smile. It infuriated the nurses even more than her glum expression. 'They're hassling me all the time. I feel anxious, isolated and ready to slit my throat.' Even her family's visit for her twentieth birthday was marred by the stifling presence of two 'guards'.

'They said those haunting yet sad words: "Happy Birthday". But I am not rejoicing. I am twenty, suspended in a wind; neither terribly young nor terribly old, but halfway to somewhere . . . I am barren. I have no child, no husband, no destination,' June wrote in her diary.

Jennifer, too, was being moulded into the stereotype of the patient/ victim. Like June, she had been confined nine months on the same ward, in York House. It was a year to the day from their trial, when their hopes for cure and comfort in the special hospital had been so high. Now, after all these months, no-one had succeeded in helping them; they felt they were being treated even more as babies or idiots, with nurses and other people talking about them and across them. For the first time, the system was winning. On their occasional meetings, the unhappy girls plotted their revenge. They decided they must take matters into their own hands – the time had come for a change.

It was 7.25 pm on 27th May 1983 when the alarm bells rang out across the gardens and airing courts on the female side of Broadmoor hospital. Nurses were seen running between the blocks. One or two charge nurses from the male side followed. Upstairs in Lancaster Ward 2, June looked at her watch. Yes, it was the exact time. 'D-Day. The rockets are launched. She has done it. Well done, Jen. You're braver than me.' She heard a noise and scuffle as the nurses dragged a patient across the yard towards Lancaster 1. She heard a voice shouting, 'Freedom. I want my freedom!' June was sure it was Jennifer. She thought about her with warmth. 'God bless you, Jenny. You're on Lancs. with me now. I wonder what you did?' June could not find out what her sister had done; she knew she had rung the alarm bell, but she was not sure what else. It was part of their scheme that they would either attack at the same time and therefore get together in the intensive-care unit, or, if the separation policy was still in force, when June was moved to intensive care in Lancaster House, the staff would have to move Jennifer to York House. They would keep switching houses to manipulate and confuse the system.

The first moves had gone well. June and Jennifer had contrived to meet on the day Jennifer pulled the alarm bell, at the locked doors linking the two wards. They had whispered through the keyhole and slipped letters under the door. But June had been caught before her part of the plan had been finalized.

Jennifer was put in room 23, Lancaster 1, the bottom of the ladder again. She had committed two unforgivable crimes; she had set off the alarm bells and she had attacked a nurse, by grabbing her keys and rushing for her face. For a week she was kept locked up in seclusion. The morning after the attack, June went to her locker and found it empty. Her diaries, letters, poems and clothes had been removed. She attempted to smuggle a letter to Jennifer, using a girl from her ward who used to clean on Lancaster 1. The letter, clearly written with the enemy in mind, was as she suspected, intercepted and read.

Dear Jennifer,
They seem to be taking vengeance on me, because you turned the world upside down. What on earth did you do? No-one will tell me. The bitches seem to think we had the whole thing planned? Do you recall talking about it to me? Did we set a time to do it? Are we mind-readers? They don't know what to believe. I will not react to these slags. They want me, I suppose, to turn around and smash them up. I'm too clever for that, aren't I? They're angry it's not me on Lancs. 1. Why don't they take me now? I could do with a long, long rest. I wonder when I will see you again? I wonder a lot of things, particularly why the 'wheels' have stopped or why I've missed the bus. It's the end of a chapter.

That night June dreamed of green snow and bicycles, both ill omens. She knew she should live up to her sister's resistance, but lacked the courage. Jennifer guessed as much and despised her sister. Had she failed to keep her side of the bargain? Was she such a coward that she not only had to wait for Jennifer to move first, but then did not follow?

A week later, Jennifer was promoted from room 23 to a superior room. Her possessions were returned, except the diaries and silver and gold bangles Rosie had given her for her birthday. She was allowed to eat in the dining hall of Lancaster 1 and spend a few hours in the day room. Unknown to her, June was now locked in another seclusion room down the corridor. In order to regain any self-respect, June knew her attack on the nursing staff had to be even more dramatic than her sister's.

But this time the authorities had the trump card. Dr Le Couteur visited both girls in their rooms. He was holding some papers which he told them he was filling in, to arrange for the transfer of one of them to Rampton special hospital if they continued to misbehave. This threat achieved its aim – to unhinge the twinship and set the girls into renewed competition against each other instead of the system. Le Couteur decided that if they played on the twins' fear of separation, each would blame the other. 'If we move one onto a better ward so that she bypasses her twin, the other girl may co-operate,' he explained to me on my next visit.

By the autumn of 1983, June and Jennifer were in eclipse. With the threat of Rampton always present, they had settled into the hospital routine, skilfully avoiding chores such as cleaning, washing and iron-ing. Jennifer made some attempts to communicate with the staff, but June sat in her room, still as stone. By now they were both on medication: regular injections of Depixol, one of the major tranquil-lizers, usually administered to people suffering from schizophrenia or other severe mental illness, but occasionally used to make aggressive patients more co-operative. They both wrote to me complaining that the drug gave them blurred eyesight and spoiled their concentration so much that they had almost given up reading and wrote only short poems or diary entries. Dr Cyril Levin, one of the medical officers for the female side, and Dr Le Couteur told me that the twins were only using their knowledge of side effects and the dosages were insufficient to harm.

On 19th September 1983, I visited June and Jennifer. Jennifer looked plump in the face and her eyes were dulled, but she quickly came alive at the talk of using their diaries for a book and the possibility that some of her writings might get published. June was still in the intensive-care unit. Her face looked swollen, her hands were shaking and she scarcely spoke, but she handed me a book of poems she had written. When I read them on the train back to London, my eyes were stinging. The 'September Poems', sometimes three or four in one day, were filled with a poignance and melancholy which seemed far from what I would have expected of a dangerous psychopath.

> I am immune from sanity or insanity
> I am an empty present box; all
> unwrapped for someone else's disposal.
> I am a thrown away egg-shell,
> With no life inside me, for I am
> not touchable, but a slave to nothingness.
> I feel nothing, I have nothing, for I am

transparent to life; I am a silver
streamer on a balloon; a balloon
which will fly away without any
oxygen inside. I feel nothing,
for I am nothing, but I can
see the world from up here.

Neither girl was attending English class any longer. They had missed the date for their exam and, for all the interest they had shown, the teacher found it hard to believe they were capable of stringing words together into coherent sentences, let alone writing stories, poems or books. The typewriter which Aubrey had brought down from their home stayed in the quiet room, untouched. Dr Le Couteur told me he was not surprised. He had hoped that my visits might stimulate them into creative writing again, but they had produced only one short story each, apart from the poems and diaries which he had not read but had been told by the nursing staff were filled with erotic fantasies and obscenities. 'They're not getting therapy,' Le Couteur said. 'The speech therapist is finding no response. If they want to talk to me, I'll listen. But I'm not going to waste time.'

The nursing staff were equally disaffected. Lennie Dunn, the charge nurse for Lancaster Ward where Jennifer had been transferred, told me how much trouble they had been having with her. 'She hasn't talked to me or other staff except in monosyllables, when she wants something. We tried withdrawing their diaries when they behaved badly, but they don't seem to care. They play games with us as they have with everyone all their lives. They move us around on their chess board.'

Inside their minds, the twins' ancient battles raged. Jennifer was furious that June would not talk and co-operate. June blamed her sister for the unhappy turn of events. Jennifer stayed upstairs on Lancaster 2, June below her on Lancaster 1. It was like Furzy Park and Puckle-church all over again, only this time the country's most expensive custodial institution was using its resources to keep them apart.

In the year that followed, June and Jennifer moved to more privileged rooms and better wards. They were kept on regular tranquillizers and appeared to be more at peace with themselves and the institution. But when I last attended a case conference where the staff were discussing whether they should remain separate (it was a unanimous decision that they should be kept apart), the prognosis was still disheartening. Although the twins told me they had decided to 'talk themselves out' and were beginning to make some voluntary efforts, they had laid their other talents to sleep. Their letters to me were filled with the social life and the daily trivia, but there were no poems, no stories, and no plans for new books. 'I don't read much now,' Jennifer told me. 'I read a few pages after lunch.'

'What have you read recently?'

'June's "Pepsi-Cola Addict".'

'But you've read that hundreds of times.'

She grinned, knowing as I knew that her decision to be a good patient had its repercussions. 'I don't concentrate and my eyes get blurred.'

'Do you write?'

Again the same grin. 'Only my diaries. How's your book about us getting along? Why don't you call it *Rag Dolls*?'

'What else do you do? Do you go to English or art class?'

Again, Jennifer shook her head. 'Occupational therapy. I'm allowed to go to the activity centre with the male side. I've a boyfriend . . .'

'What do you do there?'

'I make toys, and do colouring in.'

'But you were good at art, don't you ever draw your own pictures?'

She shrugged and smiled.

The nurses explained that Jennifer had co-operated more than June and had just started a proper behaviour-modification programme whereby she was asked to write down her feelings and reactions to everything that happened in the day. I remembered all the diaries she had given me, as I knew she did. 'She's doing very well,' said the sister. 'She's beginning to express some feelings. It seems to be helping her.'

Despite their apparent progress, Dr Le Couteur predicts that it will be a long time before they are sufficiently independent to live apart and sufficiently cured so that they no longer represent a threat to society.

The twins, too, hold out little hope for their immediate future. After spending the whole of their lives trying to be outstanding, to break away from the mediocrity of their surroundings, they have been forced to conform. They realize that as they get more content with their hospital lives, they will lose touch with the outside world and the world will abandon them. June reflected in her diary:

We are forgotten, faded away, never to be seen again. What sort of day will it be when I walk free? What kind of weather? How old will I be? It sends shudders down my spine. J. and I are two twins of history; coloured girls. Life will go on outside, passing away; memories of our trial, of our case. Where are we now, they will say? What do they look like now? And one day we will be quietly, secretly released; mature women. All things must end. New things begin.